ODD COUPLE

ODD COUPLE

International Trade and Labor Standards in History

Michael Huberman

Yale

UNIVERSITY

PRESS

New Haven & London

Published with assistance from the Mary Cady Tew Memorial Fund.

Yale University Press books may be purchased in quantity for educational, business, or promotional use. For information, please e-mail sales.press@yale.edu (U.S. office) or sales@yaleup.co.uk (U.K. office).

Set in Electra type by Westchester Book Group, Danbury, Connecticut.

ISBN: 978-0-300-15870-0 (cloth)

Library of Congress catalog control number: 2011944443

A catalogue record for this book is available from the British Library.

This paper meets the requirements of ANSI/NISO Z39.48–1992 (Permanence of Paper).

There is a part of everything which is unexplored, because we are accustomed to using our eyes only in association with the memory of what people before us have thought of the thing we are looking at. Even the smallest thing has something in it which is unknown.

—Gustave Flaubert in a letter to Guy de Maupassant

CONTENTS

PREFACE

I once met a senior colleague who asked what I was working on. "Another book on the welfare state? Another book on globalization? Can we squeeze more juice out of these old lemons?" I persisted, perhaps out of stubbornness or some other reason, but I took my colleague's complaint seriously. I have attempted to narrow my project down to a simple observation. My point of departure is that historians have considered globalization and the welfare state as separate events. This is odd. It is hard to imagine that a pair of social, economic, and political movements of this magnitude, arising in the same historical conjuncture in the last quarter of the nineteenth century, did not somehow form a couple either operating in concert or locked in discord—an interdependence that has persisted into the present century.

The book is designed for readers receptive to the idea that the past informs the present and that the present informs our reading of the past. Today, globalization challenges us to revise our views of the benefits and costs of social policy; at the same time, the extent of the safety net prompts us to reconsider our attitudes toward international integration. We want to know how our social entitlements and labor standards match up against those of trading partners. We have also come to appreciate, sometimes belatedly, that decisions taken elsewhere on employment conditions have repercussions on our own. How do we adapt to weaker labor standards abroad? Do we have confidence that the development process eventually includes latecomers? Or do we respond aggressively and unilaterally, imposing a code of working conditions on others and, if so, how? Do we raise tariffs or impose sanctions against rivals tolerating or encouraging slack regulatory environments? Alternatively, do we exchange ideas for goods, granting market access to trading partners who have resolved or consented to improve labor standards?

In this book I relate how workers, firms, and states in the first wave of globalization responded to these questions. In many ways, conflicts among the period's social actors prefigured modern debates on trade and labor standards. But my claim goes further. Not only did early concerns mirror our own anxieties, but initial responses have contributed to defining our actions (or inaction) today. The historical resolution of trade and labor standards goes a good way in explaining how and why the European social model differs from that of liberal North America, and why the Latin American model is still different.

The problem I have set out for myself required I consult primary sources, national histories, and comparative studies in economics and political science. The project became a Leninist effort: one step forward, two steps back. To make the task manageable, I have selected three countries, Belgium, Brazil, and Canada, whose experiences were representative of the economies and politics of Old and New Worlds. I cannot say I am a master in any of these areas, or of any particular country for that matter—this will become painfully clear—and I ask readers to forgive my excesses. My aim was simply to rescue an idea, the interdependence of globalization and the welfare state, that was popular a century ago, but has been too long ignored. This connection is as relevant today as it was in the past. It remains for readers to judge whether I have succeeded in making lemonade out of those old lemons. *Bonne dégustation.*

ACKNOWLEDGMENTS

In preparing this book, I am three times lucky. First, a cast of creative, talented, and dependable coauthors (in order of appearance)—Denise Young, Wayne Lewchuk, Christopher Minns, and Christopher Meissner—has had a significant part in formulating and implementing many of the ideas I have come to rely on. I have learned a great deal about research strategies, and much else, from my coauthors. I thank them for granting permission to use our joint research. I am of course responsible for the versions found here.

Second, colleagues generously commented on my research at conferences of the Economics History Association and Cliometrics Society. I benefited as well from discussions at seminars at Harvard, Lund, Rutgers, and Stanford Universities, the London School of Economics, and the University of Toronto. Robert C. Allen, Concha Betrán, Michael Bordo, George Boyer, John C. Brown, Frank Lewis, Peter H. Lindert, Aldo Mussachio, Kim Oosterlinck, Kevin O'Rourke, Jaime Reis, Eugene White, Jeffrey G. Williamson, and Gavin Wright contributed to the making of this book. At the Université de Montréal, I appreciate sincerely the support of Emanuela Cardia, Leonard Dudley, Baris Kaymak, Lyndon Moore, and Benoît Perron.

I began imagining this book when I was a visitor at UCLA in 2007 and am grateful to Naomi Lamoreaux and the late Ken Sokoloff for that opportunity. Jérôme Bourdieu and Gilles Postel-Vinay invited me to Paris in the spring of 2008 where I started writing. Portions of chapters of this book have appeared in the *Economic History Review, European Review of Economic History, Explorations in Economic History*, and the *Journal of Economic History*. I thank the editors and publishers of these journals for permission to use this material. The bibliography contains full references to these articles. Several grants from the Social Science and Humanities Research Council of Canada assisted in the preparation of this book. The SSHRC-INE-TARGET research team based at the University of British Columbia and headed by Thomas Lemieux gave me an opportunity to speak to an interdisciplinary audience. Peter Solar and Peter Scholliers directed my access to Belgian materials. Manoela Pedroza conducted my way in Brazilian archives. At the Université de Montréal, students Marie-Pierre Busson, Carolina Corral, and Mathieu Grandmaison provided excellent research assistance.

At Yale, I thank Michael O'Malley for his unfailing optimism about the project, William Frucht for guiding the manuscript through all stages of publication, and Katherine Scheuer for her excellent editorial assistance. Two anonymous referees read and reread the manuscript. I am sincerely grateful for their reports.

Lastly, my greatest debt goes to Sally Cooper Cole, and Isabella and Samuel Cole Huberman, who have indulged me. I dedicate this book to my father, Leon Huberman, on whose ninety-second birthday I delivered the final manuscript.

ODD COUPLE

The Virtuous Circle of Trade and the Labor Compact

During the [nineteenth century] two great discoveries have been made in the science of government: the one is the immense advantage of abolishing restrictions on trade; the other is the absolute necessity of imposing restrictions on labor. And so the Factory Acts, instead of being excused as exceptional and pleaded for as justified only under extraordinary conditions ought to be recognised as in truth the first legislative recognition of a great Natural Law, quite as important as Freedom of Trade, and which, like this last, was yet destined to claim for itself wider and wider application.

—*George Campbell, Eighth Duke of Argyll*, The Reign of Law, *page 367.*

Globalization does not rule out all egalitarian interventions.

—*Samuel Bowles*, Globalization and Egalitarian Redistribution, *page 121.*

LABOR AND FREE TRADE IN THE FIN DE SIÈCLE

A hundred years ago, the *patron* of the Belgian Labor Party, Émile Vandervelde, rose in parliamentary debate and endorsed with conviction his country's free trade policy. In France, Germany, the United Kingdom, and elsewhere, labor leaders followed suit.[1] In the shadow of labor's opposition toward free trade in the twenty-first century, how can we understand Vandervelde's and his comrades' enthusiasm?

The labor historian (Van der Linden 2003) might argue that Vandervelde was extolling the virtues of a transnational workers' organization, centered on the socialist Second International, a movement in which he himself played a leading role. Was his message a mere shibboleth? In the factories and in the mines, however, international socialism had made few gains, and most workers saw that their fate was attached to national movements. Contrary to expectations, international trade unions were strongest in North America, and only the ideologue would consider the mass of U.S. or Canadian workers revolutionary vanguards. In Europe, socialists had abandoned Marx for Richard Cobden, the British liberal free trader whose philosophy Vandervelde referred to as *le manchestérianisme*. But this does imply that workers and their leaders were prepared to embrace free trade wholeheartedly as liberal economists did. Free trade was part of a larger project to improve labor's well-being.

The economist (Stigler 1982) and economic historian (Gerschenkron 1943; Bairoch 1989) would answer that workers benefited from free trade because of cheap grain imports. By opening up markets, Belgium would reap the benefits of its comparative advantage. It was a labor-abundant and land-scarce economy, and workers would move out of agriculture and into labor-intensive industries like textiles. As manufacturing exports increased, so would have the demand for labor. The problem with this line of reasoning is that Belgium had had low tariff barriers since the 1860s. Why did it take organized labor a generation to support free trade? Was its adoption tied to other social and political projects?

The political scientist (Gourevitch 1986; Rogowski 1989) may suspect that Vandervelde was a fair-weather free trader, representing a narrow group of self-interested workers in the export sector demanding immediate attention. The trouble with this argument is that by the 1880s, Belgium had an integrated labor market, the fate of all wage earners rising and falling together. Vandervelde embraced free trade because workers across regions and industries had something to gain by it. The reason why labor endorsed free trade lies elsewhere.

Vandervelde's own explanation, simple and direct, forms the backbone of my study. As Belgium integrated into the world economy, workers in the tradable sector confronted increased dislocation and uncertainty. Vandervelde's support of free trade was conditional on the adoption of a package of labor regulations and social entitlements, what I refer to as the labor compact, providing insurance against these hazards. Because these reforms required cross-class support, the argument had a political dimension. Free trade in the Old World marked the end of the ancien régime and the power of landowners, an outcome that aroused the support of liberals and manufacturers because of their overlapping interests. The collapse of agricultural tariffs would compel the state to tax land to finance newly created redistributive programs without sacrificing the benefits of trade.

Vandervelde grasped the two-sided relation between trade and the labor compact. By raising the price of labor, the new labor laws altered cost structures and induced firms to invest in modern technologies and upgrade product lines. The increase in wages caused improvements in labor productivity, firms and workers emerging as better exporters. Anticipating the line of reasoning of European social democrats after 1945 (Eichengreen 2007), Vandervelde concluded that international economic integration promoted social and political equality, and that egalitarianism would fasten workers' attachment to openness.

The primary objective of this book is to relate how Vandervelde's vision, shared by an international movement of reformists and social activists, came to be realized before 1914. I propose to show that trade served as a main pathway in the spread of the labor compact. I demonstrate that the feedback between trade and the labor compact was much stronger in Europe than elsewhere. I conclude that the first great wave of globalization had enduring effects in the development of 'social Europe' and 'liberal America' (Pontusson 2005).[2]

The historical relation between trade and the labor compact resonates today. For the period since the 1960s, Dani Rodrik (1997, 1998, 2011; Cameron 1978) observed the positive relation between international exposure and state intervention.[3] But there is a competing view. Lawrence Summers (2008), for one, remarked that "global considerations constrain competitiveness," raising the costs of providing social protection. While the verdict will never be known with certainty, history serves as jury to the ongoing deliberations.

WELFARE STATE FUNDAMENTALISM

Certain components of the labor compact, like limits on work time, are not considered typical welfare-state benefits because governments commit fewer resources in their provision than in the delivery of unemployment insurance and other social entitlements. Still, labor regulations and social policy have similar effects on well-being. They restrict labor supply and compress wage distributions, redistributing income as a result. Historically, the labor compact is seen as a precursor to greater and direct state intervention. As such, it is useful to begin with an overview of the conventional treatment of globalization and the welfare state.

The dominant narrative explains the rise of the welfare state as a response to the dislocation resulting from industrialization. Before the extension and deepening of market forces, the story goes, workers and families could rely on the church, benevolent landowners, and local authorities to support them when they were without work, fell ill, or met some other hazard.[4] But these institutions proved to be insufficient in the wake of the industrial revolution that brought with it new kinds of exposures and risks. These risks emanated from the creation of the factory system—its long hours of work, exploitation of children and women, and unsanitary conditions—and the concentration of industry in urban centers where workers found themselves cut off from customary social networks when they became ill, unemployed, or too old to work. Markets do not always provide adequate insurance for these outcomes, and state intervention was the logical response to the changing dynamic.

Karl Polanyi (1944, 250) is chief standard bearer of this approach. "The congenital weakness of nineteenth century society was not that it was industrial, but that it was a market society." But while Polanyi insisted that the market was inherently a social institution, his views have been recast in a fundamental dialectic that opposes markets and states. In the blunt words of Gøsta Esping-Andersen (1990, 157), the doyen of comparative social policy, the welfare state sought to "emancipate individuals from market dependence." The success of state intervention is conventionally measured in its ability to thwart and roll back the market.

The narrative is written as a chapter of national history in which domestic forces and actors, workers, employers, or the state, are forefront.[5] Although disentangling the many explanations is bound to be unsatisfactory—and beyond my purposes—, several strands of thought can be identified. A main thread is the struggle between classical liberalism and the modern state. For instance, the advent of French social policy was the outcome of a local "ideological struggle between the defenders of laissez-faire liberalism and the diverse forces of socialists, social Catholics, and solidarists, who favored varying levels of state intervention to promote the common welfare" (Dutton 2002, 5). In the power resources model, the spread of the franchise and the rise of organized labor are leading protagonists. In Britain, after 1900, the "new mass political culture" (Harris 1993, 193) influenced the direction of social legislation. Domestic affairs differed in North America and Australia, because the numbers of voters were initially higher and the process of democratization was not tied directly to a program of social reform. Comparative approaches in this vein have built on national histories, grouping countries, as in Esping-Andersen (1990), by the success or failure of labor to oppose capital and moderate workers' dependence on wage compensation.

The welfare state as the offspring of domestic forces is common currency. From an economic historian's perspective, Peter H. Lindert (2004) evaluated the determinants of social spending from 1880 until the present, the long twentieth century, for a large sample of poor and rich countries. He attributed the rise in spending to domestic forces: the growth in income, the expression of new political voices, and the aging of the population. In the U.S., while spending on education was considerable before 1914, the ratio of persons actually voting in the enfranchised population was lower than in Europe. Ever the optimist, Lindert concluded that the welfare state was not a European construct, since population movements and democratization have comparable effects on emerging economies today. Lindert's approach, like other comparative studies, juxtaposed national histories without entertaining their likely interdependence.

It is a puzzle that the main narrative has tended to downsize the impact of external or international forces on the rise of the welfare state. Polanyi (1944) himself devoted attention to the rise and fall of the period's gold standard. And trade was a staple of life, exactly in the decades that saw the rise of the labor compact. Jeffrey G. Williamson (1998, 2002, 2006) and coauthors (Hatton and Williamson 1998, 2005; O'Rourke and Williamson 1999; Taylor and Williamson 1997) have forcefully demonstrated the role of the great transport revolutions of the period in promoting the movement of labor, capital, and goods across Old and New Worlds.[6] Table 1.1 gives the external exposure of a sample of countries. As distances were cut short, the trade content of GDP increased, by about 400 percent between 1870 and 1914 (Findlay and O'Rourke 2007, 412). It may well be that the simultaneous rise in the welfare state and in trade was mere coincidence. But this proposition is difficult to sustain. They were intertwined since both were related to structural changes in the economy and the rise in income.

To be fair, historians (Rodgers 1998) have remarked on the cross-border and trans-Atlantic exchanges of social policies. In the 1880s, Bismarck's compatriots criticized his reforms for being "too French" (Berger 2003, 78), while Lloyd George was full of praise for Germany's social programs after his visit in 1908, the year before he introduced unemployment insurance legislation in London (Hay 1977, 51). Still, the focus is squarely on the transnational movements of ideas, referred to as the "transfer of social technology" (Hennock 1987). The consequences for social policy of international flows of workers, goods, and capital—the nuts and bolts of globalization—have received less attention. And so has the fact that all social actors cared about the regulatory environment of their trading partners, which may have been perceived to provide them with seemingly unfair advantages. These forces would certainly have affected the design of the labor compact. The history of the welfare state has remained staunchly, almost triumphantly, national in scope and purpose. Even Peter Katzenstein (1985, 133–34), whose body of research is devoted to the centrality of external pressures and opportunities on policy making, upheld 'the welfare state in one country' view: "Domestic compensation responds primarily to the logic of domestic politics; it is not a deliberate response to the logic of the international economy."

Table 1.1. Trade openness in Old and New Worlds, 1870–1914

	1870	1880	1890	1900	1913	MANUFACTURE share of EXPORTS
Austria	13.1	25.5	25.2	26.8	24.1	56.0
Belgium	35.6	53.2	55.6	73.4	76.1	62.0
Bulgaria	12.2	15.2	15.0	15.0	17.0	n.a
Denmark	35.7	45.8	48.0	52.8	61.5	4.0
Finland	31.7	50.8	39.3	47.6	56.2	n.a
France	23.6	33.5	28.2	26.8	30.8	60.0
Germany	36.8	32.1	30.1	30.5	37.2	67.0
Italy	18.3	18.3	15.9	19.0	23.9	26.0
Netherlands	115.4	100.5	112.3	124.1	179.6	n.a
Norway	33.9	36.1	43.6	43.4	50.9	26.0
Portugal	33.7	43.8	45.3	48.9	57.4	8.0
Russia	5.6	14.4	15.0	11.4	13.8	4.0
Spain	11.7	13.9	19.2	21.9	22.7	25.0
Sweden	32.0	37.3	44.9	39.4	34.7	25.0
Switzerland	47.0	78.2	52.0	67.2	47.0	25.0
UK	43.6	46.0	46.6	42.4	51.2	83.0
Argentina	25.2	32.8	35.8	35.2	42.6	1.0
Australia	27.8	32.8	31.2	42.6	36.8	3.0
Brazil	28.9	42.8	46.6	44.1	41.8	0.0
Canada	17.2	25.2	22.6	36.6	25.6	5.0
Mexico	6.2	8.4	10.2	10.8	16.7	0.0
US	9.5	13.4	12.6	14.8	13.2	20.0
Old World	33.1	40.3	39.8	43.2	49.0	36.2
New World	19.1	25.9	26.5	30.7	29.5	4.8
World	29.3	36.4	36.1	39.8	43.7	26.3

Sources: Bairoch (1976); Daudin, Morys, and O'Rourke (2010); Estevadeordal (1987). Manufacturing exports from Williamson (2006). Belgium is from Degrève (1982).
Notes: Mid-point values where estimates differ.

Other political scientists (Berman 2006; Silver 2003; see also Tilly 1995), motivated by the recent wave of globalization, have extended the fundamental dialectic to accommodate international integration. Nonetheless, they have retained the familiar trope of states versus markets in which globalization is construed as an added layer of risk and dislocation. But attitudes to domestic and international trade are not identical, because the challenges they pose are different.

In autarky, the fate of social actors is tied to local demand and supply, but in an open economy global markets determine rewards for labor, land, and capital.[7] This distinction gave pause to contemporaries. "It is no exaggeration," a British worker lamented, "to say that the wages of an English weaver may be determined by the conditions existing in Japanese mills."[8] While the accuracy of this claim was and is controversial (Clark 1987), more unanimous was the observation that loose operating rules and regulations abroad were a source of unfair competition. Workers may have accepted similar discrepancies within their own borders, if only because they never appeared to be that large. Similarly, workers separated the effects on their livelihoods of internal migration and cross-border movements. The responses of labor, as well as those of business and states, to foreign and domestic challenges were therefore not always the same. For the key social actors, globalization was conceived as something more than and different from structural change in the domestic economy.

GLOBALIZATION BACKLASH: ONE SIZE FITS ALL?

In the Polanyi framework, the historical response to globalization was its rejection. Welfare states are perceived to be stronger in closed and isolated economies. Where globalization forces cannot be resisted, welfare states unravel in a race to the bottom.[9] The adoption of social legislation, Polanyi (1944, 204) wrote, went hand in hand with trade protectionism. "Internal and external, social and national protectionism tended to fuse." The inference is that by 1914 states everywhere had successfully turned back competitive forces. Economic historians have offered support for this line of reasoning. In his classic study Paul Bairoch (1989) sought to document the rise of protectionism in the developed world from 1870 on. In the Old World, agrarian and industrial interests aligned to raise tariffs, and in the New, producers sought protection against manufacturing imports.[10]

The backlash to globalization was ubiquitous, as if one size fits all. Immigration restrictions complemented tariff protection. The fall in transport costs had precipitated waves of immigration. From 1870 until the Great War, more than 50 million Europeans emigrated overseas and roughly a similar number moved elsewhere on the continent. In receiving countries, the complaint was that migrants put downward pressure on wages and increased employment insecurity (Hatton and Williamson 2005). Everywhere governments responded by placing restrictions on new arrivals.

The standard formulation is inadequate because there were alternatives (Adserà and Boix 2002). Tellingly, protectionism around 1900 was on the decline in Europe and parts of the Americas (Dormois 2009, 136); immigration restrictions were lax in the Old World and uneven in the New. More than enabling, globalization broke down existing political alliances and created a propitious environment for the emergence of new coalitions and policy experiments. For one, labor regulation was conceived to provide workers wage and employment security, without sacrificing the gains of trade. Labor would benefit from improved factory conditions and have their free trade 'loaf' too (Trentmann 2008). While the threat of rivals operating with inferior labor standards was real, the response was not necessarily closing doors to trade. To safeguard the labor compact, states had the option of convincing rivals to adopt more and tighter regulation in exchange for greater market access, a phenomenon David Vogel (1995) has appropriately termed "trading up." Of course, the adoption of labor regulation and free trade was more likely if labor was relatively abundant, where states were less dependent on custom duties as a revenue source, and when the alliance of labor and manufacturers came to dominate agricultural interests. But the upshot is that there were policy options to the backlash, the decisions to open markets and to implement redistributive programs being simultaneously determined and not mutually exclusive (Boix 2006).

Conceived as a reaction to trade, the one-size-fits-all view resurfaces in a narrative of growth in which protectionism was the period's dominant, if not unique, strategy of state policy, even if the evidence of its success is mixed (O'Rourke 2000; Irwin 2002). The adoption of labor laws provided an alternative growth strategy, because like the welfare state, cost structures changed, and hence comparative advantage. To be sure, Price Fishback (1998, 2007) and others (Moehling 1999) maintained that much of the period's legislation codified existing practice and, as a result, did not have much effect. But this claim is embedded in a closed economy framework in which local interests determined the timing and nature of reform. In the open economy before 1914, external pressures mattered too, foreign rivals often dictating the legislative agendas of trading partners (Putnam 1988). In this scenario, local producers had to adapt to the larger playing field or close down. The causal link was then from labor law and higher wages to labor productivity. Business may have adjusted by moving up the product chain, by substituting capital for labor, or both; as young workers withdrew from the labor market and years of schooling rose, so did levels of human capital. All together, improvements in labor productivity promoted an increase in the variety and number of goods exported to new markets abroad. Arthur Lewis (1978, 74) proposed a similar interpretation of European economic growth: "The engine of growth was technological change with international trade serving as lubricating oil and not as fuel."

There are many histories of the welfare state. I reject the categorization of states versus markets because it is too narrow a framework, a false choice. In my version there were alternative responses to globalization, from protectionism and immigration restrictions on the one hand, to the reduction of trade barriers and the adoption of the labor compact on the other—and various combinations in between. These decisions, in turn, affected the flow and direction of trade. In the remainder of this chapter, I examine how contemporaries perceived the different options to the backlash, and then introduce the details of the labor compact.

ORIGINS OF AN IDEA

Contemporaries did not share the view that states and markets were antagonists. They saw that labor regulation was complementary to free trade. The formal divorce between free trade and laissez-faire had to wait until the contributions of Mihaïl Manoïlescu and James Meade in the mid twentieth century, exactly at the time of Polanyi's writing (Irwin 1996, 87–100). These authors showed that domestic distortions caused by, say, an externality in the employment of labor, are most effectively treated by policies that address market failures at their source. Trade interventions such as tariffs are quite unlikely to be first best solutions, since they create another set of distortions. Although lacking comparable rigor and crispness of argument, British and continental political economists had arrived at a similar result. Because I refer to the contributions of theorists and practitioners throughout the book, it is useful to begin with a brief outline of the origins and the diffusion of notions reconciling labor regulation and free trade.

In the U.K., the proposition linking free trade and factory legislation had its origins in the period after 1850. The two were clearly separate in debates on the repeal of the Corn Laws. The mounting pressure for repeal in the 1840s coincided with Chartism, the great movement for social change and universal suffrage. The Free Traders sought the backing of the Chartists to bolster their cause in Parliament. John Bright (cited in Schonhardt-Bailey 2006, 101), a leading spokesperson for Manchester liberals, had invoked standard trade theory in his address to the workers of Rochdale in the heartland of industrialized Lancashire:

> Your first step to entire freedom must be commercial freedom—freedom of industry. We must put an end to the partial famine which is destroying trade, the demand for your labor, your wages, your comforts, and your independence. The aristocracy regard the Anti-Corn law League as their greatest enemy. That which is the greatest enemy of the remorseless aristocracy of Britain must almost

of necessity be your firmest friend. Every man who tells you to support the Corn Law is your enemy. Whilst that inhuman law exists your wages must decline. When it is abolished, and not till then, they will rise.

To George Stigler, interests invariably trumped ideas, and all members of the "manufacturing class," workers and employers alike, naturally supported free trade.[11] Yet the Chartists balked. It may be that the social movement cleaved along sectoral and regional interests and, since labor mobility was restricted, there was no common basis for supporting free trade. But more fundamentally, interests were not expressed independently of ideology, which in the case of Chartists was both backward and forward looking, their articulated demands an amalgam of artisanal and 'working class' influences (Stedman Jones 1983). Free trade was perceived as a threat to their long-held belief in a 'fair' wage determined by the Old Poor Law, itself a relic of the Elizabethan period. In the end, the Corn Laws were repealed without support from workers.[12] Indeed, Bright comforted the agrarian interests in Parliament arguing that free trade would postpone demands for universal suffrage and greater redistribution. British wages did rise, although the uncertainties and hazards of factory work did not abate. Indeed, the first factory laws were put in place not because of free trade, but in spite of it, the Ten Hours Act being carried by a left-right coalition to punish the repealers of the Corn Laws (McLean 2001, 120). It was a half-century later, in 1904, that the British Labour Party officially supported free trade.

Sometime between Chartism and the formation of the British Labour Party, political economists began to conceive differently the basic identity between laissez-faire and free trade. Free Trade had become a pillar of British civil society (Trentmann 2008), and social reformers adjusting to the new landscape began to circulate the idea that libre-échange could be decoupled from laissez-faire. The Webbs (1902, 868) ascribed paternity to the political philosopher and Liberal cabinet minister George Campbell (1867), eighth Duke of Argyll, who saw the marriage of factory regulation and free trade as innately "natural." More pragmatic in their beliefs, the Webbs proposed the idea of national, if not universal, standards to correct for market failures without abandoning the principles of free trade, although they themselves were less than dogmatic on its virtues. "Unfettered freedom of competition" had created a class of sweating or "parasitic" trades, an informal sector of low-paid occupations with poor working conditions.

We can now see that the economists of the middle of the century only taught and the Free Trade statesmen only learnt one-half of their lesson. The proposal for the systematic enforcement, throughout each country of its own national minimum of education, sanitation, leisure and wages, becomes necessary completion of the free trade policy.

On the continent, the twinning of free trade and labor regulation had different intellectual origins. Schooled in Ricardian economics and Malthusian pessimism, Marx (1977, 270) himself was an early devotee of laissez-faire, declaring in 1848 in a celebrated address in Brussels that "free trade hastens the social revolution," and saw social policy as an obstacle to its progress.[13] Ever the pragmatist, Engels reasoned that protective tariffs would bolster jobs and membership in trade unions, and in the 1880s, his opinion prevailed among Germans socialists—the leading and most influential movement on the continent.

By the end of the century, on theoretical and empirical grounds, socialists had overthrown these ideas.[14] The Berliner Eduard Bernstein was a bridge between the U.K. and continental schools of thought. While Bernstein's contributions were not pathbreaking, he gave immense credibility to the idea of joining trade and redistribution. Exiled in London in the 1890s, Bernstein made contacts with the Webbs and other Fabians, although he seems to have gone beyond them in his fervent support of free trade.[15] Bernstein (1901) laid out a trenchant critique of Bismarckian social and commercial policy.[16] Protectionism had not offset domestic distortions caused by industrialization; rather, as Meade claimed a half-century later, it only created other types of inefficiencies. Tariffs had raised the cost of living of German workers, and a good part of the social insurance they did receive was paid for out of their own pockets. The domestic market was too small to support modern German industry. Free trade meant an increased purchasing power, while direct taxes would come to replace custom revenues, providing resources for a more extensive safety net. Upon returning to Germany, Bernstein maintained close links with the British Cobden Club, sending an enthusiastic message on the virtues of free trade to its 1908 meeting attended by Asquith and Churchill, and reformers like Lujo Brentano (*Report of Proceedings* 1908). As one historian (Fletcher 1983, 571) concluded, "Bernstein was, in fact, more an unreconstructed Cobdenite than were many of his English radical contemporaries."

The fin de siècle saw a formal break with orthodox Marxism. Bernstein's prescription became standard fare of the left. At their Stuttgart conference in 1899, the German socialists embraced a free trade platform identical to that adopted by the Belgian Labor Party earlier in the decade.[17] In the U.K., Lloyd George's fiscal program of 1909 was known as the 'Free Trade Budget'—although it is now referred to as the People's Budget—because of its link between redistributive policy and traditional trade policy, and stood in opposition to the attempt by conservatives to initiate tariff reform to protect jobs.[18]

The New World was not immune from ideas in the air.[19] In New South Wales, B. R. Wise, educated in the U.K. and a student of the new Cobdenism, was an architect of the coalition of export interests and labor groups supporting free trade and redistribution in the 1880s, which lasted until federation. Educated in Germany, Richard Ely (1888, 214–22) was a representative of continental philosophy in the U.S. Ely wrote that the value of the tariff had "long passed," and never did serve the interests of American laborers anyway. "Factory legislation is preferable to a social protective tariff." Ely's natural audience was smaller than it would have been in Europe, because labor was relatively scarce and, consequently, support for free trade was weaker, especially among unions. Still, Democrats in the U.S. Congress in 1913 insisted on and succeeded in reducing tariffs and introducing an income tax simultaneously. Woodrow Wilson's Secretary of Agriculture echoed the terminology of Vandervelde: "Think of it—a tariff revision downwards at all—not dictated by the manufacturer. A progressive income tax! I did not think we would live to see these things."[20]

Globalization was a purveyor of ideas. From 1900 on, the coupling of free trade and the labor compact had wide reception. It is difficult to ascertain whether ideas had an independent effect on the spread of policy, and trade itself, as I will show, was a conduit of their diffusion. Countries trading similar goods with each other had comparable labor laws, but it is also clear ideas were more than "simply hooks on which politicians hang their objectives and by which they further their interests" (Shepsle 1985, 233). Reformers presented their views in a new vocabulary, giving voice to emerging interests and preparing common ground essential to constructive coalitions (Hall 1997, 199). The mix of free trade and regulation was a staple of social democratic platforms throughout Europe, and orthodox Marxists and liberals could be swayed as well. The idea was dormant in the interwar years, but resurfaced in the immediate postwar period, becoming a pillar of the European miracle. Still, memory is selective.[21] Theoreticians and social activists of the original labor compact would be perplexed by the less than enthusiastic response those on the left today have demonstrated for globalization.

THE LABOR COMPACT: BASIC DATA

Table 1.2 gives dates of adoption—as opposed to the dates when laws came into effect—of eleven major pieces of legislation dealing with conditions workers faced inside the factory (labor regulations) and the benefits they received if they became ill, unemployed, or unable to work (social insurance). Together, this legislation comprised the labor compact forming the basis of this book. Although other elements, like compulsory schooling, could be included, my choice was determined by the availability of comparable laws for a wide sample of countries, since I am interested in the interdependence of regulation. My intention is to be forward looking. Thus I have omitted the Poor Law and other earlier types of assistance, because they varied considerably across countries and because they belonged to another historical epoch. Lastly, my choice corresponds as closely as possible to the OECD's (1996) definition of labor standards as the norms, rules, and conventions that govern the work environment.

The shortcomings of my procedure deserve mention, although I leave a full discussion to the appendix. When it comes to labor laws, the devil is in the details. For some pieces of legislation, like minimum age laws, authorities fixed different cut-off points. To ensure comparability across jurisdictions, I chose standards established at the international conference on labor legislation held in Berlin in 1890.[22] In the case of child labor, the standard was 12 years of age. But Berlin did not cover all details of legislation; in Britain, for instance, children under 12 years were permitted to work half days if they attended school part-time before 1901. Generally, any international comparison of legislation is compromised because labor laws by their very nature were not identical across jurisdictions, owing to differences in coverage, application, and compliance. There was great variation across the sample in the size of manufacturing and mining sectors, the labor force participation of women and children, and the number of inspectors hired to enforce the laws and their duties.

The federal structures of the New World, Germany, and Switzerland complicate issues of comparability because sub-national authorities held responsibility for labor legislation. The bias varied across countries. While Canadian provinces and Australian states adopted legislation a very short time after their neighbors, there were substantial differences in dates of adoption and in the heterogeneity of laws across U.S. jurisdictions. To adjust for this, the table gives two dates for the introduction of each piece of legislation in the U.S., the first when ten states achieved the level set at Berlin, and a second, in parentheses, when the ten most populated states achieved this norm. The considerable lags in dates of introduction using these two methods serve as a reminder of one of the possible hazards of the procedure I use.

Across countries and sub-national units, many dimensions of the regulations tended to converge after their passage, and policy makers perhaps expected this development when they considered adoption. The same pressures promoting diffusion of the idea of legal protection also affected the various dimensions of these laws. Table 1.3 reports the number of factory inspectors per establishment,

Table 1.2. Labor compact: Dates of adoption

	LABOR MARKET REGULATION							SOCIAL INSURANCE			
	Introduction of factory inspection	Introduction of first factory acts	Minimum age 12	Ten-hour working day youths	Night work children prohibited	Night work women prohibited	Eleven-hour working day women	Accident insurance	Unemployment insurance	Sickness insurance	Old age insurance
Austria	1883	1842	1885	1883	1842	1895	1895	1887	*	1888	1906
Belgium	1889	1889	1889	*	1889	1909	*	1903	1907/1920 (V)	1894	1900 (V)
Bulgaria	1905	*	1905	*	–	1909e	1913	1908	*	*	*
Denmark	1873	1873	1901	1901	1891	*	*	1898	1907 (V)	1892 (V)	1891
Finland	1889	*	1889	*	–	*	*	1893	*	*	*
France	1874	1841	1871	1892	1892	1892	1892	1898	1905 (V)	1898 (V)	1900 (V)
Germany	1853	1839	1853	1839	1839	1891	1891	1884	*	1883	1889
Hungary	1893	1842	1884	1893	1884	1909e	*	1907	*	1891	*
Italy	1906	1886	1907	*	1902	1907	*	1898	*	1886 (V)	1898 (V)
Netherlands	1895	1874	1889	1913	1889	1889	1889	1901	*	1913	1913
Norway	1892	1892	1892	1892	1892	1909e	*	1894	1906 (V)	1909	*
Portugal	1893	1891	*	1891	*	1909e	*	1913	*	*	*
Russia	1882	1882	1907	*	*	1905	*	1903	*	n.a	*

Spain	1907	1873	*	*	1900	1909	*	1900	*	*	*
Sweden	1889	1881	1881	1890	1892	1909	*	1901	*	1891 (V)	1913
Switzerland	1877	1877	1833	*	1837	1894	1894	1911	*	1911 (V)	*
United Kingdom	1833	1833	1901	*	1833	1844	1850	1897	1911	1911	1908
Argentina	*	1905	*	*	*	*	*	1915	*	*	*
Australia	1885	1854	1885	1885	1896	1896	1873	1914	*	1907	1901
Canada	1888	1888	1885	1885	1910	1910	1910	*	*	*	*
Mexico	1913	1913	*	*	*	*	*	*	*	*	*
United States	1893	1879	1889	1879	1909	1913	1892	1911	*	*	*
	(1911)	(1911)	(1912)	(1912)				(1914)			

Sources: See appendix.

Notes: *Indicates did not enact regulation. V stands for a voluntary scheme. Values in parentheses for U.S. are the dates when the ten largest states adopted law.

Table 1.3. Dimensions of labor legislation

| | FACTORY INSPECTION 1914 | | NIGHT REST FOR WOMEN (HOURS) | | MINIMUM AGE (YEAR) | | AGE RESTRICTION NIGHT LABOR WOMEN (YEARS) | ACCIDENT INSURANCE cost as share of wages (%) |
	Inspectors	Workers ('000)/ inspectors	1910	1919	c1900	1919	1910	1910
Austria	80	8.75	11	11	14	14	18	0.72
Belgium	33	12.12	8	11	12	14	21	3.10
Bulgaria			8	9		12		
Denmark	75	5.33		11	10	14	18	0.75
Finland	30	8.63		11				
France	121	6.61	9	11	13	13	18	2.10
Germany	279	10.75	9	11	13	14	18	1.08
Hungary	43		9	11	12	12	16	
Italy	29	51.72	9	11	9	12		1.95
Netherlands	92	4.35	10	11	12	13	16	
Norway	35	4.40	11	11	12	14	18	1.63
Portugal			8	11	10	12	21	
Russia	201	11.51	8	11	12	12	15	1.36
Spain	61	6.56	8	11	10	10	14	1.50
Sweden	45	4.44	11	11	12	13	18	1.21
Switzerland	20	5.00	10	11	14	13	18	

							all	
United Kingdom	206	12.14	12	12	11	14	all	0.73
Argentina						10		
Australia	50	6.72	12	12	14	14	18	
Canada	58	8.62	12	12	14	14	18	
Mexico						12		
United States	114	10.53	14	14	14	14	16	1.56

Sources and notes: See appendix for details. Employer compensation for accidents as share of wage bill.

specifics of restrictions on women's night work, age limits for children, and the actual contributions employers paid out for accident insurance (measured as a percentage of the wage bill). Despite different legal frameworks and administrative practices, and even before pressures to harmonize labor regulations which can be traced to the establishment of the International Labour Organization in 1919, dispersion across these dimensions was remarkably small—a testament to the forces of convergence in policy that I will describe below. There is only one obvious outlier in the table: the factory inspectorate in Italy was poorly staffed, a finding that is entirely consistent with contemporary observation and gives credence to other values in the table.

Were these laws observed? In several countries, factory inspection was in place from an early date. In Britain, institutional and class actors developed vested interests to defend the factory laws (Fuchs 2001)—a body of legislation that Marx (1981, 416) referred to as the Magna Carta of the industrial revolution. In Germany, which hired 25 percent more superintendents than the U.K., inspection was conceived as a substitute for extensive factory regulation. In many countries, accident insurance was critical in promoting compliance.[23] Since governments had guaranteed the funds of private insurers, or had set up their own insurance plans, they had an incentive to monitor working conditions closely. States received the compliance of employers who did not want to see their premiums rise and sought an official seal of approval as enterprises offering good working conditions.[24]

Appealing to national stereotypes, surviving vignettes on the diligence of inspectors and government officials need to be treated with circumspection. Typically, Canadian inspectors used mediation and exhortation to ensure compliance (Webber 1995, 169). In Germany, enforcement was under the jurisdiction of the police (Price 1923, 7). Russian inspectors, according to one study (Volodine 2007), were fair and diligent and surprisingly numerous. Franz Kafka's career summarizes the ambiguity of evidence on diligence. As an administrator for the Austro-Hungarian accident compensation program, he managed to fulfill his obligations before lunch, leaving the rest of the day for his writing.

Putting aside these claims, compliance ultimately depended on whether or not there was widespread acceptance of the new social norm of regulation. Edward Glaeser and Andrei Schleifer (2003, 408) argued the attitudes evolved when it became too costly to go before the courts to enforce individual and complex contracts between firms and workers. As the monetary value of settlements rose, liable parties had an incentive to subvert justice and to corrupt judges and officials. Legislation was intended to put an end to these abuses. In contrast to court decisions, regulatory systems handed out small fines. They functioned relatively well since as more laws appeared on the books, the probability of detection rose. National authorities could also draw on external support. If my claim that the labor compact was an international project is close to the mark, countries had an interest overseeing whether or not their trading partners maintained their commitments. The threat of sanctions or the promise of increased market access incited countries to ensure that the laws were observed.

THE *ODD COUPLE*: ORGANIZATION

Inspired by Vandervelde, I divide my study in two parts: Part 1 asks how globalization caused the labor compact, and Part 2 how the labor compact caused trade. The subject is addressed thematically, drawing on large international datasets I have collected on working conditions and labor market outcomes. Many other comparative histories limit their reach to the club of OECD countries, a type of sample selection bias. My focus provides a comprehensive and global history of the welfare state that consists of 'successes' and 'failures'—across three continents—whose histories were interdependent.

The welfare states of Belgium, Canada, and Brazil, which I have selected to study in detail, were typical of the labor compacts that had emerged in 'small' open economies in labor-abundant Europe, land-rich regions of recent settlement, and New World countries harboring enclaves of cheap labor. Their experiences cast light on the roles of domestic and external forces in the adoption of the labor compact not evident in existing studies of large and rich countries. Certainly, in Europe and regions of new settlement, other policy outcomes were possible. For instance, Australia had initially a more extensive safety net than Canada, and Germany's welfare state had different origins than that of Europe's smaller countries. Disparities in social policy persisted within regions into the twentieth century. Nonetheless, by 1914, the social models of Europe and its offshoots had diverged.

Like other areas in Latin America, Brazil was a latecomer to labor regulation, its first substantial laws being adopted in the interwar period. The standard explanation of the region's failure to expand regulation and social spending beyond a select group of clients has privileged domestic politics (Haggard and Kaufman 2008). But the Brazil case is informative precisely because it showcases the role of external markets, or better the lack thereof, in the development of the welfare state. While Belgium established the labor compact in a world of expanding trade, the binding constraint in Brazil was the collapse in world markets. Timing may not have been everything in establishing the welfare state, but almost.

Chapter 2 introduces the conceptual framework I use to study the adoption and spread of the labor compact in an interdependent world. In the spirit of models of open economy politics, domestic (demand) and external (supply) factors were entangled. On the demand side, the decline in trade costs ought to have made the labor compact redundant, since the extension of markets operated as an insurance mechanism. But globalization had not delivered the gains that, in theory, it promised. Everywhere, labor clamored for better working conditions and social entitlements in an attempt to reduce income and employment uncertainty. This cannot be a complete account of the rise of the regulatory state, however. Individual countries were hard-pressed to uphold their regulatory environments, since capital mobility had the potential of initiating a downward spiral in social policy. As it happens, the evidence points in the other direction. On the supply side, states acquiesced to pressures emanating from trading partners to harmonize regulatory environments. If states failed to emulate the superior labor regulations of their important partners, they were vulnerable to embargos and sanctions on their specialized exports. These forces were stronger in the Old World because of the importance of trade in differentiated and brand items in the region. Trade in primary resources was resistant to these pressures. International trade, therefore, had an asymmetric effect on the rise of the labor compact.

Next, I examine demand and supply in more detail. Chapter 3 compares the rise of the labor compact in Belgium and its relative absence in Canada. The labor compact was designed to provide insurance against the dislocation and volatility of the new world order. The trouble was that the adoption of stabilization programs was not assured, even if the franchise was large or if mobilization for greater democratic participation was tied to the demand for labor legislation. Labor required partners to see through the reform agenda (Rueschemeyer, Stephens, and Stephens 1992). Globalization, itself, promoted coalition building because, by reconfiguring the alignment of political forces, social actors with different interests emerged and shaped commercial and social policy. In the Old World, labor used strategically its endorsement of free trade as a lever to gain a better labor compact, Vandervelde's Belgium being the template of the reform process. Politically isolated, Canadian workers failed to realize demands for regulation and shifted resources to restricting immigration instead.

I contrast the success and failures of international and bilateral accords to harmonize regulation in chapter 4. Transnational movements of social reformers actively disseminated the ideas behind and models of labor regulation, but they made recommendations only. Bilateral labor accords were more successful since they tied the adoption of labor regulation to guarantees of market access. A country that unilaterally tightened its labor regulation imposed a cost upon itself. But if a trading partner lowered tariffs or gave the country's exports preferential treatment it would be more inclined to adopt regulation. These accords originated as a response to the cross-border movement of workers, which, contemporaries observed, had the potential to undercut social policy. To safeguard their side of the labor compact, states were compelled to extend benefits to migrant workers. In exchange, foreign countries agreed to raise their own standards, thereby conserving market access of commercial partners. In this fashion, labor standards before 1914 spread in the absence of a centralized authority. The greater the trade between countries, the more likely the pair had comparable regulatory environments.

But if global markets promoted the adoption of social policy, they were also affected by it, and, in Part 2 of the book, I evaluate the effects of the labor compact on trade. I begin with an assessment of the effects of labor regulation on wages and hours of work in chapter 5. The labor compact had teeth in the Old World, but small or no bite in the richer countries of the New World. The findings deepen the debate between globalization optimists and pessimists. I decompose inequality into between and within components. Between the Old and the rich New World, inequality, broadly defined to include leisure, narrowed. Within countries, the labor compact promoted egalitarianism, and in Europe wage differentials between skill groups and between women and men grew smaller. In the rich New World, changes in hours of work were relatively unimportant and inequality persisted, and perhaps intensified, in the wake of globalization. The labor-abundant regions of Brazil prove to be an exception, regulation in the Southern Cone in the 1920s having the same effects on wage inequality as in labor-abundant Europe.

In chapter 6, I study how the labor compact shifted sources of comparative advantage. The increase in labor costs induced firms to replace machinery and equipment for workers, and firms emerged as better exporters. Here the comparison between Belgium and Brazil is telling. In response to regulation, Belgian companies developed new product lines that they sold to an expanding number of destinations. The labor compact was certainly not a drag on growth. The upward pressure on labor costs in Brazil paralleled developments in the Old World. As elsewhere, firms responded by substituting capital for labor and shifted toward higher value items. But the international landscape had changed. Foreign outlets were closing down, and firms could only dump their new items on home markets. The association between the extension of the market and productivity enhancements was weak in Latin America. As a result, Brazil's welfare state was piecemeal at best.

In chapter 7, I bring the labor compact up to the present. I consider economists' claims that worktimes diverged between Europe and the rest of the world after 1970, or later. A common explanation is that Europeans work less because they are taxed more, a result of the social model they have come to enjoy. I challenge this view. Hours of work declined more rapidly in the Old World than New well before the introduction of modern tax schedules. Pursuing the findings of the previous chapter on the wage effects of the labor compact, I find that inequality was the main driver of long hours over the long twentieth century. As the distribution of income widened, North Americans toiled long hours since the reward was great. Egalitarian Europe had more regulated labor markets and the gains of long hours were limited. Even before the war, Europeans had twice as many vacation days as North Americans. The long-term trends are evidence of the indelible legacy of the labor compact.

By 1914, globalization had driven a wedge between Old and New World social models. The relation between markets and welfare states was certainly more complex than Polanyi and others imagined. Welfare states did not necessarily rise in opposition to markets. If certain countries, like Canada, opted for protectionism and immigration restrictions, elsewhere, as in Belgium, workers and liberals chose free trade and labor regulation. Still others embraced a hybrid, combining, as in Brazil, isolation and regulation.

Impressions to the contrary, one would be mistaken to read this book as a panglossian history of the European welfare state. A cogent critique of the European model is that inequality has been reduced at the expense of higher tax rates that, in turn, have cut back the supply of labor in the form of lower effort and reduced participation rates. There are other social policies that produce lower levels of unemployment. This is a choice Europeans have made, and the evidence on preferences toward hours of work that I introduce points to this possibility. Another explanation is that the labor compact was the outcome of mere historical contingency defined by the particular social, economic, and political context of Europe's belle époque. Regardless of these claims, it does not follow that the labor compact was and remains the privilege of the Old World. The prospect that the gains of globalization can be redistributed more equitably provides an alternative roadmap for policy across time and space.

Part One

How Globalization Caused the Labor Compact

CHALLENGE AND RESPONSE

Canada will adopt climate-change regulations comparable to those of the United States—including new rules for oil sands producers and refiners—to avoid punitive 'green' tariffs. The Canadian environmental minister vowed to be as tough on Canadian industry as the U.S. government is on its big emitters. He suggested that Canada would have little choice but to match the U.S. measures, despite resistance from Alberta, which worries that costly new regulations would impede development.

—The Globe and Mail, *July 1, 2009, B3.*

THE CONCEPTUAL FRAMEWORK

The contrast between 1870 and 1914 was stark.[1] In 1870, labor protection was scarce; by 1914 it was common in the Old World and uneven in the New. Yet, during these decades degrees of openness actually increased. How can we square globalization and the rise of social protection?

The well-rehearsed response is that labor laws were the stepchild of development, "the consequences," Stanley Engerman (2003, 60) wrote, "of higher national income, with accompanying changing preferences regarding work time and work arrangements as income rose." In the power resources model, the timing of adoption is tied to the rise of organized labor and the extension of the franchise. Curiously, while Lindert (2004) and others (Aidt, Dutta, and Loukoianova 2006) have found a relation between income and voter turnout and social spending, the basic data reveal only a weak correspondence between these key determinants and the adoption of labor laws. Among Old World countries, the dispersion of income was large, as was voter turnout, but even the poorest and least democratic countries, Bulgaria, Italy, Portugal, Russia, and Spain, had some laws on the books. In the New World, Canada was relatively wealthy and had a large male electorate, but it was a laggard compared to Europe, and Mexico after the revolution had pretty much the same level of regulation (Bortz 2000; Gómez-Galvarriato 1999).

The calendar of adoption was also inconsistent with the income and voice model. Germany, Switzerland, and the United Kingdom were early movers. But, beginning in the 1880s, no obvious leader emerged and any systematic ordering in laws adopted is difficult to detect.[2] Even the early adopters were followers. Germany was ahead in social entitlements, like accident insurance, but it introduced restrictions on women's work a decade later; the U.K. was an innovator in factory inspection and protection of women, but a laggard in regulating child labor; an early mover, Switzerland adopted limits on women's work only after its continental neighbors.

Figure 2.1 presents a competing perspective on the spread of labor laws showcasing their diffusion over a narrow time frame. The adoption of minimum age legislation of 12 years traces a classic S-shaped logistic curve, a pattern representative of other laws in table 1.2, and similar to that which has been documented for the diffusion of democracy and economic and social policies, from Keynesianism to neo-liberalism, across a range of countries in the late twentieth century (Simmons, Dobbin, and Garret 2008). The first movers behind age limits, Germany and Switzerland, were decidedly early. For this precocious club, regulation may have had different origins than for countries in the middle years. This next phase, which had no obvious leader, saw the bulk of adoptions in small and large, and poor and rich countries alike. In the last period, adoptions leveled off and were restricted to latecomers in the periphery. The pattern of diffusion puts paid to the widely held view of labor regulation as a chapter in national history. My claim is that, beginning in the 1870s, pressures emanating from international markets were part of the story.

This chapter introduces a framework to study the effects of domestic and foreign factors on the adoption of labor laws.[3] The standard approach of policy formation in an open economy begins with the local interests of key protagonists, firms, sectors, or factors of production, whose preferences toward policy are defined by their location relative to others in the international economy; in the next phase, domestic institutions and politicians, whose objective may be to maximize support, broker competing interests and determine policy; in the final stage, the state, as if it were a unitary actor, brings these outcomes to the international level. My view, which is in the spirit of studies in "open economy politics," captures the likelihood that causality also runs in the other direction, from

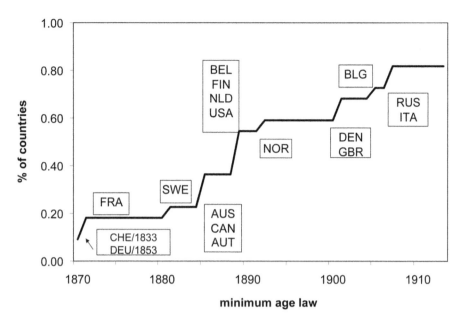

Figure 2.1. International diffusion of minimum age law, 1870–1914
Dates of adoption from table 1.2. Minimum age is 12 years. Adapted from
Huberman and Meissner (2010).

international institutions and pressures to domestic interests.[4] In this case, states do not take domestic and foreign interests as given, because the international context structures bargaining and affects outcomes relevant to constituents. Since states must contend with a complex and shifting amalgam of interests, they are anything but unitary actors. Robert Putnam (1988, 427) put the problem simply: "Domestic politics and international relations are somehow often entangled. It is fruitless to debate whether domestic politics really determine international relations or the reverse. The answer to that question is clearly both sometimes."

HOW LABOR PERCEIVED GLOBALIZATION

The specter of international competition haunted labor in the first wave of globalization. The evolving fortunes of cotton textiles, the flagship global industry, provide a window on the risks an average worker confronted, since trade was based on comparative advantage and product differentiation.[5] Two spinning technologies were in use by the 1870s, rings (continuous) and mules (intermittent).

The choice of technique mapped loosely onto the supplies of labor and raw cotton. Rings were more adept in the manufacture of coarse grades, or low numbers, and where there was an abundant supply of cheap labor and long-staple cotton; they were often found in emerging economies. Mules produced yarns of various fineness mixing different varieties of raw cottons and lengths, and were most often located in regions like the U.K. with an established history of spinning, including a complement of skilled spinners.[6] Until the last quarter of the century, markets for the products of these two technologies had small overlap.

The U.K. industry benefited from economies of scale connected to the agglomeration of skilled labor, merchants, bankers, insurance agents, and satellite industries collected in Lancashire. Into the 1880s, if not later, the British maintained their export share on the continent and elsewhere, selling brand items at both low and high ends. European producers, like those in France and Germany, were not perceived as a threat to the British, although they had begun exploiting market niches for their own specialty items, a trend that gathered momentum in the decades before 1914 (Brown 1995). Based on trade patterns circa 1870, world distribution of cotton textile manufacture was not pinned down by labor abundance exclusively, since countries with comparable factor intensities exchanged different varieties of yarn. Operating mules, France and Germany had similar wages, energy, and material costs, and they exchanged specialty items with each other. Trade of this sort enabled producers to spread fixed costs over larger markets. Under these strict conditions, the challenge of foreign competition based on low wages was of no consequence.

Beginning in the 1880s, low-wage producers began to cast a long-term shadow on industry in the European core. Ring and mule spinning technologies improved, enabling greater overlap and flexibility in types of yarn spun. Although quality was a continuous source of contention, these near-goods were price competitive, and producers, from Spain to Japan, began to encroach on markets previously beyond reach (Saxonhouse and Wright 2004, 2010). For instance, Brazil was able to capture most of its home market by the early twentieth century. With the fall in transport costs, factor abundance increasingly had a role in the location of the industry. This wave of competition was supported by machinery exports from Lancashire and the complementary displacement of British engineers, millwrights, and foremen around the world. In Brazil, mechanics sent by British machine makers erected most of the spinning and weaving equipment, and the early mills operated under foreign supervision (Clark 1910, 46–48).

Figure 2.2 depicts what an industrial worker in Lancashire perceived of international competition. To show this, I replicate Krugman's (2008) study of late

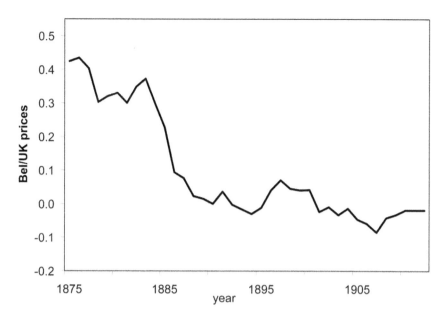

Figure 2.2. Belgian and U.K. export prices, 1870–1914
Belgian series is for no. 20 (Van Houtte 1949, 269–71); U.K., no. 32 (Jewkes and
Gray 1935, 211). Log prices centered on 1900 = 0.

twentieth-century Chinese imports to the U.S., using Belgian and British
prices one hundred years earlier. I assume that Belgium exported labor-
intensive items, while the U.K. exported relatively skill-intensive goods; the ratio of prices should provide a measure of the price of labor-intensive goods
workers in advanced countries confronted.[7] The figure gives the log of the ratio
of prices of Belgian coarse yarn imports to the price of British yarn exports,
normalized so that 1900 = 0.[8] Three phases can be identified. Initially, import
prices were high and rising, a finding consistent with the observation of the
U.K. trade representative in Ghent that Lancashire "manufacturers have nothing
to fear from their rivals in Belgium" (UK PP 1871, 8, 24). In the mid 1880s, and
lasting until the late 1890s, there was a sharp decline in prices of labor-intensive
imports, a trend that was not lost on British textile operatives of coarse fabrics.
Belgium's entry in Lancashire's home market was based on low wages, long
hours, and "industriousness" (UK PP 1893–94, 193). Belgium was no Asian tiger,
but it had access to the latest vintages of technology and imported managerial
talent. In the third period, from 1895 on, the price ratio declined at a slower
pace. I will argue that adoption of labor regulation in the century's last decade

in Belgium and on the continent ushered in new trade patterns. But this is getting ahead of my story. The bottom line is that for a good part of the period, Lancashire had grounds to raise concern about the harm of cheap foreign imports to its livelihood.

SOURCES OF VOLATILITY AND EARLY RESPONSES

In theory, the expansion in international trade acted as an insurance mechanism because of increased specialization and market size. But as trade costs fell, employers and consumers exchanged foreign labor and resources for domestic ones, either by investing overseas or by importing products made or grown abroad. In markets where domestic and foreign goods were close substitutes, international competition made the demand for labor very responsive to changes in its price, with the result that shocks in labor demand generated much greater fluctuations in both earnings and hours worked than had appeared in the closed economy of the first half of the century (Rodrik 1997, 19–20).

In cases where exports and imports were imperfect substitutes, the benefits of specialization may have outstripped the downside effects of trade on wages. But there was a drawback to intra-industry trade. Foreign outlets were notoriously fickle, prices and wages responding to sudden and unanticipated changes in tastes, commercial policy, or the entry of new rivals. For highly differentiated goods, like the case of Swiss cheese which I discuss later, trade wars had detrimental consequences for labor markets. If earnings in the tradable sector deviated in any way from the market wage, because, say, of collective bargaining, sizeable changes in pay resulted.[9]

In markets for brand goods, unfair trade practices and outsourcing magnified degrees of risk. Unfair competition emerged when big countries discriminated between home and foreign markets. Providing a textbook study, Belgian woolen manufacturers accused German firms of pricing exports lower than identical goods sold in their home market—a practice referred to as *le dumping*. Since their domestic market was small, the Belgians had no means of reciprocating (Mahaim 1905). The re-export trade, a type of outsourcing, exposed workers' sense of vulnerability, because the labor supply available to capital was effectively increased. Ghent was a hub of the international textile trade. Fine flax was sent to England and returned for finishing; wool yarn was exported to Saxony, mixed with cotton, and subsequently delivered to Scotland.[10] As intermediate goods production shifted abroad, demand for labor shrank at home.

Large and unanticipated shocks in demand were manifested in terms of trade fluctuations (Rodrik 1997).[11] Figure 2.3 portrays the relation between

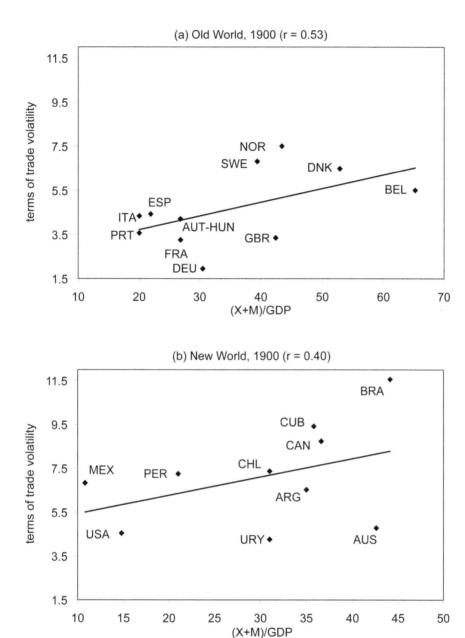

Figure 2.3. Trade openness and volatility, 1900
Trade from table 1.1. Volatility defined as changes in terms of trade and measured
as the decadal standard deviation from trend taken from Blattman, Hwang,
and Williamson (2007).

openness, measured by the trade content of GDP, and uncertainty, represented by the variation in terms of trade. I have separated the New and Old World because volatility in the export prices of resources was of a different order of magnitude.[12] Nonetheless, regardless of the type of trade, instability rose everywhere as economies became more open. The period's gold standard shifted the burden of trade shocks onto wages. Given fixed exchange rates, when demand and prices contracted, wages had to be cut (Frieden 2006, 121). Evidently, the expansion of markets did not necessarily serve as an insurance mechanism and source of income stability.

The early responses to rising insecurity depended on customary forms of assistance. But these measures proved ineffectual or even counterproductive in the new world order. Expenditures on poor relief were actually declining in Europe from 1830 on (Lindert 2004). Anyway, poor relief provided inadequate benefits for short spells; it was not organized to meet the demands of agricultural laborers displaced by imports of cheap grain and relocating en masse to cities. The gold standard and the dominant liberal ideology of the period restricted states' use of deficit spending to subsidize and enlarge existing social programs. A handful of paternalist employers may have eased the pain caused by unanticipated changes in demand, but their strategies tied workers down to specific sectors and regions—competition in export markets depended on the flexibility and mobility of workers and firms.

Labor mobility, in principle, moderated the effects of trade shocks on wages and employment. Short-distance migration was a customary response to job loss and as transport costs collapsed regions of new settlement became accessible to millions of Europeans. But while migration addressed the harm caused by idiosyncratic shocks, it did not necessarily eliminate the distress of industry-wide shocks. In the manufacturing sector of the New World, immigrants were not isolated from the aftershocks of volatile primary products prices. In Europe's export industries, migrant workers were susceptible to the general misery of trade wars; in fact immigration augmented the likelihood of conflict over markets. It may have been the case that individual immigrants accepted higher levels of risk and preferred less state intervention than those they had left behind.[13] But if immigration had any negative effects on wage levels, the livelihoods of all workers in receiving countries suffered, and widespread demand for some form of support would have ensued.[14] Social policy was a collective, not an individual choice.

Confronted by the failure of customary means of assistance to contain the uncertainty and insecurity of the first great wave of globalization, labor and social reformers proposed new measures to stabilize wages and employment.

These were the domestic origins of the labor compact. Before examining more closely the determinants behind its adoption, in the next section I discuss how business responded to labor's demands.

CAPITAL'S QUANDARY

Summers (2008) contrasted capital's attitude toward labor in the closed and open economies of 1950 and 2000. In the postwar period, business had a huge stake in the quality of the national workforce and infrastructure because profits hinged upon it; in the current wave of globalization, firms have abandoned the concept of workers as stakeholders, because they can combine more easily capital with lower-priced labor elsewhere. Companies in the latest wave have been prone to simply pack up and leave or outsource parts of production. Was 1900 closer to 1950 or 2000?

The evidence is mixed. Capital mobility, encouraged and safeguarded by the gold standard, was certainly on the rise in the decades before 1914 (Obstfeld and Taylor 2004).[15] Capital flows made economies interdependent, regardless of the trade content of GDP. Initially, investment in railways and other infrastructure projects in resource-exporting regions bulked large, but as financial markets developed, a greater share of foreign investment was directed to manufacturing interests. Calling on an international mix of capital and labor, investments in large units of more than 1,000 workers served markets in Europe and beyond (Hannah 2008). For instance, mining and steel companies based in Germany sought to take advantage of the lower wages and poorer working conditions in Belgium (Strikwerda 1997); in textiles, the International Trade Union Congress in 1886 condemned the "action of certain English capitalists" who, in the wake of labor unrest in Lancashire, moved plant and equipment to France (Potter 1910, 351).[16]

As long as capital was mobile, labor could not count on its support for reform. Challenged by rivals operating in more 'favorable' regulatory environments, capital exploited the exit threat. Was this mere rhetoric or did regulation actually bite into profits? There was a bit of both. Capital made the most of its opposition to reform, warning against a slippery slope and large-scale changes in the distribution in income. But the disadvantages of an uneven playing field were real. Consider the effects of unforeseen changes in the regulatory environment on the balance sheet of a representative cotton textile mill in Alsace-Loraine. After it passed from French to German authority in 1871, the mill used identical equipment and workers, and incurred the same energy, raw material, and wage costs. However, France operated its factories for one hour per day more. When the mill became German, its manufacturing costs increased by 10 percent, and profits fell by the same order of magnitude.[17]

Putting aside these estimates, any constraints on labor contracts resulted in idle plant, thereby lowering the marginal efficiency of capital and causing a misallocation of resources. Certain Alsatian manufacturers petitioned Berlin for an exemption from German law (Hagemann 2001, 159); other producers relocated their plants back to France (Clapham 1961, 246). Drawing on this lesson, Bismarck was reluctant to extend the labor compact beyond social entitlements. If states acquiesced to labor's demands, the response would be capital flight. Isaac Hourwich (1911, 640), a prominent twentieth-century observer of U.S. social policy, summarized capital's quandary:

> It must be remembered that capital is international: production is advanced by such rapid strides in the United States because capital has had a sufficient supply of labor. If an artificial scarcity of labor were created resulting in a rise of wages that could cut down the profits below the average of other countries, more American capital would seek investment abroad. American goods produced by better paid American labor could not compete in the world's markets with the products of Mexican or Siberian labor directed by American capital.

So much for the claim that pits employers and their representatives against workers and social activists. A parallel and equally compelling narrative is that competitive forces pressured firms to develop 'stakeholders' (Baldwin 1990; Iversen 2005; Swenson 2002). Isabela Mares (2003) provides the most complete account of this view. She maintains that as technology became more complex firms needed to make continuous investments in workers and develop strategies to retain them. Business would not resist the new social programs because they effectively tied workers to firms, and if their cost was spread widely—or if it could be shifted entirely onto agricultural interests—the burden would be small relative to the benefits. Comparing experiences in the European core, Mares concluded that the introduction and the design of the welfare state depended on the local 'risk' environment, by which she meant the size of firms, investments in equipment, and dependence on skilled labor. If all countries in the industrial core went through a similar process, levels of regulation would increase everywhere. In this scenario, foreign investment, counterintuitively, promoted the diffusion of labor laws.

The two faces of capital can be reconciled. In the short run, capital could not abandon its plant and equipment.[18] In the near term, firms were resigned to the new laws. Over time, capital regained its bargaining power, if not its dominance. In order to equalize profits to be earned at home and abroad, companies adapted to the labor compact, enhancing investments in physical and human capital, or they closed down and shifted operations abroad. To be sure, resistance to the labor compact was weaker (and adaptation smoother) the lower the labor force participation of women, the higher the school attendance of children, and the smaller the degree of substitution between domestic and foreign trade.[19] Certain employers may have endorsed regulation in order to drive out domestic competitors. A common ground for cross-class coalitions was therefore not improbable, even if capital and labor remained adversaries. Still, coalition building was not guaranteed since the partners had to demonstrate commitments to each other along multiple dimensions of social and commercial policies. In the Old World, labor was abundant and the coalition was built around a shared interest in free trade; in the New, labor was scarce and the two antagonists overlapped on protectionism. In chapter 3, I take up this theme further.

THE DEMAND SIDE: A PRELIMINARY ANALYSIS

The labor compact was conceived with the dual objective of satisfying domestic concerns related to the structural change and the needs of workers in the new global order. The conventional view of the welfare state regards big and rich countries, Germany and the U.K., as role models. This select group pioneered state-wide programs, like social insurance, which they could fund more easily than smaller and poorer European states resigned to less costly regulation, like factory inspection (Mulligan and Shleifer 2004). The demands of labor in export- and import-competing sectors coincided with the domestic reform movement for better conditions, but workers confronting global competition had their own concerns. Such needs were more pronounced in small countries because they traded more than larger ones. In this section, I present preliminary evidence of the separate and distinct role of trade on the origins of the welfare state.

To begin, I divide the legislation in table 1.2 into three components: factory legislation and inspection, laws restricting the supply of children and women, and social entitlements. In many countries, the demand for early factory legislation had its origins in the decades before the expansion of trade and was related to long-term structural change, the general movement of workers out of agriculture into full-time industrial activities. This demand, as I discussed in chapter 1, was joined to calls to protect the most vulnerable laborers.

Restrictions on children's and women's labor met concerns of workers in all sectors of activity. At the most basic level, these regulations provided insurance because they reduced total labor input, and, as a result, they raised wages at the lower end of the distribution relative to the average.[20] As wage distributions compressed, workers had a built-in guarantee their welfare would not fall below some minimum level.[21] In the face of uncertain markets and shocks in demand, state regulation guaranteed workers that their entitlements to job conditions and their station in the wage distribution were transferable across firms and sectors. Increased mobility meant that workers shared in the gains of trade and were, as a result, prepared to make investments in skill.

Social entitlements benefited all workers, but they had special resonance in tradable sectors. Pensions reduced lifetime uncertainty about the flow of income and smoothed consumption expenditure. The adoption of accident insurance provided firms and workers an incentive to upgrade skills. But external exposure had an independent influence on demand. Social insurance served as a direct policy response compensating workers relocating across sectors because of import competition, caused, say, by cheap grain imports in the Old World and cheap manufacturing goods in the New. We would expect these types of programs to be prevalent in small countries since they were more open than larger ones.

Table 2.1 reports regression results on the determinants of policy outcome. I am interested in the relative importance of risk factors: the hazards associated with broader structural change and the insecurity induced by trade forces.[22] To be clear, these risk factors operated through domestic channels. I leave the effects of foreign entanglements to the second half of this chapter. The dependent variable is the total number of pieces of legislation each country adopted from 1880 on, using dates in table 1.2. I examine the determinants of the labor compact in model 1 and then of its sub-components: factory legislation and inspection (model 2); children's and women's work (model 3); social entitlements (model 4). The percentage of agriculture in GDP is a proxy for long-run development, while export shares and terms of trade volatility stand in for the risks of openness: the flatness of and fluctuations in the demand curve respectively. Regardless of the source of demand, I would expect that the number of laws adopted was dependent on voter turnout, defined as the ratio of persons actually voting to the adult population (of the relevant enfranchised gender). I have included GDP and population to appraise different claims on the relation between country wealth and size and the various components of the labor compact. Education levels stand in for firms' investments in human and physical capital, along the lines suggested by Mares. Finally, the regressions include controls for year and country.

Consider the effects of the usual suspects: structural change, wealth, population size, and voter turnout. Across models, with the exception of social entitle-

Table 2.1. Determinants of the labor compact, 1870–1914

	MODEL 1 All Labor Standards			MODEL 2 Factory Conditions			MODEL 3 Regulation on Child and Women Labor			MODEL 4 Social Insurance		
	(1)	(2)	(3)	(4)	(5)	(6)	(7)	(8)	(9)	(10)	(11)	(12)
Export share of GDP	7.419	6.918	2.501	1.601*	1.488	0.145	5.818	5.430	2.355	11.778	11.746	12.011
	(1.89)***	(1.84)***	(2.40)	(0.92)	(0.91)	(1.21)	(1.48)***	(1.44)***	(1.85)	(1.14)***	(1.14)***	(1.52)***
Turnout		0.095	0.109		0.019	0.034		0.076	0.074		-0.008	-0.008
		(0.03)***	(0.03)***		(0.01)	(0.01)**		(0.02)***	(0.02)***		(0.02)	(0.02)
Share of labor in agriculture		-5.969	-5.920		-1.322	-0.746		-4.646	-5.175		-0.252	0.149
		(1.07)***	(1.09)***		(0.53)**	(0.55)		(0.84)***	(0.83)***		(0.66)	(0.69)
Terms of trade volatility			-7.112			-0.117			-6.995			-0.649
			(2.67)**			(1.35)			(2.05)***			(1.69)
Terms of trade volatility x export's share			50.05			-5.140			41.907			23.85
			(24.15)**			(12.19)			(18.57)**			(15.30)**
ln (Population)	1.070	1.030	0.417	0.334	0.328	0.133	0.736	0.701	0.284	-2.953	-2.934	-2.559
	(0.69)	(0.67)	(0.68)	(0.34)	(0.34)	(0.35)	(0.54)	(0.53)	(0.53)	(0.42)***	(0.42)***	(0.43)***

(continued)

Table 2.1. continued

	MODEL 1 All Labor Standards			MODEL 2 Factory Conditions			MODEL 3 Regulation of Child and Women Labor			MODEL 4 Social Insurance		
	(1)	(2)	(3)	(4)	(5)	(6)	(7)	(8)	(9)	(10)	(11)	(12)
ln (GDP)	−1.523	−1.394	−0.836	−0.342	−0.319	−0.087	−1.181	−1.075	−0.749	−0.144	−0.172	−0.396
	(0.44)***	(0.43)**	(0.45)*	(0.21)	(0.22)	(0.23)	(0.34)***	(0.34)**	(0.35)**	(0.26)	(0.27)	(0.28)
Primary and secondary school enrollment	−12.836	−11.302	−15.095	−5.193	−4.836	−6.717	−7.642	−6.465	−8.378	9.769	9.938	9.670
	(2.87)***	(2.83)***	(2.98)***	(1.39)***	(1.41)***	(1.50)***	(2.24)***	(2.21)**	(2.29)***	(1.73)***	(1.76)***	(1.89)***
constant	6.447	8.152	9.529	1.049	1.452	1.058	5.398	6.700	8.472	25.947	26.171	25.233
	(3.50)*	(3.46)**	(3.51)**	(1.70)	(1.72)	(1.77)	(2.74)**	(2.71)**	(2.70)**	(2.11)***	(2.15)***	(2.22)***
Observations	792	792	704	792	792	704	792	792	704	792	792	704
Within R-Squared	0.725	0.741	0.728	0.549	0.554	0.530	0.666	0.686	0.683	0.653	0.653	0.631

Sources: Trade data from table 1.1; GDP and population from Maddison (1995, 2001); labor force and turnout from Mitchell (1981) and Lindert (2004); terms of trade volatility measured as the decadal standard deviation from trend in Blattman, Hwang, and Williamson (2007).

Notes: The dependent variable is the sum of laws adopted. Population and GDP are log values. All regressions include year and country dummies. OLS estimates. Robust standard errors in brackets. *significant at 10%; **significant at 5%; ***significant at 1%.

ments, the number of laws adopted increased as the size of the agricultural sector shrank and voter turnout grew. Size and wealth (columns 4–9) had no effect on factory laws and limits on labor supply. GDP may perform poorly because of correlation with other determinants, but the weak relation between income and the labor compact also shows up in other specifications I discuss later in this chapter.[23] Small countries (columns 10–12) were more likely to adopt social insurance. The number of social entitlements was also related to levels of education. At least for this component, capital was labor's ally.

Trade had a discernible imprint on the number and type of laws adopted.[24] While voter turnout, structural change, and the degree of openness rendered limits on children's and women's work more likely (columns 7–9), trade mattered exclusively in the case of social entitlements (columns 10–12). Interestingly, the instability of export demand captured in terms of trade volatility had a negative effect on adoption. One interpretation is that price volatility was a proxy for region, the New World generally having a weaker labor compact than the Old. However, the coefficient for price shocks interacted with export share is positive and significant, with the exception of model 2, a result Rodrik (1998) found for the current wave of globalization.

Overall, the results indicate that trade had a separate effect on the labor compact and its subcomponents. Small countries were more exposed to international forces than larger states, and the demand for social insurance overrode the fact that they were often poorer. The contrast between Denmark and Germany is informative. In the supposedly classic example of the rise of the welfare state, Bismarck introduced social legislation to appease labor—and not because of trade exposure. Germany had considerable tariffs from the 1870s on, but the bulk of excise taxes and custom revenues were in the hands of individual states (Hennock 2007, 342). The incidence of social policy fell heavily on workers themselves (Khoudour-Castéras 2008).

The Danish labor compact seems closer to the more idealized European model and from an early date (Lindert 2004). As in Germany, factory regulation was relatively weak, but the similarities ended here. A small and open economy, Denmark favored social insurance to subsidize labor relocation from contracting to expanding sectors. Indirect taxes funded redistributive programs, the incidence of which fell on urban workers whose wages were rising (Baldwin 1990, 63–64).[25] Denmark, it should be added, resisted the protectionist backlash of the period.

Table 2.1 provides evidence that trade mattered, but it does not address the process behind adoption. A cross-class coalition, as Mares claimed, was not unlikely, however. For instance, in the case of social entitlements the level of education was a significant and positive factor, but voter turnout was exceptionally unimportant.

The inference is that labor had the potential support of capital, at least for part of the labor compact. More problematically, table 2.1 gives the domestic or demand side view only. There were alternative sources of the labor compact, including the social policies of neighbors and trading partners. In the next section, I examine the international transmission mechanism of the labor compact.

OPEN ECONOMY POLITICS

In today's global economy, the claim is (Bartolini and Drazen 1997; Swank 2006) that national authorities care what social and economic policies get adopted elsewhere, because they want to keep exports competitive, contain imports, and maintain home markets open to foreign investment.[26] Of course, in the long term, certain regulations may increase the capabilities of local workforces, but policymakers are driven by short-run considerations, and assume rivals vie for a fixed quantity of trade or investment. Polices adopted to harmonize markets across jurisdictions have tended to weaken local controls. Everywhere, the argument goes, global competition has unleashed a race to the bottom in all types and dimensions of regulation.

The late nineteenth century, the heyday of globalization, saw comparable competitive pressures. The Swiss National Council, despite the early leadership of several cantons in legislative action and the sustained demands of labor groups and social reformers, delayed passage of the first set of federal labor laws in the early 1870s.[27] The association of cotton textile employers had lobbied against proposals for limits on hours in order to preserve foreign and domestic markets. The industry employed about 25 percent of all workers in manufacturing, with 50 percent of its production being exported, principally to its closest neighbors. At the time, imports comprised about 20 percent of Helvetic consumption of yarn and unfinished woven goods. The industry had no clear cost advantage. Its wage levels were the same as those in Germany and France, and because it relied on imported coal, profit margins were narrow. Its capital stock was old, and machinery was run at slower speeds than its rivals used. With the value of cotton production at about 5 percent of GDP in 1883, the Swiss government heeded the demands of employers and did not move ahead with protective legislation.

Others have found direct evidence of a downward spiral in labor regulation. In 1891, Finland extended the length of the work day of minors (aged 12–14 years) to 8.5 hours from the level of 6.5 fixed in 1889, after its export firms found they had lost their competitive edge. Following the decision of its neighbor to loosen standards, Sweden reciprocated and lengthened the working day of 13-year-olds from 6 to 10 hours (Rahikainan 2001). For the U.S., Jacob Hacker and Paul Pierson (2002) claimed that capital's threat to divest locally and move enterprises across state borders stunted, if not delayed, the development of the welfare state. Canada, in turn, postponed legislation to limit women's work to meet the competitive North American environment (Drummond 1987, 234–47).

There is an opposing way to conceptualize the role of competition. Countries imported and exported labor standards as they did goods. Globalization, in this view, was an effective deterrent and not the cause of a race to the bottom. Kyle Bagwell and Robert Staiger (2001, 2004) developed a model in which countries are motivated to preserve market access, the combined shares of exports they have acquired in foreign markets, and of imports they have come to accept.[28] A country that unilaterally raises its labor standards will find its domestic market more vulnerable to imports and its exports less competitive, since adopting stricter laws is the equivalent of reducing trade barriers. Bagwell and Staiger empower any country in the WTO, as set in GATT Article XXIII, to impose sanctions on trading partners that fail to reciprocate because they have reneged on raising labor standards or lowering tariffs. There is no presumption that labor standards will be harmonized internationally, only that the newly established level of regulation will preserve market access, thus giving politicians discretion to raise standards as they see fit.

In light of this model, consider the interdependent world of 1914 facing support-maximizing politicians. Their objective was to supply benefits, like regulation, to supporters, groups of labor, reformers, and even capital, while spreading costs as much as possible. To reduce the burden on constituents, policymakers would naturally prevail upon commercial partners to harmonize regulation. Under certain circumstances, foreign countries had legislation imposed on them, regardless of local labor market conditions and how domestic forces lined up in support of or in opposition to regulation. The upshot is that domestic and foreign reform agendas were entangled.

Even in the absence of international oversight, states had options to harmonize the regulatory environment. Until 1900 or so, coercion prevailed over persuasion and negotiation.[29] States threatened import restrictions on selected products of trading partners; failed to renew or abrogated commercial treaties and most-favored-nation clauses; or, in extreme cases, initiated trade wars to cut off competitors' entry into their markets (Conybeare 1987; Lazer 1999; Pahre 2001). The risk of market loss was credible in established and thick trading networks, like the bulk of countries grouped in the middle period of figure 2.1. Conversely, low degrees of integration reduced enforcement of labor standards, and latecomers at the tail of the logistic curve, the handful of countries that did not play by the rules or did not know them, were more likely to defect.

International associations used soft coercion or moral suasion on these countries, but in the absence of sanctions the incentive to cooperate was weak. Russia, where the state "stood ahead of public opinion of employers and workers," was exceptional (Von Laue 1960, 348).[30] It upgraded its labor standards to attract more foreign investment and in anticipation of securing new export markets, but elsewhere countries would not initiate more intervention unless their major trading partners had done so.

The distinction between types of trade is relevant to the history of labor regulation because countries exporting differentiated goods were more susceptible to retaliation if they failed to bend to the dictates of their chief markets. While the hallmark trade in the period was exchange between the resource-abundant New World and labor-abundant Old, trade in manufacturing was sizeable within the European core.[31] In the allegedly iconic world industry, cotton textiles, Europe was the foremost producer and largest consumer. Specialization across countries was based on the type of machinery operated, the quality and treatment of cotton fibers, the final dressing and preparation of goods, and economies of scale. Into the 1880s, many producers were dependent on restricted outlets, for instance Belgium on France, and Italy on France and Germany, and found themselves exposed to threats of market loss. Certainly, manufacturers could have modified or upgraded products to find new customers, but, in the short run, if states did not acquiesce to demands for a level playing field, they had to dump their goods at steep discounts.

Again the Swiss experience is illustrative. Recall Switzerland was reluctant to adopt limits on hours, fearing the loss of export markets if it introduced legislation ahead of major partners. Germany and France did introduce limits on women's work in 1891 and 1892. As it happens, the French National Assembly had initiated an inquiry into compulsory accident insurance in 1893, and opponents claimed that exporters and import-competing industries would not be able to pass on the increased costs (Fuchs 2001, 321; Jay 1891, 1910). The timing of the reform debate was propitious. Rejecting France's offer of the minimum rates in the Méline tariff schedule in exchange for import concessions, Switzerland initiated a trade war.[32] French exports fell, but the conflict was relatively more costly for Switzerland.[33] It could not find alternative outlets for its major exports to France, high-end cotton textiles and silks, clocks, and specialty cheese. The French had an incentive to prolong the conflict since it provided the import-competing sector a respite to adjust to the new reforms. It was the Swiss who backed down first. Even before the end of the trade war in 1894, Switzerland agreed to restrictions on night work and an 11-hour working day for women.

In the New World, domestic concerns trumped external pressures. Regions of recent settlement mainly exported foods and raw materials whose prices were fixed in world markets. The pressure to comply with standards of major trading partners was less keen, because exporters could shift outlets without severe loss. Canada's wheat exports did not contract when Germany launched a trade war between 1903 and 1910 to protest Ottawa's preferential agreement with London; in fact, it was the U.K. that feared collateral damage.[34] Exceptionally, by 1914 the U.S. had begun exporting manufactured goods, although these were mainly standardized items (Sabel and Zeitlin 1985). Anyway, international trade played a small role in its total production. Overall, the New World was insulated from external pressures to emulate the European model. Trade patterns reinforced the primacy of domestic factors in areas of recent settlement. There was a structural disconnect in the New World between commercial access negotiated at the national level and labor laws passed by subnational jurisdictions. In some regions, like Australia, labor succeeded in mobilizing in key states and used the ballot box to see through legislation; in North America this was less common. The aphorism that all politics is local was appropriate to the New World.

THE SUPPLY SIDE: TRADE AS A PATHWAY IN DIFFUSION

So far, I have identified demand (domestic) and supply (international) forces behind the rise of the labor compact. In this section, I go a step further and study their joint effects. Did countries converge on social policy because of common domestic forces like the rise in income and voter turnout, or because countries adopted polices of trading partners, or both?

For this exercise, I implement an event history analysis in which the unit of analysis is the country-pair-year (or dyad-year). I seek to explain why country "A" converges to the labor standards already adopted by another country "B." Convergence does not imply that policymakers emulate exactly the other country in the dyad. The dichotomous dependent variable takes on the value one if country A adopts *at least one* out of five labor standards given that B had already adopted that (those) particular standard(s) prior to the current year, and zero otherwise.[35] When A converges to *all* standards in B, this particular dyad is dropped from the sample, since no further convergence is possible. The appendix gives other details on method and research strategy.

The control variables consist of external and internal determinants of labor standards. For trade integration, I use the measure of trade costs developed by David Jacks, Christopher Meissner, and David Novy (2008, 2010). The term can be interpreted as the extent to which foreign trade is more costly than domestic trade; it falls as countries trade more together. The estimated coefficient will have a negative sign if increased trade encourages A to adopt B's policy.

The baseline model includes the share of the labor force in agriculture of country A to control for the level of development, and wealth and size (the logarithms of GDP and population) of each country in a pair. Country A's demand for labor regulation may have risen with income per capita (a positive marginal effect of GDP for a fixed level of population). Big countries may have been less prone to imitate neighbors because they naturally traded less internationally and were more shielded from foreign competition. A proportional increase in GDP and population (an increase in size) would lower the likelihood of adoption. I also include real GDP and population of country B to identify the roles of wealth and size in policy diffusion and emulation: was A compelled to adopt if B was big or rich?

The other determinants follow from previous discussion. Union density and voter turnout, measured as the ratio of persons actually voting to the adult population (of the relevant enfranchised gender), stand in for the key determinants of the power resources and voice models. Since convergence may have differed across regions, a dummy variable indicates whether country A is in the New World or not. I have included an interaction variable between the presence of a New World country and voter turnout. This variable disentangles the roles of resources and political economy factors behind regulation. The decision to adopt might also be dependent on the number of standards already in place, measured by the total number of laws (out of the five considered) A and B shared in the prior year.

Table 2.2 gives results of a series of logit regressions for the policy convergence model.[36] In the baseline specification of column 1, which includes all relevant independent variables, the trade cost marginal effect is negative and significant. Trade was a conduit of convergence. Contrary to claims, international competition did not lead to a downward cascade in social and labor policy. Wealthier, larger, or more democratic countries were not more likely to play leadership roles. It would appear that the impact of Germany's advanced legislation on British policy had as much to do with Lloyd George's storied visit to a large country as with the fact that the two were major trading partners.

In the baseline regression, domestic factors in A, with the exception of union density, have the expected signs, though their impact was not significant. The positive marginal effects of A's GDP and population are insignificant.[37] The overall size of A was unimportant. Proportionally increasing GDP and population did not lead to a change in the probability of convergence. The transmission of the labor compact, it appears, was not mediated by the relative size of

Table 2.2. Determinants of convergence in labor regulations for country pairs, 1881–1914

	(1) BASELINE	(2) SHORT BASELINE	(3) EUROPE ONLY	(4) NEW WORLD ONLY
International forces				
Trade costs	−0.04	−0.057	−0.067	0.065
	(0.024)*	(0.020)***	(0.038)*	(0.066)
In (GDP B)	−0.027	−0.033	−0.039	0.004
	(0.018)	(0.015)**	(0.027)	(0.072)
In (Population B)	0.022	0.027	0.035	0.011
	(0.019)	(0.017)	(0.030)	(0.065)
Turnout B	0.025	0.021	0.015	0.017
	(0.018)	(0.018)	(0.028)	(0.042)
Domestic forces				
In (GDP A)	0.019	0.013	0.031	−0.038
	(0.024)	(0.014)	(0.020)	(0.193)
In (Population A)	0.002	0.001	−0.019	0.088
	(0.026)	(0.015)	(0.021)	(0.208)
New World A	−0.123	−0.153		
	(0.040)***	(0.026)***		
Turnout A	0.005	0.006	0.000	0.262
	(0.013)	(0.013)	(0.016)	(0.135)*
New World A x Turnout A	0.286	0.273		
	(0.063)***	(0.054)***		
Union density A	−0.003			
	(0.002)*			
Share of labor in agriculture A	−0.019			
	(0.080)			
Share of population 65+ A	0.002			
	(0.006)			
Lagged level of similarity in labor standards	−0.01	−0.01	−0.022	0.034
	(0.006)	(0.005)*	(0.009)***	(0.019)*

(continued)

Table 2.2. *continued*

	(1) BASELINE	(2) SHORT BASELINE	(3) EUROPE ONLY	(4) NEW WORLD ONLY
International Forces: Robustness Checks				
Absolute value of ln (GDP per capita A) - ln (GDP per capita B)	−0.021 (0.016)			
Absolute value of (turnout A) - (turnout B)	−0.007 (0.020)			
ln (Distance km. between capitals)	−0.015 (0.006)***			
Shared border	−0.022 (0.011)*			
Observations	2875	2875	1661	375
Pseudo-R-Squared	0.05	0.05	0.04	0.2

Sources: Dates of adoption from table 1.2; trade costs, distance, and border from Jacks, Meissner, and Novy (2008, 2010); union density from Friedman (2003); other variables from table 2.1.

Notes: Standard errors in brackets clustered at the country pair level. Estimation is by maximum likelihood for a logit model. The dependent variable is 1 when there is convergence on any of five labor standards. I report average marginal effects. Quinquennial dummies are included but not reported. *significant at 10%; **significant at 5%; ***significant at 1%.

trading partners: neither were large and democratic countries leaders, nor small countries followers.

The salience of domestic and international factors varied across regions. In the Old World, voter turnout, while positive, is not significant. Domestic voice appears to have been insufficient to achieve the goals of social activists, although it may have interacted with other internal or external forces to advance the reform agenda. In one scenario, capital in B sought to form cross-border and cross-class coalitions with labor and reformers in A to harmonize regulation across trading partners. These types of pressures may be captured in the trade costs term itself. Putting aside this explanation, the dynamic was different in the New World. Countries were less prone to converge, but sufficiently high levels of voter turnout offset the obstacles to regulation posed by the region's specialization in primary products and other idiosyncrasies.

The sign of union density may appear to be counterintuitive, but worker organization was strongly correlated with the presence of a New World country. Other studies have reported a positive relation between the share of population above 65 and social spending, a finding repeated in column 1, although the marginal effect is statistically insignificant. As Lindert (2004) observed, older workers were less mobile than younger ones and more dependent on social entitlements. Populations were younger in the New World, thus deepening the divergence between regions. Countries with relatively weaker regulation were more prone to adopt new laws. The negative sign on the lagged number of shared standards has, at least, two interpretations. Stragglers may have wanted to signal to residents and foreigners their willingness to move toward the new international norm of greater regulation, albeit at a slower pace; alternatively, they may have adopted legislation later than others because the cost of doing so was less.

Did countries resembling each other have the same regulatory outcomes? Neither differences in GDP nor turnout had a perceptible effect. I cannot conclude, as did Markus Lampe (2009) and Robert Pahre (2007, 247–79) in separate studies of MFNs, that democracies were any more prone to emulate each other than autocracies. I also consider in the baseline whether close neighbors were more likely to copy each other. The answer is mixed. A common border actually exerted pressure to diverge, but a smaller distance between capitals implied a greater chance of adopting a similar labor standard. Emulation effects, derived from culture—common language and legal origins, and shared histories—cannot be excluded even after controlling for trade relations.

In the remaining columns, I explore the robustness of these findings. I exclude unionization, agricultural share of the labor force, age distribution, differences in turnout and income per capita, and geographical variables. These variables did not prove to be robust determinants, and, in the short baseline of column 2, the trade cost coefficient actually increases in significance. The geographical variables are highly co-linear with trade costs as the literature on trade and gravity models shows. The income and turnout differences are essentially controlled for already since A and B's respective levels are entered separately. The other structural variables are poorly measured across the sample, and I am hesitant to rely on them further.

Columns 3 and 4 compare estimates of an Old World sample and another which restricts country A to being in the New World. For European pairs, the results are in line with column 1. The dynamic was different in the New World: the trade cost term is positive but not significant, and the marginal effect of voter turnout is statistically significant. Recall Rodgers's (1998) assertion that blueprints of social reform flowed across the Atlantic and in both directions; international trade, however, was not the channel of transmission to the Americas and Australia. Voice was the main determinant of policy diffusion in the region.

CONCLUSION: THE LABOR COMPACT WAS A DOMESTIC AND FOREIGN AFFAIR

Putnam's claim was on the mark. Domestic and foreign forces were entangled in the rise of the labor compact. The extension of the franchise, the rise in organized labor, and the increase in income levels created necessary conditions in individual countries behind the adoption of new laws. They were not sufficient, however, when rivals operated under different or weaker sets of rules. Trade itself proved to be an effective backstop against a race to the bottom. A type of whipsawing effect ensued. States accommodated domestic interests because they were coerced by rivals to do so. The stronger local pressure groups were, the more likely foreign intervention counted, but the opposite was also the case. External pressures incited workers and activists to demand better conditions.

The balance of domestic and foreign factors varied by region. Local forces prevailed over global pressures in the New World, the obverse holding in the Old. From its origins, trade pulled welfare states apart. Exporters of primary products were isolated from trading partners with more advanced labor regulation, forcing New World workers to depend on local pressure groups for reform. In the Old World, voice, while not unimportant in policy adoption, was more effective when backed by trade.[38]

In the next two chapters, I explore the demand for and supply of the labor compact. On the demand side, I relate how Belgian labor came to form alliances with business to advance the reform agenda—a coalition which globalization had made possible. Cross-class alliances did not adhere in the New World. On the supply side, states put aside costly trade wars and turned instead to collaboration, guaranteeing market access at home in exchange for improved labor regulation of trading partners. Again, this outcome was more prevalent in the Old World.

MARKETS AND STATES IN OLD
AND NEW WORLDS

Braves fermiers de modeste culture,
Vous vous plaignez tout haut et justement;
Mais l'argent pris à notre nourriture,
On pourrait bien vous le rendre autrement;
Vous payez tout sans mesure et sans trêve;
Le sol, l'outil; l'habit, le mobilier;
Demandez donc plutôt qu'on vous dégrève
Sans renchérir le pain d'ouvrier.

RESPONSES TO GLOBALIZATION:
ALTERNATIVE ROADMAPS

Can the welfare state survive globalization? Will globalization outlive the nation state? While an either-or construction dominates twenty-first-century discourse on globalization and the state, advocates of the original labor compact saw beyond these stock phrases. Start with workers' responses in the Old World. As trade expanded, the price of labor-intensive exports rose and the price of imports from land-abundant regions fell. The movement in prices ought to have translated into increased real wages. Though in principle workers had an incentive to leap onto the free-trade bandwagon, they had good reason to be skeptical about international integration. Market forces were not always predictable and reliable as the basic trade model supposes, the adoption of free trade being neither natural nor inevitable.[1] Wages moved sluggishly and markets did not provide adequate insurance for the uncertainty and volatility created by the steep rise in trade exposure (Newbery and Stiglitz 1984; Stiglitz 2006).

The New World faced opposing pressures. Industrial workers were seemingly natural allies of protectionist interests in manufacturing, since trade expansion squeezed their earnings relative to returns of resource exporters. But commercial barriers, like their obverse, free trade, had not delivered wage gains and secured employment as anticipated. Tariff protection was uneven, its modest beneficial effects on earnings being undone since any rise in workers' rewards attracted waves of immigrants, many unskilled (Dales 1966; Hatton and Williamson 2005). Contrary to plan, protectionism in the New World had made countries more integrated in the world economy, not less.

Everywhere the labor compact was conceived to provide wage and employment insurance. The rub was that labor needed coalition partners to realize its reform agenda, regulation being adopted as part of a package of social and commercial policies. The policy mix varied across and within Old and New Worlds. This chapter contrasts Belgian and Canadian experiences. Belgian workers demanded a mechanism to redistribute the benefits and share the costs of greater trade integration that did not contravene the logic of comparative advantage. The labor compact enabled workers, turning their backs on the familiar 'either-or' construction, to exploit globalization to their benefit. Specifically, I identify three phases in the development of the Belgian labor compact: first, the development of an integrated labor market; second, the adoption of a free trade platform by the Parti Ouvrier Belge (POB; Belgian Labor Party); and the final act, labor's endorsement of globalization as a political lever to improve working conditions.

In Canada, redistributive programs developed slowly. Linkages between commercial and social protection were slack. Workers' proposition to business of trading off support for tariffs in exchange for capital's backing the labor compact was rebuffed. It was unlikely that labor could have forged an enduring alliance with free-trade agriculture. In any event, the Canadian state was dependent on tariff revenues and was reluctant to endorse free trade. Eventually, workers turned their attention away from labor reform toward measures to control immigration, a position for which they found allies in industry, the state, and the wider society. By 1914, Old and New Worlds had developed distinct social models coexisting side by side. Immigration quotas were married to tariffs in the New World, as the labor compact was coupled to free trade in the Old.

DID ATTITUDES TOWARD TRADE CONFORM
TO THE TEXTBOOK MODEL?

Workers in Belgium, a small Old World country, rich in labor relative to land, were in a good position to benefit from the wave of globalization before

1914.[2] Belgium was an active player in the movement toward free trade initiated by the Cobden-Chevalier treaty of 1860. It signed its own trade agreement with France in 1861, followed rapidly by treaties with Britain (1862), the Netherlands (1863), and later with Prussia (1865).[3] Based on measures of tariff revenues as a percentage of imports, Belgium's commitment to openness was stable throughout the period.[4] Fearing reprisals from more powerful commercial partners, the country shunned trade wars. As transport and trade costs fell, labor-intensive industries like textiles ought to have prospered, and on the import ledger the country would benefit from cheap foreign grains. Belgium was also rich in capital relative to land. Because of its factor endowments and degree of openness, Belgium would have escaped the "curse of diminishing returns," growth continuing unabated (Helpman 2004, 14–35).

Belgium was engaged in intra- and interindustry trade, but the classic Stolper-Samuelson model—rising wages in labor-abundant activities and falling rents in agriculture—serves as a starting point to consider the effects of trade on factor returns.[5] While the model assumes factors are immobile internationally, it depends upon internal labor mobility. Wages of workers with the same skills are identical. This assumption is powerful. It assures that regardless of the portion of the economy engaged directly in trade, its effects will be felt everywhere. For nineteenth-century Belgium, this implied that real wages would have converged to levels in labor-scarce and land-rich countries.

The trouble is that factor rewards in Belgium did not move as predicted. The grain invasion ought to have engendered a price shock, lowering rents and promoting a transfer of resources to the labor-abundant sector. Arable prices did contract by about 30 percent from 1870 until 1914 and production fell by about 25 percent (Blomme 1993, 396, 418–19). However, exports of labor-intensive goods scarcely progressed before the tariff revision of the mid 1890s. Some resources were transferred to dairy production, but sheltered behind a tariff wall this sector produced mainly for the domestic market. Clearly, the grain invasion did not precipitate significant changes in the distribution of employment as theory predicted.

It is customary (Witte, Craeybeckx, and Meynen 2000) to demarcate Belgian 'fault lines' along linguistic and regional boundaries, but in the late nineteenth century these divisions sat athwart an occupational division between agriculture and industry. The concentration of immobile labor in agriculture was not lost on contemporaries. Vandervelde, who conducted doctoral research on agrarian conditions before assuming the leadership of the POB, documented the overcrowding of the countryside. He (Vandervelde 1895, 12) reported that the number of tenants doubled between 1846 and 1880, amounting in the later year to 68 percent of the rural population. Land rents spiked upwards. Into the 1880s, pull factors attracting laborers into industry remained weak. Internal migration to urban centers had slowed down after 1850, and, while Belgians had a long tradition of short-distance relocation to France, emigration to the New World was comparatively rare. The result was "a substantial degree of hidden unemployment [in the countryside] which, certainly in the middle of the nineteenth century, must have assumed grotesque proportions in certain regions" (Blomme 1993, 23).

In general, real wages stagnated. Workers in all sectors, tariff protected or not, benefited from the fall in the price of bread, a major item in their diets. Urban industrial workers, isolated from the pool of immobile workers in the countryside, ought to have seen their real wages rise. Skilled labor in the capital-intensive sector did see pay increases, but the story in semi- and unskilled industries was different. With the exception of mining, demand for workers in the labor-intensive manufacturing sector was not forthcoming. All totaled, the growth of average industrial wages was held back, certainly compared to other open economies of the period (O'Rourke and Williamson 1999).[6]

The evolution of land rents and earnings affected the attitudes of the key social groups toward trade. In principle, where labor is relatively abundant it had much to gain from supporting free trade, while landed interests would oppose it, but Belgium's unbalanced economic development made for an awkward mapping from factors of production to attitudes toward commercial policy.[7] Despite the growth in international exposure far exceeding that of other small countries, its rural population—landlords and tenants—retained an important economic and political weight similar to that of France and Germany (Van Molle 1989, 361–68). Conservative and Catholic parties had a stronghold in the countryside. Lacking comparative advantage in agricultural production, rural interests were favorable to tariff protection. Urban and liberal Belgium was less than unanimous about the merits of free trade. Antwerp, whose fortunes were based on its external commerce, had a strong predisposition to laissez-faire, but Ghent cotton-textile manufacturers demanded protection from foreign competition (Scholliers 2001, 134–35).

At this stage of its development, the left was not sold on the merits of openness. Although the vision of a socialist international was honored and the benefits of falling grain prices certainly embraced, the left had more than a wistful attachment to rural demands and protectionist sentiments of selected groups of workers. Belgian socialists were more inclined than their German comrades to uphold rural values, supporting tenants and small landholders who had a keen attachment to the land.[8] Certain groups of urban skilled workers had a strong interest in maintaining the status quo. Apart from the benefits of cheaper consumption goods, the labor aristocracy did not object to the fact that hordes of cheap laborers remained confined to the countryside, not least because it made city housing affordable. Workers in import-competing sectors, such as weaving, campaigned actively alongside employers for greater protection against cheaper imports. These divisions splintered labor along trade and economic issues that were superimposed on deep-seated fault lines of language and region. Unsurprisingly, confronting diverse and competing interests, the left was divided on the benefits of free trade. Many of these fissures were present in the POB, even after it proclaimed its support for free trade at its founding conference in 1885.

The divergence in attitudes toward commercial policy does not sit well with Stolper-Samuelson. Recall that the basic model depends critically on the assumption of perfectly mobile factors within the domestic economy. Mobility assures that trade affects labor, capital, and natural resources in the same way, no matter where they are employed in the economy. The implication is that owners of the same factor share the same preferences with respect to trade policy. However, into the 1880s, Belgian labor was hardly mobile out of agriculture and from contracting to expanding industrial activities. The country seems to have been closer to the fixed-factor world of Ricardo-Viner, in which the gains of openness are not distributed evenly to the abundant factor (Hiscox 2002, 12–34). In these models, where factors are immobile, attitudes to trade policy cleave along industry as opposed to class lines, exactly as they did in Belgium until 1885.

THE MAKING OF THE BELGIAN WORKING CLASS

Some time before the turn of the century, workers tended to forsake sectoral interests and began to share common ground on economic issues. The turning point, Belgian historians (Cassiers 1980a, 1980b; Polasky 1995, 18–22) assert, was the extension of the rail network and the widespread use of subsidized transport that allowed workers to commute non-trivial distances on a daily basis. The standard account (Mahaim 1910) is as follows. In 1870, the state began to buy up private lines, leading to the establishment in 1884 of the Société nationale des chemins de fer vincinaux (SNCV). Initially, groups of employers, especially in the iron and steel and mining industries in the south had demanded state intervention to assure a plentiful and steady supply of labor. They received backing from Catholic groups and even liberals who believed that the rail system would stem the rise in urban support for socialism (Van den Eeckhout, 1992, 190). A dense, secondary train network linking rural villages with larger conurbations was built rapidly over a small land mass. Workers could stay in the countryside but have jobs in the city, thereby breaking down regional and sectoral divisions.

A national labor market took root in which "commuting workers regulated supply and demand" (Mahaim 1910, 175). Socialists, originally hesitant in their support for the expanded transport network—they preferred that workers congregate in urban centers for electoral reasons—came to see the emergent culture of the trains as instrumental to the early fortunes of the fledgling labor party. The network resolved the agrarian question and, although historic divisions persisted, the salutary effects of bonding hardscrabble miners, proletarian weavers, and master glaziers on a daily commute were an effective counterweight. The various groups became receptive to new ideas in political economy that they filtered through their own experiences. Vandervelde and Jules Destrée (1898, 308) wrote:

> They [employers] had hoped to severely weaken unions, to flood the market with cheap labor, and to thereby lower workers' 'standard of life.' But, contrary to expectations, the opposite occurred. Flemish coalmen—who travel as long as two hours a day to work in the mines of the Borinage and in central Belgium—and masons, carpenters, and plasterers who come to Brussels every morning are in daily contact with other groups of workers. They have acquired the same needs, make the same demands, and they argue the same opinions. Every night, we hear socialist songs in the trains bringing them back home, and the electoral progress of our party can be attributed to them.[9]

The extension of the network was part of the global transport revolution that reduced trade costs in the movement of people, goods, and capital.[10] In Belgium, train transport accelerated structural change that was partly achieved elsewhere in Europe by emigration. Wage evidence confirms the unifying effects of the network. For a broad sample of occupations, the dispersion of wages fell markedly after the mid 1880s, as farm wages closed the gap with the pay of industrial workers (Huberman 2008, 342). The new transport system had transformed an immobile into a mobile labor force, the crucial assumption underlying Stolper-Samuelson. The Belgian workers' party, the POB, was founded precisely in the period in which the forces of convergence in wages across the country were strongest. The question remains as to whether the newly formed party was able to channel this transformation in the labor market to its advantage.

The new workers' party seized the initiative. Beginning in 1886 a broad-based movement of protest, or "social upheaval" according to Belgian historians (Witte, Craeybeckx, and Meynen 2000, 13), swept the country. Before 1890, Belgium was notorious for its poor working conditions and social entitlements were unknown.

The country was, in Marx's phrase, a "capitalist's paradise," and in Vandervelde's eyes, a "workers' purgatory."[11] The demands of the masses were multiple and interlaced: the right to vote, better working conditions, and a more egalitarian distribution of income. The authorities responded first with a show of force and then with piecemeal legislation, including the introduction of limits on child labor in 1889. As trading partners recognized, even this legislation was far behind the European norm, and militancy was not appeased. Finally, to put an end to the protest, elites acquiesced and extended the franchise to male workers in 1893.

Daron Acemoglu and James Robinson (2006) provide a model of the transition. To prevent social unrest, elites extend the franchise as a signal of their commitment to incorporate workers into civil society. Minor and haphazard reforms directed at narrow interest groups are not sufficient because, unlike democracy, they are not perceived as credible commitments to widespread change. The transition to democracy occurs when elites recognize that losses from redistributive policies are less than costs of potential revolution. The rate of enfranchisement and the timing and nature of the social and political reforms depend on the initial level of inequality and the costs of revolt.[12] Greater inequality means that democracy is costly for elites, so that repression becomes more likely.

In these types of models, globalization can tip the balance toward extending the franchise. In theory, the increase in trade in a labor-abundant country reduces the gap between incomes of labor and capital. While the rise in median wages reduces pressures for a larger franchise, it also makes elites less resistant to change. The costs of redistribution would be lower because the new middle class would shun policies that raise their own tax burdens, and because international capital mobility shelters business from assuming the incidence of the new reforms (Boix 2003). Finally, globalization raises the costs of disruption caused by repression or by revolution, and democratization is more likely as a result.

BELGIAN WORKERS ENDORSE FREE TRADE

Globalization may have opened the door for greater democratic participation, as Acemoglu and Robinson asserted, but there was no assurance that the benefits of trade, however modest, would trickle down. By themselves, economic forces did not assure better working conditions and wage security. Anyway the causal link from globalization to democracy was not tight because international trade was on the rise for several decades before electoral reform. Another reading is that the democratization process itself was a catalyst for greater attachment to external exposure.[13] The extension of the franchise created a vacuum in which emerging pressure groups aligned themselves on commercial and social policies (O'Rourke and Taylor 2007). In principle, new political voices representing abundant factors of production, capital and labor, had an incentive for reducing trade barriers. And while the expanded train network was the ticket to trade for the Belgian working class, in practical terms the POB faced the dilemma of crafting a program of labor and commercial policies that satisfied its diverse membership and coalition partners. The outcome was the coupling of the labor compact and free trade.

The tariff debate of 1894 was a turning point for the budding coalition in support of labor reform. During the first parliamentary session after the extension of the franchise, the governing Conservatives introduced a bill intended to make comprehensive changes to Belgium's tariff structure. Faced by the renewed protectionism of its two main trading partners, France and Germany, the Belgian government was under strong pressure from employers in key sectors and from landlords to retaliate, but it also feared the consequences of trade wars with its larger neighbors. The Belgian government was in a weaker position than its continental neighbors because the various pressure groups behind protectionism were split across religious and linguistic affiliations, confronting a collective action dilemma as did the free traders. In this environment, government leaders maintained that tariff changes were necessary because of declining state revenues. The government proposed to harmonize the tariff system, which meant rates of around 5 to 10 percent across a broad range of manufacturing and agricultural products.

At the outset of the 1894 debate, citing the examples of its larger neighbors, the government anticipated that voters would endorse the increase in tariffs.[14] However, contrary to calculation, more democratic representation was not necessarily antithetical to free trade. Although parliamentary exchanges did not always reveal cleavages along class lines, by the end of the debate the parties had moved in this direction.[15] Among Liberals, defenders of laissez-faire came to dominate employer groups expressing protectionist sentiments, and the Conservative Party emerged as the spokesperson of protectionist landlords and rural values at the expense of its urban clientele.

Organized labor's stance in support of free trade balanced the competing interests of its supporters. The POB had to reckon with pockets of workers retaining strong regional connections, skilled labor in capital-intensive industries who had sorted themselves from the mass of unskilled, and still others tempted by the appeal of Catholic unions. In Parliament, as on the commuter trains, the POB sought to convince workers of the benefits of free trade based on their immediate needs as consumers and producers. Earlier proponents in Belgium had rehearsed these arguments. Workers' well-being was inextricably tied to international markets ever since the cooperative movement had established *Maisons du Peuple*—the first branch was founded in Jolimont in 1872—the goal of which was ensuring a cheap and ready supply of bread. Trade reform would deepen this attachment, incorporating dairy and meat products in workers' diets, and providing a supplementary source of calories to sustain them over their long workdays. As food prices fell, a larger part of families' budgets became available for household expenses and lodging. Henri Denis, a member of the POB caucus and pioneer in the international movement for labor standards, calculated the salutary effects of reform on clothing purchases. On the production side, the POB observed that existing tariffs on inputs like wood and raw materials had increased building and equipment expenditures unreasonably. And echoing Manchester liberals, parliamentary socialists claimed that lower consumer prices would translate into reduced wage pressures on employers. Lastly, taking a page from basic theory, the POB saw that free trade was a 'wake-up call,' compelling employers in export-challenged industries to modernize plant and equipment.

While these arguments were standard fare, the POB's innovative contribution was to link these claims to the extension of the labor compact.[16] Globalization had accelerated structural change of the economy. Existing relief programs, like those provided by the cooperative movement, proved insufficient. Workers in the countryside had home gardens to fall back upon, but the new jobs they now commuted to had created an additional set of risks and uncertainties, arising in part from their long hours and dangerous conditions. And selected groups of skilled workers, for instance in glass manufacturing, and less skilled labor in import-competing industries like spinning lobbied hard to maintain levels of protection. Like any political party, the POB was sensitive to demands of this type and favored some modest degree of protection.

Protectionism, however, was a temporary reprieve. In response to the government's policy of using custom revenues to fund its planned social spending, the POB insisted the country's external exposure could not be compromised. The proposed tariff changes benefited landlords and selected employers at the expense of workers, widening already large gaps in income. Socialists maintained that tariff policy was inherently inequitable, and the security against dislocation it provided was uneven across regions and sectors, depending as it did on the lobbying power of key pressure groups.[17] Protectionism was a pillar of the ancien régime, an obstacle to the functioning of the new participatory democracy.

The vocabulary and substance of the POB's project rallied both liberals and workers. The POB anticipated that the reduction in general tariffs was a first step to fiscal reform. After removing trade barriers, the government, although constrained by the gold standard, would need additional revenue, and, inspired by the fervent free-trader Henry George, labor proposed an egalitarian system of income and property taxation.[18] Employers had concerns that the burden of new regulation and social entitlements would fall on fixed plant and equipment, but they rallied to the POB's agenda because land was immobile—certainly more so than capital—and a seemingly large and inexhaustible source of revenue. As resources shifted out of agriculture, liberal Belgium would emerge as the governing elite in Brussels.

Groups of worker had to be won over too. Rejecting the binary formulation of winners and losers—the same laborer could move rapidly between these categories—, the POB proposed channeling the new state revenues to expand existing social entitlements, like unemployment insurance, which had been managed in the past by municipalities and trade unions, and to fund new job exchanges encouraging mobility. Skilled laborers had no qualms about universal programs that did not take away from their union benefits. Workers in the tradable sectors would come to depend on the safety net to smooth income during periods of job loss and reduce search costs for new job opportunities. And access to accident compensation promoted investments in skill. For agriculture workers, the POB developed an insurance program to stabilize incomes.

In the end, the ruling party had partial success in adopting its proposed tariff changes, limited for the most part to dairy products. In the textile industry, duties on imported yarns were actually cut. All together, in 1913, manufacturing tariffs were half those in France and in Germany (O'Rourke and Williamson 1999, 98). In the decade after the debate, Belgium negotiated fifteen commercial agreements with its trading partners, resulting in bilateral tariff reductions and guarantees of market access. [19] Some of these accords, as I discuss in the next chapter, had social clauses stipulating reciprocal agreements on the provision of accident insurance and other workplace entitlements. Business could be assured that the country was not ahead of its rivals in labor regulation and that its exports remained internationally competitive.

Thus, when political opponents upbraided Vandervelde for unabashedly declaring "we [POB] demand zero protection for all industries"—although in fact labor had voted for selected short-term protectionist measures—he responded that his endorsement was conditional upon a program of egalitarianism, which he referred to as "*l'alternative*" (BAP 1894–95, 879).[20] For the left, openness was complementary to redistribution, a line of reasoning preempting the arguments of David Cameron (1978), Rodrik (1998, 2011), and others, by one hundred years. The debate on commercial policy had enduring effects on the direction of social and commercial policy in Belgium—and elsewhere. The tariff question was effectively buried, protectionism losing favor even among Conservatives.

Recall that in Acemoglu and Robinson's model (2006), elites have an incentive to extend the franchise in periods of globalization, because the median voter whose earnings are now higher has no reason to support redistribution. In Belgium, in contrast, workers saw free trade and egalitarianism as mutually reinforcing. Labor had successfully transformed debate on free trade into a project on social policy.

Workers exploited the tariff debate as a steppingstone for more and, in their eyes, better social legislation. In 1899, with the advent of proportional representation, coalition building became the norm in the legislature.[21] The moment was propitious for the POB. The debate gave the party credibility, a precondition in forming cross-party alliances, if only because it had demonstrated steadfastness in its critique of the government's commercial policy. But it was not evident, a priori, who was labor's natural partner. On social issues, except for the religious question, the POB was closer to groups of Conservatives and Catholics advocating reforms, albeit to curtail socialism; Liberals, on ideological grounds, were less inclined to support labor's demand for legislation restricting who could work and when, but they were persuaded that the left's program entailed the demise of rural power. Factory owners in the party who had successfully adapted to prior legislation were not opposed to gradual reform either. Practically, because the Liberal Party needed worker votes if it ever hoped to regain power, it moved closer to the POB.[22]

In parliamentary regimes, no party can pretend to lead a government without regard to the balance of forces in the legislature. By the mid 1890s, the Lib-Lab coalition effectively pressured the ruling Conservatives to forsake protectionism and introduce new social legislation. The move to proportional representation had opened the door to state funding.[23] Old age pensions were introduced in 1900, accident compensation in 1903, and unemployment insurance in 1907 (see table 1.2).[24] Although regulations and social insurance programs had been previously adopted elsewhere, the Belgian example is remarkable because the labor compact was achieved in a short time span. Throughout this period, I should add, there was no movement to raise trade barriers, and levels of openness surged. Vandervelde's 'alternative' policy mix was realized, labor choosing social over tariff protection.

CANADA IN THE BELGIAN MIRROR

In the fast-industrializing centers of the New World, workers demanded better employment conditions as they did in Europe. U.S. reformers had contributed to the new field of industrial relations, and innovative policies, like paid vacations, had made their way to the Old World (Hunnicutt 1988; Rodgers 1998). These accomplishments aside, the labor compact in the New World was porous. In the preceding chapter, I outlined reasons why New World states were not bound to adopt labor standards of trading partners. In this section, I focus on domestic factors limiting their adoption, in light of Belgian workers' ability in developing coalition partners.

The Canadian experience had much in common with other countries of recent settlement. As trade costs fell, there was upward pressure on prices of exports using the abundant factor, land, and downward pressure on prices of goods produced by the scarce factor, labor. Workers in the manufacturing sector had good reason to support the National Policy of 1879 that remained the framework of Canadian tariff structure until 1931 (Green 2000, 211). But protectionism was piecemeal and uneven, more often designed to meet the revenue needs of the state than to accommodate the demands of domestic industry.[25] To get workers onside, the government introduced new legislation guaranteeing trade unions' rights (Ostry 1960). Canadian labor, mainly represented by the union movement, sought to lever its coalition with manufacturers on commercial policy to improve employment conditions. But workers in the non-competing and non-tradable sectors preferred lower tariffs, although they too had something to gain from the labor compact. The point is that the presence of a strong Canadian workers' party would not have been sufficient to see through the reform agenda. As in Belgium, workers needed a cross-class alliance to bridge the demands of its diverse membership.

Labor's alliance with manufacturers failed to cohere.[26] Regulation was delayed since it was uncertain whether or not legislation was a federal or provincial jurisdiction (Drummond 1987, 234). More substantially, capital was not prepared to expand the labor compact beyond basic standards limiting children's and women's work, claiming that, in the absence of additional tariff changes, it could not pass onto consumers the costs of regulation. Organized labor's attempts to build bridges with rural interests were equally unsuccessful. Farmers expressed concern that an earlier round of regulation of the railway trades had led to increased transport costs (Wood 1924, 150–52). Faced by world markets, the export sector was compelled to absorb higher input prices. In rural Ontario, regulation was limited to the 1874 law making the owners of threshing machines responsible for ensuring that moving parts were fitted with guards (Crowley 1995, 69). As a group, farmers rejected labor's demands for limits on hours of work (Goutor 2007, 179).

The tariff commission of 1905–06, established by Ottawa to hear out various interest groups on proposed adjustments to the tariff schedule, laid bare labor's isolation, an outcome diametrically opposed to the Belgian debate on commercial policy sealing the coalition for social reform.[27] Incoherence and indecision marked labor's participation. The Trades and Labour Congress, the central federation of labor, claimed that the "tariff is high enough at present"; while stone cutters demanded further increases, labor in sugar refineries sought that, since "living was so high in Canada, articles should be free of duty." Better organized, rural interests made a compelling case for sharply reduced rates of protection—they were partially successful; manufacturers took the opposing position. But labor, to borrow the term of theorists, was not "adjacent" to the interests of either farmers or business (Axelrod 1970). Fragmented, the labor movement had little to offer either group to lever support for more and better legislation. Typically, in the historic 1911 election, when the country rejected trade reciprocity with the U.S., workers were divided on the issue (Beaulieu and Emery 2001).

Canadian labor's failure at the commission to align cross-class support for the reform agenda was indicative of a reorientation in priorities. Immigration had become the focal issue and demand for regulation took a back seat (Goutor 2007).[28] Like labor laws, limits on foreign workers provided residents a certain degree of wage and employment security. From Confederation until the 1890s, Canada lost workers to the U.S., land values stagnating in both Ontario and the west (Emery, Inwood, and Thille 2007). Wages of industrial workers increased modestly.[29] In fact, labor's limited success in improving employment conditions was restricted to the 1880s.[30] But during the Wheat Boom, which saw the extension of the frontier and strong demand for exports, immigration attained historic levels. The Canadian state took an active role in sponsoring new arrivals.[31] In the Belgian mirror, immigration assumed the role of an extended train network, foreigners selecting destinations on the basis of skills (Green and Green 1993). For urban residents, inflows of unskilled workers and imports of cheap manufactured goods were identical. While the downward effect on wages would have been relieved if labor was mobile, 2,000 kms of lakes and rocks separated the industrial belt from the prairies. The wage gap between skilled and unskilled widened. As elsewhere in the New World, when wage inequality rose, so did the demand for immigration quotas (Hatton and Williamson 2005, 174–77).

By the turn of the century, tariff and immigration policies jointly determined Canadian labor's well-being. Foreign workers were attracted by the earnings and employment security the tariff guaranteed. Into the early 1900s, Canadian wage growth was flat and labor productivity in manufacturing sectors like textiles stagnated. Immigration had other consequences. Throughout the New World, the claim was that foreign workers diluted labor organization, complicating negotiations on public goods like hours of work. For instance, in urban Brazil, conflict arose between immigrant and indigenous groups, as well as between Italian and Portuguese migrants, over the priorities of collective bargaining (Maram 1977; Butler 1998). Although American nativism had particular origins (Zolberg 2006), the backlash in the New World against new arrivals was ubiquitous.

Canadian labor would expend much of its political energies in the decade before 1914 demanding an end to the open-door policy. Unlike regulation, immigration was a federal jurisdiction, but coalition building was no easier at this level and labor found few allies in industry and agriculture.[32] In the early 1900s, the Trades and Labour Congress had threatened to withdraw its endorsement of the tariff, deeming it as important to get its voice heard on immigration. "While the government's assistance to immigration compels the labourer to sell his labor at the lowest price in competition with the whole world, the employers are protected from foreign competition by a tariff often exceeding 50 percent" (cited in Craven 1980, 277). Canadian manufacturers rejected the link. Rural interests, dependent on seasonal supplies of labor, had no reason to support immigration quotas either. New restrictions on arrivals were imposed in 1910, but like earlier laws they were limited in application and scope, as the state held to its position that immigration was a cornerstone in nation building.[33] Broad-based support for quotas had to wait until the 1920s and emerged mainly in response to U.S. policy (Hatton and Williamson 2005, 177). Any political capital expended on demands for limits on foreign workers translated into fewer resources to build a labor compact. Tellingly, Canada's welfare state was realized—unemployment insurance was introduced in 1940—only when the immigration question was resolved.

Inevitably, Canadian labor's interests located elsewhere, depending almost exclusively on industrial action to improve their welfare. Resigned to the fact that they lacked political clout to improve labor regulations, Canadian workers sought higher wages to compensate for inferior employment conditions and as a countervailing measure against immigration. The sharp contrast with Belgium in the decade before 1914 is apparent. Canadian workers mobilized in strikes more often than Belgians and had, in fact, more success in doing so.[34] And while the majority of Canadian disputes addressed wage issues and only a handful working conditions, in Belgium strikes concerning employment conditions were as numerous as those about pay. A unique union structure in which the vast majority of Canadian workers had membership in U.S.-based internationals lay behind the spike in militancy. For certain skill types, North America was a common labor market and bigger and better-funded unions increased the probability of strike success. The irony is that Canadian workers, clearly not the ideological vanguard, were more attuned to the call of internationalism than Belgians, who had put aside class conflict to secure the labor compact.

CONCLUSION: TOWARD TWO SOCIAL MODELS

The idea of coupling the labor compact and free trade had circulated in Europe since the 1880s. While it may not have been the ideal European country, Belgium was among the pioneers in making the link, and, by the turn of the century, continental reformers began to draw on Vandervelde's insights and strategies. To be sure, different coalitions and policy outcomes were possible in the Old World. In Scandinavia, agriculture interests and labor coalesced around the twin demands of free trade and social entitlements. The German case appears to have pursued another roadmap. Labor allied originally with protectionist interests in anticipation that employers would reciprocate and throw their support behind improved labor regulation. But labor grew to be disillusioned with its partners as the cost of protectionism became difficult to justify. The German left's repositioning on commercial policy toward that of its smaller neighbor, and along the lines suggested by Bernstein which I introduced in chapter 1, was testament to the power of globalization forces.

The New World, too, saw a variety of political outcomes. Pre-federation Australia provides a counter example to Canada. Union voice was stronger than in other settler economies—Melbourne stonemasons winning the eight-hour day in 1856. By the 1880s, organized labor in New South Wales developed close ties with liberal free traders and export interests, composed mainly of wheat farmers and wool shearers (Archer 2007, 43–47; Boix 2006). Even before Vandervelde trumpeted the virtuous circle of free trade and the labor compact, B. R. Wise (1892), an architect of the country's social legislation and member of Sydney's Cobden Club, had made the connection.[35] Under Henry Parke's stewardship, NSW introduced redistributive programs, funded by land tax revenues to offset the negative effects of trade on wages, although the government did exploit anti-immigrant sentiment as well to control labor supply (Lamb 1967; Hiscox 2002, 118–21). The alliance of populists and labor pushed forward legislation that was the most advanced in the New World. But after federation, which followed a steep recession in the 1890s, Victoria came to dominate social and commercial policy, and Australia converged to the Canadian model. Labor support for free trade weakened, a new protectionist coalition with manufacturers replacing the old alliance with agriculture. As elsewhere in the New World, immigration quotas and tariffs became the policies of choice.

How were these two distinct models of social and commercial policy sustained? In an open economy, all countries would feel pressure to standardize policy along the same dimensions. For the New World, T. J. Hatton and Williamson (2005) found that more restrictive immigration polices abroad, principally in the U.S., induced restrictive domestic policies elsewhere in the New World. The story in the Old World is more complex because of the larger menu of labor reforms adopted. Vandervelde recognized that while the POB had achieved the labor compact in Brussels, its extension, let alone viability, was still in doubt. Belgium's incipient welfare state could be preserved only if its major trading partners had comparable programs in place. With this objective, Vandervelde and his colleagues became tireless ambassadors of the Belgian model and were instrumental in attempts to harmonize regulation at the international level. I examine the success and failures of these initiatives in the next chapter.

4

INTERNATIONAL LABOR STANDARDS: IDEAS OR TRADE BASED?

The practicality of the idea of international labor legislation derives not so much from the fact that the assumptions on which it is based were true as that they were thought to be true.

> —*Daniel Patrick Moynihan, "The United States and*
> *the International Labor Organization," page 3.*

An increased focus of international economic diplomacy should be to prevent harmful regulatory competition. There has not been enough serious consideration of the alternative—global co-operation to raise standards. While labour standards arguments have at times been invoked as a cover for protectionism, and this must be avoided, it is entirely appropriate that US policymakers seek to ensure that greater global integration does not become an excuse for eroding labour rights.

> —*Lawrence Summers*, Financial Times, *May 5, 2008.*

IS INTERNATIONAL GOVERNANCE ESSENTIAL TO LEVEL THE PLAYING FIELD?

A debate has roughly formed between those who support the authority of international organizations to impose labor standards and those who view intervention as harmful, or at best wasteful. To some, poorer economies have an unfair trade advantage because of their weak regulatory environment. States have pursued several options to harmonize the rules of trade. They have attached social clauses in regional trade agreements to compel negligent or refractory partners to upgrade their regulatory environments. On the global stage, rich countries have appealed to the ILO, in conjunction with the WTO, to take action against latecomers to the reform movement (Mazur 2000; Finbow 2006). To others, international guidelines are a conceit, an attempt by richer countries to block trade, which would have the consequence of only slowing down the adoption of labor standards in poorer countries because of its harmful effects on income. So-called substandard working conditions in the poor countries are not trade related, but a domestic problem arising from the side effects of industrialization, similar to that previously experienced by the advanced economies (Singh 2003)

The debate pivots on the balance between national sovereignty and international authority (Rodrik 2011).[1] There is consensus on the underlying model. An increase in trade between a low-standard and labor-intensive economy and a high-standard and skill-intensive one harms the latter's low-wage earners (Ehrenberg 1994; Rodrik 1996).[2] Is the hurt large or small? Unequal labor rules may have a small effect on that part of trade pinned down by factor endowments, because, after the effects of regulation are removed, the gap in wages between rich and poor countries remains sizeable; in specialized trade, regulation makes only a small dent in costs because labor productivity differences decidedly favor the industrialized core (Bhagwati 1996). Opponents of international guidelines go on to claim that rising levels of income and increased democratization will drive labor standards in the poorer regions upward, sooner or later. Unequal rules of trade are not necessarily unfair rules.

The empirical evidence on these issues is mixed.[3] In advanced economies, the effects of international rules on wages are often conflated with those of technical change on skilled and unskilled wages. But the actual contribution of labor standards may be beside the point. Policymakers have to be seen alleviating domestic concerns and bringing pressure on international authorities to level the field. Policy cannot wait for poorer countries to move first, patience not being a remedy for groups of unskilled workers in forlorn industrial heartlands demanding immediate action. Unequal rules are always unfair.

The first wave of globalization prefigured modern debates. Reformers did not have confidence that economic development would lead naturally to better labor standards—and figure 2.1 gave credence to this belief. An epistemic community of activists and trade unions propagated the idea of an international code, but states postponed ratification, even piecemeal, until the establishment of the ILO. Multilateral accords proved to be futile because of negotiation costs, and because in the absence of sanctions governments did not have the incentive to harmonize labor rules. In the wake of these failures, states turned toward bilateral labor agreements. The origins of reciprocal accords can be traced to the cross-border movement of workers attracted to European countries harboring fledgling welfare states. To preserve their commitments to the labor compact, states expanded benefits to foreign workers. In exchange, foreign countries consented to raise their labor standards, which amounted to a reduction of tariffs. The end result was the expansion of trade and the labor compact. International trade trumped ideas in leveling labor law.

The outcome was similar to that of the Bagwell-Staiger model I introduced in chapter 2. But this model requires a central authority like the WTO to mete out rewards and penalties. What is remarkable about the early period is that, without an authority governing international coordination, decentralized forces succeeded in promoting convergence in worker protection. States had an incentive to abide by labor agreements they had negotiated with trading partners because they wanted to protect market access. Although the process was not immediately evident, farsighted states came to recognize that agreements standardizing labor laws deepened economic integration, thereby realizing further gains from trade.

WORKERS OF THE WORLD UNITE?

Robert Owen, a pioneer of factory legislation in the U.K., warned that, despite the best intentions of legislators, reforms at the national level would be ineffectual because of international competitive forces. Owen proposed the establishment of international guidelines, and while others on the continent echoed the call, the movement only gathered momentum beginning in the 1870s. The dates of the major international conferences, their objectives, and outcomes are listed in table 4.1. There were three types: conferences run by labor organizations, those run by states, and those organized by a coalition of social reformers and activists.

There are a number of possible readings of the conferences organized by labor. One interpretation is that they were driven by the ideal of an international socialist brotherhood; another is that labor acted as spokesperson for various humanitarian groups determined to eliminate child labor and reduce hours of work of women. But another reading is that workers, like employers and states, recognized that the ongoing decline in transport costs had fundamentally altered the international trading order. Workers identified their role as guardians of national interests and regulations that they themselves had helped establish.

Labor-sponsored conferences made little headway in harmonizing national standards. Initially, delegates met under the auspices of the Workers'

International, but conflicts between adherents of socialist revolution and international liberalism splintered the movement, with the result that labor's representatives began to meet along sectoral or industrial lines after 1890 or so (Donald 2001; Rodríguez García 2006).[4] Although these groups continued to exchange sermons on the benefits of international brotherhood, the imagined community they proposed did not mask underlying cleavages. In a discourse that was remarkably similar to those of their employers and their political trustees, labor was far more motivated to extract real advantages from their competitors. In the conflict between ideals and interests, the latter seem to have had the upper hand.

At the industry level, labor met informally and formally. In 1900, British cotton-textile unions invited representatives of Belgian, French, and German unions to tour Lancashire.[5] In earlier times, textile unions had been in the forefront of demands for universal suffrage and factory regulation, although they began to depend more on collective bargaining to achieve their goals. But even in Lancashire's hands, the fabric of the welfare state was woven from the weft of the local and the warp of the international. By the turn of the century, British hours of work were 20 percent below continental levels, putting the Lancashire industry—it was believed—at a competitive disadvantage since improvements in ring spinning allowed increased substitution between home- and foreign-produced goods. The objective was to demonstrate to Europeans the superior organization of Lancashire's factories and its social and moral benefits. If all went according to plan, upon their return European workers would bring greater pressure on their bosses and governments to reduce working hours. The British plan backfired. Upon visiting Lancashire, foreign unions discovered a higher proportion of children at work than in Europe.[6] They would agree to press for a shorter workday if the British unions would push for greater restrictions on youth employment. Fearful of constraining their ever-diminishing overseas markets, British (male) workers balked.

The meetings of the International Federation of Textile Workers' Associations (IFTWA) were typical of formal attempts to standardize regulation. Delegates from Austria, Belgium, Denmark, France, the Netherlands, the U.S., and the U.K. attended the first congress in Manchester in 1894, and German, Italian, Swedish, and Swiss unionists joined soon after. These were not forums of contestation against globalization. Workers had not banded together to demand tariff protection, because to reject the benefits of trade was to throw the baby out with the bathwater. Rather, they sought to defend hard-won gains, the status quo, of limits to the workday, child labor and the like, which they held to be the best fit with the type of production they had come to specialize in. At the same time, they opposed attempts by rivals to impose conditions in their own

Table 4.1. International conferences on labor standards before 1914

CONFERENCE	CITY	DATE	ORGANIZATION HOST	NUMBER OF COUNTRIES	AGENDA/OBJECTIVES	RESULTS
Geneva Congress	Geneva	1866	Working Men's International Association		Declared support for international labor standards	
International Labour Legislation (Berne)	Berne	1889	Switzerland	8	Child labor; Sunday work; night work; international standards	Discussion pursued at Berlin Conference
Berlin Conference	Berlin	1890	Germany	15	Work in mines; Sunday work; child labor; youth and women's work; factory inspection	Resolved to protect children and women and to establish a day of rest
International Labour Congress	Zurich	1897	Various trade union associations	16	Swiss Federal Council invited governments to establish an international labour office	
International Congress of Social Reformers	Brussels	1897	Belgian Minister of Commerce and Industry	3	Confirm objectives of Berlin 1890; limits to working day; international standards	Resolution to establish an International Bureau of the Protection of Labour; proceedings published
International Association for Labour Legislation–preliminary meeting	Paris	1900	International Association for Labour Legislation (IALL)	25	Consolidate reform movement; establish international labour office; circulate information on legislation; collect standardized employment statistics	Permanent organization created May 1, 1901

(continued)

Table 4.1. *continued*

CONFERENCE	CITY	DATE	ORGANIZATION HOST	NUMBER OF COUNTRIES	AGENDA/OBJECTIVES	RESULTS
International Association for Labour Legislation Congress	Basel	1901	IALL	8	Confirm objectives of Paris 1900 meeting	Establish International Office of Labour and research center; publication of official documents.
International Association for Labour Legislation Congress	Cologne	1902	IALL	12	Regulate hazardous industries; women's night work	Berne Conferences 1905–1906
Technical Conference and Diplomatic Conference	Berne	1905	IALL/Switzerland	14	Prohibit white phosphorus; women's night work	While phosphorus prohibited; women's work prohibited from 10pm to 5am; support for an international organization protecting conditions of work
International Association for Labour Legislation Congress	Lucerne	1906 1908	IALL		Eight-hour shift for coal miners	None; few industrial countries ratified Berne conventions
International Association for Labour Legislation Congress	Zurich	1912	IALL		Administration of labor laws; child labor; hours of labor; holidays; legal relations between employers and workers	None
Technical Conference	Berne	1913	IALL	16	Ten-hour day for women and children under 16 years; limit night work of adult males	Outbreak of war postponed results
Washington Conference	Washington	1919	Established at Paris Conference		Eight-hour day; unemployment insurance; women's and child's labor	ILO established

Sources: Delevingne (1934); Engerman (2003); Follows (1951); Francke (1909); Lowe (1935); Potter (1910).

mills and factories. Disparities in working conditions and rules, perceived to give competitors unfair advantage, dominated discussions. To the British, the objective of the IFTWA was limpid: "Did unionists realize to how great an extent Japan, China, and India, where the people worked for very little and kept at work as long as they pleased, were cutting them out of the markets? They would have to bring these natives up to their level" (IFTWA 1894, 304).

The various countries disputed strategies. The inexorable pressures of international competition tempered workers' expectations. Delegates from Lancashire encouraged counterparts to establish a shorter working day on the continent, while the Germans demanded the British raise the minimum age of work to Prussian levels. Smaller economies, like Switzerland and Denmark, resisted factory regulation and supported better social insurance schemes. The Belgian delegate demanded assistance from the British for political activity. "The stronger countries could help the weak," which, the Belgian recognized, "might not seem strictly trade-union work according to British ideas" (IFTWA 1894, 26).

By the end of its first decade the IFTWA had accomplished little. The British delegate (IFTWA 1908, 21) in Vienna admonished his continental counterparts:

> We are disposed to pay our [British] contributions to the International Fund without claiming any benefit. But we can't go as far as to pay for other nations without claiming any benefit. As to labor legislation, much has been done in this direction by England. It would be better if the labourers on the Continent would follow our example—fewer words, more deeds!

Eventually, British labor turned its back on its European colleagues. It held back payments to the federation's strike fund and, to the consternation of competitors, preferred to invest in a union-employer initiative to seek new sources of cheap and abundant raw cotton that would provide Lancashire some margin of adjustment to offset its superior working conditions and shorter hours. The frustration among internationalists was palpable and their vision of an international brotherhood shattered. A decade earlier, Sidney and Beatrice Webb (1902, 867) foresaw the collapse:

> If, indeed, we could arrive at an International Minimum of education and sanitation, leisure and wages, below which no country would permit any section of its manual workers to be employed in any trade whatsoever, industrial parasitism would be a thing of the past. But internationalism of this sort—a zollverein based on universal Factory Act and fair Wages clause—is obviously utopian.

THE IALL AS PURVEYOR OF SOCIAL NORMS

After Brazil abolished the slave trade in 1888, the protection of industrial workers became the calling card of social activists worldwide. By the 1890s, a broad-based movement had taken shape with the goal of harmonizing labor standards internationally. Many of the movement's leaders were Belgians and Swiss, whose small open economies had much to gain from international guidelines. Early meetings in 1897 in Brussels and in Zurich brought together an amalgam of labor representatives, socialists, Catholics, and liberal reformers, but it was quickly evident that organized labor distrusted the orientation and goals of the movement.[7] At the founding of the International Association for Labor Legislation (IALL) in Paris in 1900, social reformers had control of the agenda. After the war, the ILO was to borrow heavily from the IALL model (Shotwell 1934).[8]

The IALL was principally an epistemic community whose primary objective was evidenced-based policy and advocacy (Van Daele 2005; Keck and Sikkink 1998). Its members included leading authorities on labor conditions: Lujo Brentano (Germany), Ernest Mahaim (Belgium), and Alexandre Millerand (France). The IALL depended on national branches to collect standardized information on workplace conditions that was then disseminated across its network. Reformers did not shy from stigmatizing their own country's inferior labor laws and showcasing achievements elsewhere. European interests dominated the agenda. Japan sent delegates but had a marginal role in deliberations, while Carroll Wright, a founder of U.S. Bureau of Labor, was an occasional New World observer.

In the decades before the Paris conference, social activists (Rae 1894; Rist 1897) on both sides of the Atlantic had produced studies on workplace risks and circulated proposals for reform (Rodgers 1998). This was an informal progressive movement, but ultimately national in scope and purpose. The originality of the IALL was that it situated labor regulations in the context of globalization. Reformers contended that while trade may have increased volatility and risks of employment, labor regulation, properly designed, would secure workers the benefits of economic integration. IALL meetings did not contest globalization; delegates bashed protectionism instead, many of its leading spokespersons being ardent free traders.[9]

The IALL meetings were not always harmonious. The concept of 'core standards,' integral to twenty-first-century debates on international labor codes, was not formally developed.[10] There was bickering over the competitive advantages and disadvantages of projected labor standards and, as in the meetings of labor groups, delegates fell back on the rights of countries to legislate as they saw fit.

From the outset, activists from Italy and Norway spoke against recommendations to raise the legal age of child labor, arguing, as poorer countries do today, that international standards protected market share of richer countries. With regard to night work of women, delegates at the 1905 Berne Conference recommended 12 hours of continuous night rest for women, but Belgium (an original sponsor of the motion) demanded 10 hours of rest to protect its export interests (IALL 1907). A compromise was reached at 11 hours which Belgium and representatives of countries from the European periphery accepted, with the amendment that it was not to be adopted for another four years. There was also discussion at Berne on occupational safety, and it was agreed to limit the content of phosphorous in matches. Most countries did adopt the safety measure, but the U.S. refused, claiming that Japan, its chief competitor, had opted out of the agreement (Francke 1909).

In the face of delegates' resistance to harmonize labor standards, the powers of the IALL were limited, depending on moral suasion or soft coercion. It had no procedure in place to ensure ratification, and there was no proposed mechanism to guarantee market access. Even its leading architects saw the movement as a "chapter full of hope," restricted to the use of "moral force" (Fontaine 1920, 181). The few conventions that were actually signed, according to Engerman (2003, 37–38), had little to no effect because many of the signatories had introduced these provisions previously. Still, the IALL may have mattered as a purveyor of the reform ideal. In the five years after Berne, Belgium, Italy, Portugal, Spain, and Sweden, all latecomers to the reform movement, prohibited night work of women. National legislation converged on the maximum number of working hours for women and children (IALL 1911; Lowe 1935, 116). Attendance at conferences grew in the decade before the outbreak of war, although the commonality of purpose was strongest among countries with comparable factor endowments.[11] Even British delegates took a decisive role in discussions, unlike previous international associations where their contribution was more phlegmatic (Lyons 1963).[12]

On balance, did the IALL leave any real effect on policy adoption? There is limited statistical support for the role of the IALL as a purveyor of ideas. Returning to the model of chapter 2, I added dummy variables if both countries, A and B, attended IALL conferences in 1901 (Basel), 1905 (Berne), and 1913 (Zurich and Berne). I find attendance at all three meetings is related to a higher likelihood of adoption, but only for 1901 was it significant.[13] The effects of the 1905 and 1913 conferences may be poorly estimated because the primary objective of the later meetings was to harmonize the dimensions of existing labor regulation, as most countries had some laws on the books by this period.

It is fair to conclude that while the IALL may have spread the social norm of reform, it does not necessarily follow that regulation was adopted because of ideas in the 'air.'[14] Information networks cannot by themselves explain under what circumstances the new body of legislation was in fact adopted, especially in countries where local membership in communities in support of legislation was practically nonexistent. Yet, for a pioneer organization, the achievements of the IALL did not go unnoticed. States sending delegates to monitor proceedings came to see that the IALL was not a radical movement, hostage to organized labor's interests. Governments benefited from the scientific research conducted, since in many countries newly founded Departments of Labor were unprepared to do the necessary groundwork (Lowe 1935, 102). More importantly, states drew the lesson that multilateral agreements were costly to negotiate and defection would go unpunished. Instead, countries turned increasingly toward bilateral labor accords. Unlike IALL declarations, bilateral treaties were successful because they tied the adoption of regulation directly to trade.

HOW LABOR STANDARDS MADE STATES: EXTENDING BENEFITS TO MIGRANTS

State intervention showed a remarkable evolution in the period. The first meetings intended to bring about an international labor code failed because, like labor-sponsored associations, states wanted to protect the types of regulation they deemed to satisfy domestic interests, and hence maximize their support among their constituencies. This phase coincided with the series of trade wars discussed in chapter 2. By the turn of the century, cooperation had supplanted coercion as states became pro-active, extending benefits to foreign workers and negotiating bilateral agreements to ensure that trading partners did likewise. A conjunction of domestic and foreign interests lay behind the new attitudes toward regulation.

The Berlin conference of 1890 was representative of early state-led initiatives. Into the 1880s, Bismarck believed an agreement on international labor standards was intractable (Follows 1951, 91, 120–43). The Berlin meeting he organized had more to do with the chancellor's domestic concerns and geo-political ambitions than his interest in the welfare of workers around the world. Many countries were hesitant to send delegates, wary of offering Bismarck support in his ongoing campaign to contain labor and in his attempt to advance his country's international prestige. At the outset, Swiss delegates who had previously called for a similar conference, only to be upstaged by Bismarck, demanded "obligatory arrangements" to be signed by participating states. The outcome was predictable. Observers (Rolin-Jaequemyns 1890) saw that in the absence of an international authority to monitor whether or not countries actually complied, and to guarantee market access abroad for those countries that did, any agreement would be ineffective. To support their claim, delegates drew on comparisons with the gold standard. The exchange rate regime functioned because of London's leadership, but there was no obvious hegemon when it came to setting and enforcing labor standards. In fact, at Berlin, countries with the most advanced labor standards, like Britain, opposed a unified position. The emerging countries of northern Europe preserved their right to set labor standards according to their calendar. In the end, the achievements were minor and only Portugal which had no factory code before Berlin felt compelled to introduce labor legislation in 1891.[15] Perhaps most remarkable was Bismarck's response. He used the failure of the meeting as pretext to limit Germany's welfare state to the social entitlements he already introduced. "A normal workday could be established for Germany alone," he warned, "if Germany were surrounded by a Chinese wall and were economically self-sufficient."[16]

To explain the change in policy direction, I need to situate states' attitudes toward labor standards in the context of the period's broader social and political forces. By the turn of the century, many European states had legislated some form of labor protection, but cross-border migration threatened its effectiveness. In France, employers in border regions actively sought out Belgian and Italian guest workers (Strikwerda 1998, 125); in Germany, according to one historian (Conrad 2008, 48), migrants from Italy, the Netherlands, and Russia turned the Kaiserreich into "a country importing cheap labour on a scale only second to the United States." Almost everywhere nationals had preferential access to social entitlements and foreigners were often excluded from tax-funded relief programs or received substantially reduced benefits (Feldman 2003). Where programs were run by trade unions, they too discriminated on the basis of nationality (Strikwerda 1998, 116). Exceptionally, the U.K. permitted aliens to receive poor relief on the same terms as citizens. When migrant workers returned home, they were fortunate to have received lump-sum payments (Fahrmeir 2001, 114). Revisiting the trope of markets against states, Gérard Noiriel (2001) interpreted the first citizenship laws in France in 1889 which codified the practice of giving beneficial treatment to permanent residents, *les nationaux*, as part of the general backlash to globalization.

A two-tier system was difficult to sustain, even if superior benefits did not attract immigrants and the idea of Europe as a welfare magnate was a long way off.[17] States faced a commitment problem. In northeastern and southern France, as elsewhere, anti-immigration strikes and riots threatened social stability.

Yet, increasingly, states could not turn a blind eye to differential access to social entitlements because of the challenge it posed to the public-good nature of labor standards. Despite calls for literacy tests and hygienic restrictions, there was growing pressure to give foreign workers the same rights as nationals in order to prevent a downward spiral in social policy.[18] It was not in the interest of states to allow certain employers to play off one group of workers against another and undermine established levels of regulation. To do so would alter the equilibrium achieved in the demand for and supply of reform, and potentially unleash social unrest that the labor compact was intended to counter in the first place. Kathleen Thelan (2004, 3) summarized the problems of backsliding for all stakeholders. "Institutional frameworks provide the foundation on which (nationally distinctive) competitive advantage rests, so that key actors (especially employers) who have organized their strategies around these institutions will be loath to part with them." Consequently, states opted to incorporate foreigners in the polity. For instance, France, a weathervane of European attitudes toward migrants, modified citizenship laws after 1890, easing the integration of foreign-born workers (Noiriel and Offerlé 1997).[19]

Historians have situated social policy in the evolution of reciprocal obligations of citizens and states (Bayly 2004, 271–73).[20] Governments driven by the goal of maximizing support had to incorporate larger numbers in civil society, including, but not restricted to, those with the right to vote. Perceptively, Eugen Weber (1976, 489) wrote in his classic history that to "be in France meant to be ruled by French officials." Leonard Horner, the legendary British factory inspector, claimed that better protection at the workplace would serve to integrate workers into civil society, gradually inculcating in them the values of citizenship and patriotism (Fuchs 2005, 624). The labor compact was a symbol of the nation's reach, certainly different from military stature or a common language, but one that tied each household's well-being directly to its guarantor and trustee, which was ultimately the state.[21] There were economic externalities to the decision to uphold labor standards. Because the state was prepared to stand by the labor compact, individuals were more willing to participate in civic institutions, a key component in the formation of social capital. At the individual level, this translated into more investments by families in education and by firms in training.

The asymmetry between Old and New Worlds' attitudes toward immigration was telling. In the New World, the cry for tighter immigration controls supplanted appeals for labor regulation and social insurance. In the relatively open and more inclusive Old World, the call for better labor regulations was louder than the demand for restrictions on foreign labor. The net result was that population movements within Europe strengthened the continent's attachment to the labor compact, while elsewhere immigration weakened it.

COOPERATION TRUMPS COERCION:
TRANSNATIONAL LABOR ACCORDS

The obligations of states toward the labor compact transcended borders. An integral component in state building was establishing durable attachments, the ties that bind, to the patrie.[22] Keen to demonstrate to emigrants that they remained Italians, Poles, or Spaniards, states were compelled to assure the diaspora it had the same rights and benefits of citizenship as those staying behind. More practically, the high proportion of returning emigrants had fiscal consequences, and governments had an incentive to negotiate bilateral accords ensuring reciprocal treatment of native and foreign workers in the two countries. Some examples of these arrangements are given in table 4.2. The early transnational accords, which assured the reciprocal treatment of native and foreign workers, were conceived as backstops against a potential undercutting of labor standards. These accords served to standardize the coverage and application of labor laws reported in table 1.3 and in the appendix. Although they often revolved around single items, the expectation was, as stated clearly in the Germany and Austria-Hungary accord of 1905, that a "broader" harmonization of legislation would follow (Lowe 1935, 143–44).

There was a commercial dimension behind states' strategies, exactly along the lines of the Bagwell-Staiger model I introduced previously. Country B would induce A to upgrade its labor standards in exchange for greater access to B's markets, because in A better working conditions was the equivalent of lower tariffs. Workers and exporters in A expected to be better off or at least as well off as before. Country B anticipated reaping benefits because as the labor costs of its partner rose, so would its exports.[23] Gains for both parties may have been substantial in the presence of economies of scale. The contrast with multilateral attempts to harmonize labor standards was sharp. The epistemic communities behind the international movement had only moral suasion to put ideas into practice; bilateral accords linked adoption to the benefits of trade. In this fashion, the labor compact spread because domestic and foreign interests were entangled. Again, these forces were stronger in the Old World, where countries traded differentiated products that could not easily find new outlets if established markets closed down without warning.

States preferred negotiated bilateral labor accords rather than ratifying conventions of transnational bodies, like the IALL, because they retained direction

Table 4.2. Bilateral labor accords, 1880–1914

YEAR	COUNTRIES	AGREEMENT	MFN
1870	Great Britain – Netherlands	Emigration of Indian labor to Surinam	
1871	Great Britain – Netherlands	Labor recruitment (Guinea)	
1872	France – Great Britain	Emigration of Indian labor to French Colonies	1860/1873
1874	China – Peru	Commerce, navigation, and emigration	
1877	China – Spain	Emigration of Chinese labor to Cuba	
1880	China – United States	Emigration of Chinese labor to USA	
1882	Hawaii – Portugal	Commerce, navigation, and emigration	
1882	Belgium – France	Saving funds	
1894	China – United States	Emigration of Chinese labor to USA	
1897	Belgium – France	Saving funds	
1899	Germany – Great Britain	Colonial labor	
1899	China – Mexico	Labor mobility	
1901	Great Britain – Portugal	Labor mobility between Transvaal and Mozambique	
1904	France – Italy	Comprehensive labor treaty	1898
1904	China – Great Britain	Chinese labor	
1904	Italy–Switzerland	Accident insurance	1904
1904	Germany – Italy	Accident insurance	1904/1906
1905	Austria – Germany	Accident insurance and labor legislation	1905
1905	Belgium – Luxembourg	Accident insurance	
1905	Germany – Luxembourg	Accident insurance	
1906	France – Italy	Saving funds	
1906	Belgium – France	Accident insurance	1881
1906	France – Great Britain	Emigration from New Hebrides	1907
1906	Germany – Sweden	Accident insurance	1906/1911
1906	Belgium – Luxembourg	Accident insurance	
1906	France – Italy	Accident insurance	
1906	France – Luxembourg	Accident insurance	
1907	Germany – Netherlands	Accident insurance	
1909	France – Great Britain	Accident insurance	
1909	Great Britain – Sweden	Accident insurance	
1909	Austria – Italy	Accident insurance	1903/1906
1910	Belgium – France	Accident insurance	
1910	France – Italy	Protection of young persons	
1910	France – Italy	Social insurance laws	
1910	France – Great Britain	Accident insurance	
1911	Germany – Sweden	Accident insurance	
1911	Denmark – France	Arbitration	

Table 4.2. *continued*

YEAR	COUNTRIES	AGREEMENT	MFN
1912	Belgium – Germany	Accident insurance	
1912	Germany – Italy	Accident insurance	1904/1906
1912	Germany – Spain	Maritime accidents	
1913	Italy – United States	Accident insurance	1913
1913	Belgium – Germany	Accident insurance	
1913	France – Switzerland	Pensions	1906
1914	Germany – Netherlands	Accident insurance	

Sources: Labor accords from Lowe (1935); MFN agreements preceding and following labor accord from Robert Pahre's commercial treaty data set, personal communication.

of social policy. Moreover, because the accords were linked to market access, states had an incentive to promote and abide by them. The intuition was clearly laid out by the German Minister of the Interior, in parliamentary discussion in 1902 on Imperial commercial social and policy. Since import tariffs had reduced the purchasing power of workers, the degree of further commercial protection available to domestic manufacturers was limited. Better to persuade commercial rivals to raise levels of social protection. "If we and our neighbors agree to common charges for worker protection, we will be able to lower our commercial duties. We should consider rivals which raise their levels of protection favorably."[24] Germany had come to reject Bismarck's formulation of a "Chinese wall" in defense of social policy; instead labor regulations and economic integration were now seen as compatible. In terms of the model of chapter 2, the reduction in tariffs would lead to lower trade costs and higher likelihood of convergence.

Many of the signatories of these accords had previously negotiated most favored nation treaties as indicated in the last column of table 4.2.[25] The spike in labor accords coincided with the clustering of MFN treaties in the decade after 1904. In negotiations joining trade and these early social clauses, high-tariff countries had a discrete advantage, because they had something to give away. Germany strategically exploited its tariff structure to negotiate privileged access to its markets in exchange for better labor protection.[26] Countries agreed to raise levels of regulation because they exported more. The added incentive was that partners gained market access in countries that had MFN arrangements with Germany. In this regard, the spread of the labor compact was not independent of the decline in trade barriers before the war.

The France-Italy labor treaty of 1904 represented a comprehensive attempt by one trading partner to persuade a laggard to harmonize labor laws in exchange for greater market access.[27] France and Italy had engaged in a trade war that began in 1886 and effectively lasted into the early 1900s. The war was especially hard on Italy because of its dependence on France for its exports of specialty goods.[28] While Italian silk was a relatively standardized item and producers readily found markets in Switzerland, Italy's specialty wine producers were less fortunate and they had to dump their stock (Lazer 1999, 453). As part of the agreement ending the trade war, France demanded that Italy raise standards to international norms, allowing its exporters greater market access. In exchange, France agreed to give Italian migrant workers the same level of benefits that French workers received. It also enticed its trading partner by removing selective commercial duties on Italian imports. Italy was not opposed to the French initiative. Its history of labor legislation was recent and, because the percentage of eligible voters was low, the liberal government exploited the French initiative to circumvent vested interests who opposed labor reform.[29] The net result was that labor costs increased relatively more in Italy. In the five years after the accord, French exports to Italy rose by 61 percent; Italian exports to France increased by about 20 percent after the agreement.[30]

The strategy of linking regulation and market access was generalized across Europe. The French and Italian arrangement, which even dispassionate observers like the U.S. Department of Labor viewed as groundbreaking, served as a template for the France-Belgium (1906) accord, and Germany's treaties with Italy (1904) and Austria-Hungary (1905).[31] For the time period 1902–1914, I estimated the short- and long-run effects of the bilateral treaties (from table 4.2) on trade costs (from table 2.2) between pairs of European countries (a and b) with the regression:

$$\text{Trade costs}_{ab} = 0.0008 + 0.9248 \text{trade costs}_{ab(t-1)} - 0.0066 \text{labor treaty}_{ab}$$
$$(0.0138) \ (0.0182)^{**} \qquad\qquad (0.0029)^{*}$$

+controls (tariffs, common border, distance between capitals, year dummies),

$$N = 1868 \qquad F_{(18, 179)} = 2265.4 \qquad \text{R-squared} = 0.96.^{[32]}$$

Labor treaty is a binary variable that takes the value of 1 (0 otherwise) during the year when the pair signed a treaty. The short-run effect is the coefficient on labor treaty, −0.007, significant at the 2 percent level. The long-run effect is calculated as $-0.007/(1-0.925) = -0.089$, or a 9 percent decline in trade costs ($p = .02$). With an elasticity of substitution between foreign and home goods of

11, the point estimate amounts to a rise of bilateral exports of 35 percent for each partner.[33] Countries had an incentive to consent to converge on labor standards, because they did not wish to forsake the gains from trade.

CONCLUSION TO PART 1:
REINTERPRETING THE WELFARE STATE

Figure 4.1 summarizes the interplay of demand and supply behind the rise of the labor compact. For each year, I give the total number of labor laws adopted.[34] The maximum for the 18 countries in the sample I use is 90. I also track the decline in trade costs, calculated as the weighted average of trade costs for the sum of all trading pairs. This measure captures the general degree of openness. The decline in trade costs was steep beginning in the 1880s, as the rise in the number of adoptions was rapid. Domestic and foreign pressures operated simultaneously. Individual countries adopted labor legislation because of demand from workers confronting volatility in employment and wages; external trade pressures transmitted the labor compact internationally and established a backstop against a race to the bottom. All countries were potential leaders and followers. The net result was the growth in trade and the expansion of the labor compact.

The beginning of the welfare state was tied to the degree of external exposure. Where trade forces were strong, the labor compact was more developed. This view is distinct from, although not necessarily opposed to, the baseline narrative showcasing domestic factors. In a classic study, Esping-Andersen (1990, 22–23), relying heavily on the power resources approach pitting labor against capital, ranked OECD countries on their ability to assure "a livelihood without reliance on the market." Three categories of modern welfare states emerged: the liberal or Beveridgean model of Anglo-Saxon countries; the conservative or Bismarckian approach of continental Europe; and the Nordic, or social democratic, alternative. Welfare states were weakest in the group of Anglo-American states, and at the other extreme were Europe's small countries that had the highest "de-commodification" index. The latter's welfare states were "of very recent date," originating sometime after 1950. As for the U.S., the porous safety net was embedded in deep-seated and exceptional historical forces. I have no quarrel with the final rank ordering. Rather my concerns are that outcomes are conflated with processes and, as a result, the chronology is also suspect.

Moving beyond comparative history, economic integration had a formative influence on the rise of the welfare state. First, greater international competitiveness exposed workers to a new set of risks. These forces were strongest in

Figure 4.1. Trade costs and the labor compact, 1880–1914
Trade costs from Jacks, Meissner, and Novy (2008). Labor regulation consists of
factory inspection, minimum age law, limits on night work of women, 11-hour
working day for women, and accident compensation. Dates of adoption from table 1.2.

small and open economies. Second, the new international order reconfigured
political alliances and, in Europe, workers and capital forged coalitions supporting free trade in exchange for social protection. Again, small countries were favored, because of lower negotiation costs. Third, welfare states transcended
boundaries because countries cared about the level of regulation of trading partners. States acted strategically linking greater market access at home for greater
social protection abroad. Both large and small states were equally likely to adopt
standards of trading partners. Lastly, even before 1914, the New World had weaker
sets of labor regulation than the Old World because prices of resource exports
were set in world markets and external pressures to establish a welfare state were
weak. U.S. exceptionalism was unremarkable in light of developments in Australia and Canada.

   The process of adoption in the figure makes clear that at its origins the welfare state was not built in opposition to markets; indeed trade was a pathway in
the diffusion of the labor compact. And while historians and political scientists
(Katzenstein 1985) have dated the origins of the welfare state in Scandinavia

and in the Benelux countries to the post-1945 years, if not later, the fundamentals of the European model were well in place before 1914. Liberal, conservative, and social democratic versions of the welfare states were superimposed on the labor compact—globalization was the common denominator of the European model.

There is another reading of figure 4.1. In the preceding chapters, I have argued that causality ran from globalization to the labor compact. But the obverse also held: labor regulation because of its effects on relative wages altered comparative advantages and, hence, the nature of trade. Countries adopting regulation developed new products and varieties that were sold to new destinations. The labor compact made firms and workers better exporters and importers. My goal in the second part of the book is to examine the channels through which this occurred.

Part Two

How the Labor Compact Made Globalization

DID THE LABOR COMPACT
REDUCE INEQUALITY?

A crucial question concerns the sharing of the potential gains from globalization—between rich and poor countries and among different groups within a country. It is not sufficient to understand that the poor of the world need globalization as much as the rich do; it is also important to make sure that they actually get what they need. This may require extensive institutional reform, even as globalization is defended.

—Amartya Sen, "How to Judge Globalism," page 18.

INTRODUCTION TO PART 2: FROM THE LABOR MARKET
TO PRODUCTIVITY

So far, I have made the claim that globalization was a prime mover behind the adoption and transmission of the labor compact. The volume and type of trade conditioned responses at national and international levels. But this can only be half of the story. Globalization was not fixed. It was an ongoing process that was affected by the expansion of the labor compact itself. The causal mechanism was from higher wages to enhanced labor productivity, with the result that the regulation shifted comparative advantages across trading partners. My argument is by no means novel. Gavin Wright (2006, 158) makes the case for the effect of wages on productivity in his survey of U.S. labor market development since the 1920s. He wrote: "Of course real wages and productivity are mutually interactive, but one can point to distinct historical circumstances operating in the labor market, suggesting that the primary causal influence ran from the labor market to productivity rather than the other way around." It is the burden of this part of the book to demonstrate that the labor compact in the late nineteenth century was such a historical circumstance.[1] My argument is in two phases. In this chapter, I study the effects of regulation on wages and inequality, and, in the next chapter, I make the causal link from labor market outcomes to productivity and, ultimately, to international trade.

There are a number of competing arguments on the movement in relative wages before 1914. Lindert and Williamson (2003) claimed globalization forces lay behind changes in inequality. Relying on the predictions of standard trade theory, the rise of the wage-land rent ratio in the Old World and the opposite trend in the New World, they identified winners and losers between and within countries. Between country inequality widened since certain economies opted to be closed, forsaking the benefits of falling trade costs. Elsewhere, growth was choked off because of fundamental reasons like poorly designed property rights or low levels of democratic participation. The within component is more difficult to aggregate because of conflicting trends. In the Old World, the wages of unskilled workers, the abundant factor, rose relative to land rents and skilled wages. In the New, the gap between unskilled and skilled wages widened.

This is a partial assessment of the causes of inequality because it is based on movements in wages and incomes only. Worker welfare has many dimensions. Consider the case of working hours. Hours were very long in most countries in the mid nineteenth century and have fallen considerably, and often very abruptly, in the more than one hundred and fifty years since. They have been a significant form of adjustment. The standard competitive model of labor supply assumes that wage movements give complete information about changes in leisure. Worktimes, it is supposed, converged in tandem with wages because hours generally decline as incomes rise. Since income levels in labor-abundant and relatively poorer countries before 1914 rose more rapidly, hours in the region naturally converged to those in the land-abundant and richer countries of recent settlement in North America and Australia.

The labor compact complicates this picture. Regulation had bite, reinforcing globalization's salutary forces in the Old World, while offsetting downward pressures in the New. Thus, Lindert and Williamson understated egalitarian trends in the former and exaggerated the tendency toward inequality in the latter. But even this summary is suspect. The labor compact was ostensibly directed at the most vulnerable, women, children, and the unskilled, and the gender gap and skill premium ought to have contracted, but male workers may also have reaped a portion of the benefits because of discrimination in labor markets. As a result, the labor compact's effects on wages were uneven across and within countries, its adoption rendering the simple dichotomy of winners and losers problematic. The labor compact mediated the effects of globalization on wages.

In this chapter, I begin my examination of the labor compact in the manu-facturing sector of Brazil. In the face of longstanding inequality, did regulation succeed in narrowing the skill premium and the gender gap in the country's Southern Cone? In poor countries, biased technical change toward skilled workers exacerbated inequality since the importation of machinery from rich countries and foreign investment were complementary. But the evidence indi-cates that the bias was not severe as local producers adjusted equipment to meet local factor endowments. The implication is that the adoption of regulation in the labor-abundant regions of the New and Old Worlds had comparable out-comes, the Brazilian economy sharing in the potential of improvements in unskilled wages and enhancements in labor productivity.

My claim in this chapter is analogous to that proposed by Robert C. Allen (2009) to explain the origins of the industrial revolution. The high-wage econ-omy of eighteenth-century Britain induced the substitution of cheap capital and energy for labor. One hundred years later, the labor laws of the first wave of globalization altered factor prices in the same direction. Labor regulation trans-formed the Old World from a labor-abundant to a labor-scarce region, preci-pitating catch-up with the richer regions in the New World and Britain. I return to this theme in the chapter's conclusion.

DID LABOR STANDARDS MATTER? TWO VIEWS

Table 1.2 presented dates of introductions of the labor compact. What were the effects of the new laws on labor market outcomes? The literature on the regulation is vast and I have selected two approaches, albeit stylized, to study effects. In the spirit of the new institutional economic history, Engerman (2003, 60) wrote that changes in "legislation imposed only such standards as those that had already been achieved, or that the actual standards meant only a very small change from what was already occurring." Fishback (1998; 2007, 300) provided several examples of this process for the U.S. During the Progressive Era, an amalgam of employers, workers, social reformers, religious groups, and elected officials—"a big tent"—banded together in support of labor reform. Technical change was a force behind the new laws. Business owners of mod-ernized factories supported regulation because they adapted easily to it, and because tougher laws forced competitors using inferior technologies and em-ploying predominately adolescent and female labor forces to close down. Still other companies had an incentive to support limits on child labor and encour-age more schooling because they demanded an educated workforce. For these groups of employers, opposition to reform was primarily ideological, based on

Figure 5.1. Regulation and adaptation in Belgium: Textiles
All data from Van Houtte (1949), except for investments in ring frames in panel (e)
from Saxonhouse and Wright (2004, 144). Labor share in panel (b) is wages x
employment. Values in francs. Output in panel (c) is total of yarn and woven goods in
tons. Capital is spindles and looms. Export volumes in tons.

(b) labor share

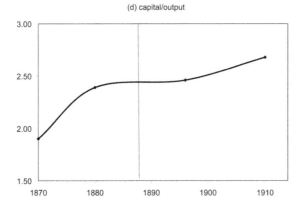

(d) capital/output

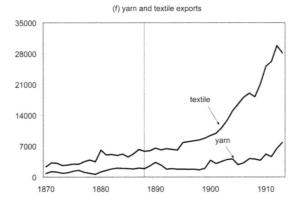

(f) yarn and textile exports

the belief that legislation in one area was the thin end of the wedge to more comprehensive legislation.

Some workers had reason to be concerned about reform as well. While men in direct competition with women and children supported limits on their supply, working families dependent on children's earnings formed a strong opposition to legislative intervention. Because skilled workers were scarce they too balked at reform, concerned that a larger pool of educated workers would flatten their premium wages (Doepke and Zilibotti 2005). Recognizing these diverse claims, activists pursued a timetable of legislation so as to prevent backsliding. The end result was that the new body of laws was diluted and its effects on labor market outcomes modest.

Studies in this vein have tended to focus on single pieces of legislation in a closed economy setting (Goldin 1990; Moehling 1999). But the argument can be extended. If economic development among trading partners was synchronized and induced the sort of changes described by Engerman, labor standards improved elsewhere and in a fairly parallel fashion, leaving relative prices and trade flows unaltered.[2] A rising tide lifted all boats. Labor standards in this view had no effect on trade because the new legislation codified best practices. This narrative is based on the strong assumption that decision makers faced no surprises. Governments were not entangled in the policy formation of trading partners, political rivals, or neighbors—the genesis of the labor compact being a domestic affair.

The alternative view claims that legislation leaves real effects. Caballero and Hammour (1998) designed a dynamic model of industrial relations in imperfect competition that was intended to track the effects of labor legislation in France of the 1970s on labor and capital shares.[3] Faced by growing social pressures, the government legislates a shorter workweek without a proportional change in weekly wages. This is a form of 'wage push.' In the very short run, the supply of capital is inelastic and militant labor is able to appropriate a larger share of the quasi-rents. There is a fall in output, market share at home and abroad contracting as firms attempt to pass on costs. The immediate loss in profits induces the substitution of capital for labor in the medium-to-long term.[4] Pressures to substitute away from labor are most keenly felt in open economies, since investors will develop or seek out new technologies (and products) to guarantee returns that they could earn elsewhere in the world. The end result is that capital's share increases along with output and reverts to its long-run level.[5] The change in capital to labor ratios has implications for the choice of technology, the nature of production, and hence trade.

In the wage-push model, unlike the big tent, labor laws are not fully anticipated. In the world of 'open political economy,' the shock to firms' cost structures can originate in domestic or external forces, or both, as they did before 1914. The adoption in Belgium in 1889 of limits on child labor provides an example of the joint contribution of domestic and foreign pressures.[6] The combination of a long period of real wage stagnation and the lag in social legislation compared to its neighbors, France and Germany, incited mobilization in the 'social upheaval.' Figure 5.1 describes the ensuing effects in the cotton textile industry where labor unrest persisted throughout the 1890s (Scholliers 1996, 225). Small firms operating a combination of rings and mules dominated the industry. The labor force was mixed. Firms had hired adolescents as apprentices to evade compliance (De Herdt 2001, 36), and others moved parts of production to the countryside where wages were up to 40 percent lower—akin to outsourcing to the informal sector (Scholliers 1996, 91). Despite these initiatives, real wages increased (panel a). Evidently, real wages were on the increase before the new law was adopted, a trend that may be partially explained by external pressure on Belgian social policy as local business became aware that labor legislation was imminent. Anyway, nominal wages, perhaps a more accurate indicator of earnings in the period of the gold standard, spiked upwards in 1889.[7] In the short term, capital's share of output was squeezed (panel b), productivity stagnated (panel c), and there was little renewed investment in the industry. Belgium's overall trade balance between 1890 and 1891 fell by more than 5 percent (Mitchell 1981).[8]

In the medium term (Blanchard 1997), capital gained the upper hand. In panel d, I track the ratio of spinning machines to yarn output (after correcting for yarn spun and type of machinery). Companies seeking to realize a rate of return available elsewhere scrapped older equipment, spinning mules, and replaced them with ring spinning machines operated by less-skilled workers, mainly women and adolescents (panel e).[9] I return to the long-term implications of the new investments on trade in the next chapter.

WAGES AND HOURS OF WORK AROUND THE WORLD

In this section, I use the *Fifteenth Annual Report* (hereafter the Report) of the U.S. Department of Labor (1900) to contrast the effects of the labor compact across regions. Under the supervision of Carroll Wright, the Report published data on weekly work hours and daily wages for the period 1850 to 1900. Compared to series that rely on observations for a small sample of businesses, usually textile mills or mines only, the Report is well suited for international comparisons. The project was not modest. The department consulted over seven hundred official publications covering eighty-eight countries and territories, ranging from Algeria to Venezuela. The Report included both manufacturing

Table 5.1. Wages and hours of work around the world, 1870–1900

Country/region	Hours per week			Wages (cents/hr)				
	n (s.d)	1870	1900	n (s.d.)	1870 (.25)	1870 (.50)	1900 (.25)	1900 (.50)
European core								
Austria-Hungary	923 (5.7)	64.3	58.6	1393 (0.31)	2.15	2.8	3.89	6.04
Belgium	172 (5.9)	72.9	64.2	136 (0.19)	3.29	4.86	4.11	5.61
Denmark	46 (6.0)	68.2	56.2	67 (0.39)	2.64	4.66	9.29	10.89
France	650 (5.5)	66.1	65.6	478 (0.41)	3.45	4.36	5.76	7.77
Germany	672 (7.2)	67.6	63.4	468 (0.36)	2.75	5.15	7.29	8.99
Great Britain	2448 (5.0)	56.9	56.0	2448 (0.33)	11.6	13.18	14.89	15.64
Italy	274 (5.4)	63.7	63.7	547 (0.32)	1.88	3.67	3.67	5.27
Netherlands	178 (6.3)	65.0	60.5	183 (0.31)	4.43	5.35	5.06	8.33
Norway	5 (10.3)		66.0	476 (0.26)			4.91	6.00
Sweden	22 (4.0)	67.1	56.8	121 (0.34)	2.41	5.01	4.33	7.61
Switzerland	140 (5.7)	70.0	59.0	255 (0.42)	2.14	3.17	4.58	7.93
mean		66.2	60.9		3.7	5.2	6.2	8.2
European periphery								
Ireland	284 (7.3)	63.8	58.6	232 (0.29)	3.29	3.57	4.51	5.94
Portugal	23 (64.2)		64.4	258 (0.37)			3.73	4.94
Russia	235 (7.9)	68.8	64.5	843 (0.45)	1.92	2.44	2.98	4.00

Spain	77 (7.3)	64.7	59.1	156 (0.56)	3.25	3.8	4.47	5.58
Med. islands	140 (2.9)	58.3	56.0	175 (0.39)	3.09	4.01	4.18	6.21
mean		63.9	60.5		2.9	3.5	4.0	5.3
North America								
Canada	505 (4.3)	57.2	62.6	505 (0.69)	12.48	16.05	13.51	16.58
United States	1570 (5.6)	62.0	57.2	1570 (0.89)	15.97	20.61	19.93	25.49
mean		59.6	59.9		14.2	18.3	16.7	21.0
Other settler countries								
Australia	189 (3.8)	56.2	48.1	949 (0.80)	11.96	16.33	17.71	26.44
New Zealand	110 (7.9)	57.2	49.8	497 (0.69)	9.55	18.36	21.81	25.90
South Africa	133 (6.9)	59.4	58.5	685 (0.97)	9.09	11.72	19.28	21.85
mean		57.6	52.1		10.2	15.5	19.6	24.7
Central America								
Bahamas	3 (3.5)		56.0	34 (0.30)			3.43	7.18
Belize	17 (0)		54.0	23 (0.44)			5.56	8.67
Cuba	57 (3.6)	59.2	59.4	96 (1.03)			6.36	10.4
Dominican Republic	7 (0)		60.0	18 (1.58)			2.20	6.20
Jamaica	5 (0)		55.0	24 (2.04)			5.24	7.85
Mexico	65 (6.7)	60.6	69.0	209 (1.22)	2.57	3.96	3.04	6.00
Cen. Am. countries	16 (6.4)	62.0	62.8	60 (1.14)			5.92	9.36
mean		60.6	59.5		2.6	4.0	4.5	8.0

(continued)

Table 5.1. (continued)

Country/region	Hours per week			Wages (cents/hr)				
	n (s.d)	1870	1900	n (s.d.)	1870 (.25)	1870 (.50)	1900 (.25)	1900 (.50)
South America								
Argentina	31.0 (1.1)	60.0	60.2	90 (1.07)	7.3	12.3	12.66	16.94
Brazil	93 (4.6)	61.2	60.6	169 (0.91)	6.37	8.53	9.31	12.87
Chile	6 (8.2)		68.0	56 (0.88)			5.56	8.91
Colombia	46 (5.1)	64.4	64.2	116 (1.35)	5.12	8.94	6.54	10.28
Ecuador	58 (2.0)	60.0	58.5	110 (0.96)			7.69	11.08
Guyana	20 (14.6)	59.2	60.3	48 (0.62)			6.17	9.25
Peru	19 (4.1)	55.3	55.2	95 (1.22)			8.7	14.57
Uruguay	6 (4.1)	61.2	61.7	33 (1.28)	5.49	14.31	13.71	17.02
Venezuela	50 (5.2)	56.1	53.0	112 (1.16)	7.70	11.98	9.74	19.25
mean		59.7	60.2		6.4	11.2	8.9	13.4
Middle East & North Africa								
Algeria	56 (6.5)		64.5	114 (0.28)			4.47	7.26
Iran	1 (0)		66.0	129 (0.21)			1.55	2.73
Morocco	30 (0)		66.0	41 (0.38)			2.55	4.36
Turkey	80 (5.1)		66.3	229 (0.85)			3.89	3.62
mean			65.7				3.1	4.5

Sub-Saharan Africa								
Sierra Leone	16 (0)	48.0	48.0	22 (0.16)			2.88	6.75
Southeast Asia								
India	38 (7.9)	56.0	50.6	897 (0.24)	0.75	1.29	0.95	1.54
Sri Lanka	37 (1.8)		53.6	67 (0.60)			2.57	4.48
mean		56.0	52.1		0.8	1.3	1.8	3.0
Far East								
China	37 (2.0)	60.0	61.8	198 (0.15)	1.10	1.70	2.04	2.43
Japan	17 (11.3)	59.3	65.6	246 (0.11)	0.91	1.32	1.55	2.1
mean		59.7	63.7		1.0	1.5	1.8	2.3
Pacific islands								
Hawaii	32 (1.6)		54.2	64 (1.52)			7.31	12.4
Philippines	1 (0)		68.0	40 (0.42)			6.26	7.24
mean			61.1				6.79	9.82

Source: U.S. Commissioner of Labor (1900).

Notes: Values in U.S.$. See appendix for details.

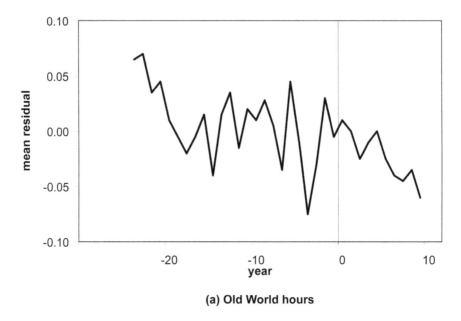

(a) Old World hours

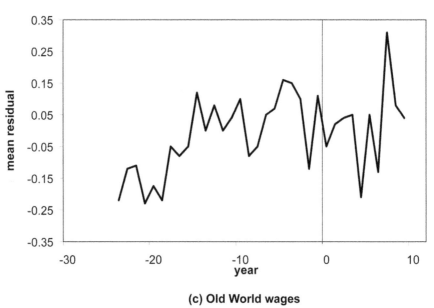

(c) Old World wages

Figure 5.2 Wages and hours of work: Before and after legislation
Residuals of regressions of wages and hours on sex, occupation, country, and year.
Residuals centered on dates of adoption of limits to female and children's work.
Year 0 represents date of adoption. Old World is Belgium, France, Germany,
and the Netherlands; New World is Australia and Canada. Adapted from
Huberman and Minns (2008).

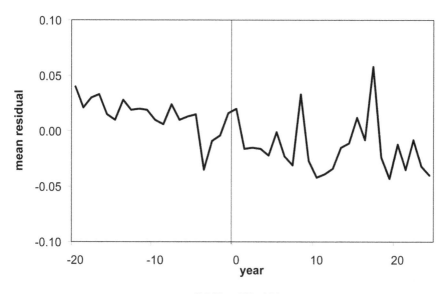

(b) New World hours

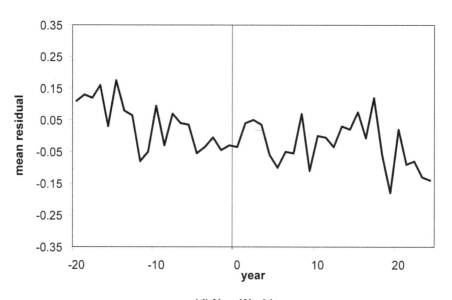

(d) New World wages

and non-manufacturing sectors for male and female workers. There is no information on agriculture; for instance, data for Brazil are from the industrial enclaves in the Southern Cone. Because of data limitations for the early years, I restrict myself to the period between 1870 and 1900. The appendix gives additional information on the Report.

Table 5.1 presents average hours of work and wages in 1870 and 1900 for nearly 50 countries and territories.[10] Because country-wide wage distributions are skewed at the top end, I report figures for the 25th and 50th percentiles, which give a better idea of the earnings of unskilled and semi-skilled workers, those groups who would be most affected by the adoption of labor regulation. Wages are in cents (U.S.$) per hour, converted at the nominal exchange rate by the Department of Labor.[11] Wage growth was strong in the Old World. In the European core, earnings of unskilled workers rose by 67 percent between 1870 and 1900, and that of semi-skilled by 57 percent. Changes were more modest in the New World. While wages rose in industrializing Brazil, earnings rose by 10 percent in Canada, a pattern consistent with that reported in chapter 3. Australia, India, New Zealand, Sierra Leone, and Sri Lanka had toiled the fewest hours in 1870; the middle-income Old World the longest. From 1870 to 1914, hours declined markedly in Europe and, with the exception of the settler economies outside of the Americas, they remained stable everywhere else. Within Europe, Belgium, Denmark, Sweden, and Switzerland experienced the biggest reductions. The correlation between wages and hours would appear to be loose. Rich and poor countries had similar workdays. The inference is that changes in wages do not give full information about movement in hours. Something else, like regulation, may be driving outcomes in the labor market.

The Report permits a closer look at the impact of the labor compact on wages and hours. To start, I (Huberman and Minns 2008) took the micro data from the Report and used regressions to control for various factors (sex, occupation, country, and year), isolating any unspecified factor causing changes in wages or hours, such as labor regulation. Next, I centered the residuals of the regressions on dates of adoption on limits to female and children's work. I then aggregated all pieces of legislation in Old and New Worlds to get a preliminary sign of the effect of legislation across the two regions.[12] This procedure allows me to describe the evolution of wages and hours over a selected time horizon and circumvent the measurement problems related to the lag between adoption and application of the new laws.

There was a marked difference in the response of wages and hours to legislation in my sample of countries. In Europe, hours of work (figure 5.2 panel a) declined in the decade after the introduction of legislation compared to the ten years prior, but in the New World (panel b) the trend in residuals is pretty much the same for five- and ten-year intervals before and after year o. Hourly wages also diverged (panels c and d). Wages spiked in the five years after legislation in the Old World; the trend is actually negative in the New. The imposition of the labor compact affected the bottom end, where earnings were low and hours long. The dispersion of hours fell by slightly more than 20 percent and wages by 12 percent in the Old; the corresponding distributions in the New were unchanged.[13] All together, the labor compact promoted greater egalitarianism in the Old and had small effect in the New. For this dataset, immigration to the New World seems to have lowered wages.

The exercise reported in the figure is partial. The wage and hour data are uneven and I cannot properly control for factors like establishment size. Nonetheless, the scale and scope of regulation affected labor market outcomes differently across countries and regions, along the lines of the models of regulation I discussed previously. The Old World was more prone to wage push, emanating from internal and external sources, and adopted more laws than elsewhere. Combined, the various pieces of legislation had teeth. In regions of recent settlement, the new institutional economic history is vindicated since the limited pieces of legislation would appear to have codified existing trends in income and technology, leaving no substantial traces on labor market outcomes.

THE LABOR COMPACT AND BETWEEN COUNTRY INEQUALITY

Between 1870 and 1914, world inequality increased (Bourgignon and Morrison 2002). To assess causes, Lindert and Williamson (2003, 246) decomposed global inequality into between and within country components.[14] With regard to the between component, they found that globalization had opposing effects: on the one hand, migration and trade from the labor-intensive and low-wage Old World to the labor-scarce and high-wage New World narrowed income gaps; on the other, capital flowing primarily to the rich New World had the contrary effect. Lindert and Williamson concluded cautiously: "Globalization looks like a force equalizing average incomes between the participating countries." World inequality increased because certain states chose to isolate themselves, and other factors, like schooling, secure property rights, and government quality, pushed countries apart.

Did the labor compact add, subtract, or have no effect on between country inequality? The answer appears to be that regulation complemented globalization forces and the effect was sizeable. GDP per capita underestimates workers' welfare because it does not include gains to workers owing to increased leisure time. Fewer hours worked by the employed implies greater leisure, which presumably adds to workers' utility. This is not true for the unemployed—of whom I will say more below—or for those working fewer hours than they would prefer to, like workers feeling constrained by regulation. Still, standard neo-classical analysis suggests that adults in countries with fewer hours worked will be better off relative to those in countries with more hours worked at the same level of GDP per capita.

To get an idea of how much better, I follow a standard approach and measure leisure-adjusted income in period t as the sum of income in period t and the difference in hours worked between t and the base year o, valued at the wage rate in t.[15] For Belgium, table 5.2 reports GDP per capita of $4,130 in 1913, and a decrease of 212 hours per person between 1870 and 1914. Assume, following Crafts (1997), that labor's share of income was 70 percent; the gain in leisure is then 0.7 x $3.45 (GDP per hour worked in 1914) x 212 = $512. Thus, leisure-adjusted GDP per capita is $4,642 (last column of the table).

Adjusting for leisure, Denmark's workers were about 20 percent and Germany's 5 percent better off than indicated by conventional GDP per capita; while Britain's and Italy's positions declined relative to the average, Belgian workers had a higher standard of adjusted welfare than Canadians in 1914. I interpret these figures to be the net addition of the labor compact to well-being, since the contribution of trade is already included in the income measures. I have not included Latin America in the tables because of the lack of employment numbers, but since hours showed little to no change it would be fair to say the two measures of GDP were about the same.[16] While labor market outcomes varied across countries, the bottom line was that the gap between New and Old Worlds was roughly $400 (30 percent) less for adjusted GDP than for GDP. The core was catching up to the settler economies, but from the optic of poor countries in the periphery, global inequality was widening.

Taking into account the decline in hours, aggregate measures of welfare improved significantly in the Old World, but individuals were worse off if they were let go and could not find work. Labor regulation and in particular job protection, according to a prominent view (Blanchard 2004), have caused levels of unemployment in Europe and the U.S. to diverge since the 1980s. The effects of the labor compact on unemployment in the first wave of globalization are less obvious. Although a proper treatment requires different types of evidence, existing data show comparable unemployment rates in social Europe and liberal America. Unemployment was under 5 percent in Belgium (Buyst 2007), France (Villa 1993), and the Netherlands (Smits, Horlings, and Van Zan-

Table 5.2. GDP adjusted for leisure, 1870–1914

Country/region	GDP per Hour		Hours per Person		GDP per Capita		GDP 1913 LEISURE AUGMENTED
	1870	1913	1870	1913	1870	1913	
Belgium	1.84	3.45	1463	1251	2640	4130	4642
Denmark	1.34	3.22	1492	1169	2008	3764	4490
France	1.28	2.52	1467	1370	2059	3452	3623
Germany	1.34	2.87	1355	1269	1913	3833	4005
Great Britain	2.76	4.06	1155	1157	3263	5032	5026
Italy	1.01	1.79	1481	1399	1467	2507	2610
Netherlands	2.20	3.55	1252	1112	2640	3950	4298
Spain	1.22	2.31	1129	977	1376	2255	2501
Sweden	1.05	2.44	1587	1271	1664	3096	3635
Switzerland	1.45	3.16	1514	1333	2172	4207	4608
Australia	3.50	6.15	994	892	3801	5505	5942
Canada	1.68	3.83	953	1101	1620	4213	3816
United States	2.16	4.43	1133	1154	2457	5307	5242
Old World	1.55	2.94	1390	1231	2120	3623	3944
	(0.56)	(0.68)	(159.1)	(128.8)	(586.6)	(858.2)	(855.5)
New World	2.45	4.80	1027	1049	2626	5008	5000
	(0.94)	(1.20)	(94.3)	(138.5)	(1,100.3)	(695.9)	(1,083.5)
World	1.76	3.37	1306	1189	2237	3942	4188
	(0.73)	(1.12)	(214.0)	(148.3)	(713.5)	(962.3)	(979.3)

Sources: GDP values from Maddison (1995). Annual hours are from appendix and table 7.3. Hours per person calculated with data from Crafts (1997).

Notes: All GDP values are in 1990 international dollars. Values in brackets are standard deviations.

den 2000), a figure corresponding to American levels (Weir 1992).[17] For the U.K., George Boyer and Hatton (2002) found that that the numbers of jobless ratcheted upward in the decades before 1914, but the dispersion in unemployment was similar to that of the U.S.

One interpretation of the weak relation between regulation and unemployment is that the labor compact was not as extensive as its modern version. Today governments make significant outlays on social entitlements, but before 1914 spending of this type was unimportant. But another reading goes back to an original role of the labor compact. Markets were incomplete and did not provide adequate protection or insurance for workers. Regulation enabled markets to come closer to the competitive ideal than otherwise would have been the case (Freeman 2007). As levels of risk diminished, labor supply adjusted to meet demand, leaving unemployment unaffected.

Notwithstanding the impact on unemployment, the exercise in table 5.2 probably underestimates the effect of the labor compact on welfare. Boyer (2007) has taken the analysis one step further, integrating literacy, schooling, and life expectancy in a broad measure of well-being. Many of these indicators rose more rapidly in the Old World. The expansion of leisure time I have detected must have been correlated with many of these improvements. The labor compact made Europeans better off at the expense of the rest of the world.

THE LABOR COMPACT AND WITHIN COUNTRY INEQUALITY: THE SKILL PREMIUM AND GENDER GAP

Has twentieth-century globalization alleviated poverty in the poor world? Ann Harrison (2007) gives a mixed report card. She observed that obstacles to labor mobility have limited gains in trade to narrow sectors of activity, mainly in urban enclaves. But even in cities, she added, the most vulnerable—women, low-wage workers, and the poor—have shared in globalization's rewards only when they have had access to a social safety net. Did the original labor compact serve this function?

To Lindert and Williamson (2003, 241) declining trade costs were sufficient to bring about non-trivial changes in the distribution of income. As is customary, because of data limitations they equate the gap between the rich and the rest with the skill premium.[18] In the Old World, increased trade and emigration reduced wage gaps between, at one end of the distribution, landlords and skilled workers, and at the other end, the unskilled; in the rich New World, trade and immigration augmented inequality, and the effects were similar in the poor, primary product–exporting countries.

Labor regulation offset and reinforced these changes. As countries introduced and extended protective legislation, limits on hours worked and minimum age laws contracted labor supply and raised wages of unskilled workers. In the New World, regulation would have offset some of the pain caused by immigration and cheap goods, while in the Old, the labor compact moved wage distributions in the same direction as did trade forces. The Report gives comfort to these claims. Egalitarianism, measured as the difference between wages at the 25th and 50th centiles in table 5.1, was on the rise in the European core and periphery, and it worsened in North and Central America. The wage gap between the median and poor worker narrowed in the Far East and India as these regions were integrated in the international economy. Elsewhere the story is mixed. In Latin America, inequality narrowed overall, with the exception of Brazil, whose experience I will return to later in this chapter. The gap widened in Australia, but closed in New Zealand and South Africa.[19]

Lindert and Williamson were not directly interested in the gender gap, but since female workers in the Old World were concentrated in labor-intensive sectors and the derived demand for these workers increased along with exports, the fall in trade costs ought to have narrowed wage differences.[20] I would expect the opposite outcome in New World manufacturing. In the global economy, market forces prevailed over social constraints in wage determination. Along the lines of Gary Becker's canonical model, discrimination against women was difficult to sustain, international competition driving non-profit maximizing firms out of the export sector, and thereby increasing female wages and employment (Ederington, Minier, and Troske 2009). Again these forces were stronger in the Old than in the New World.

In principle, the labor compact complemented globalization's effect on the gender gap in the Old World and attenuated its effects in the New. However, while legislation was directed ostensibly at children and women, it does not follow that these groups internalized its benefits. Regulation may not have been gender neutral. Men, it is believed, pushed for reforms and won a shorter workday 'from behind the women's petticoats.' There are a number of variants to this argument.[21] Some (Stewart 1989) have claimed that men supported regulation of the most vulnerable to curtail competition, creating a dual labor market in which women were increasingly segregated into low-paying and precarious jobs, while men concentrated in high-wage and stable employment. Still others (Rose 1992) have asserted, more strongly, that patriarchal employers, unions, and the state used legislation to rid factories of women and return them to the domestic sphere.

An alternative view is that the labor compact was gender blind. Men wanted the same benefits as women, but the courts and the state had denied them these rights. A "bandwagon effect" (Goldin 1990, 193) beginning in textiles spread into non-regulated activities. To be sure, historical forces predating labor regulation had constructed gender relations inside and outside the factory, but it does not follow that labor regulation added to existing inequalities. In this light, men gained relatively because they bargained better in unionized and non-unionized activities, and not because they actively sought to penalize women or segregate them in the labor market, which was already highly segmented prior to the adoption of limits on their employment. B. L. Hutchins and A. Harrison (1903, 197), in their pioneer history of factory legislation, expressed this argument:

> The process of men taking over women's work is so rare as to be absolutely inconsiderable. The idea that 'trade union jealousy' may cause women to be excluded from industry through and by means of the Factory Act, does not bear verification, for in well-organized industries it is the trade union that sets the pace, and trade union regulations require somewhat shorter hours than those permitted by the Act. The trade union supports the Act for women and children because these last do not, or cannot, combine for self-defence.

To sort through ideas, start with a model in which male and female labor markets are perfectly segmented.[22] Limits on women's hours shift the labor supply curve inwards and have the direct effect of pushing up their wages. Consider a second model in which female and male workers are substitutes. Legal limits have modest effects on both female and male wages, as the female supply shock is spread across both types of workers. Male earnings improve since their hours may be unaffected, while female earnings, although they may increase, fall relative to men because of reduced worktimes. Both models are applicable to Old and New Worlds, but waves of immigration in the latter push labor supply outward, thus minimizing the salutary effects of the labor compact on wages and hours.

There are related scenarios. Hours of men fall and wages rise, if their work is coordinated with that of women. Employers may have their say as well. Confronted with the rise of women's wages, they may turn their back on hiring them or restrict their activities. Occupational crowding is the result. So, if labor markets are integrated, tasks are coordinated across sexes, or the demand for women falls, some of the benefits of legislation will accrue to men.

Figure 5.3 presents pay and hours of work ratios for women and men at a Ghent cotton textile mill.[23] With the extension of the Belgian train network and increased labor mobility, unskilled wages trended upwards and, begin-

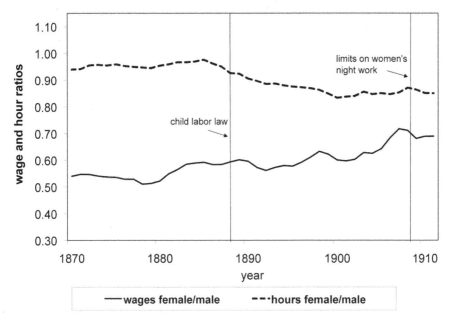

Figure 5.3. The gender gap in Belgian cotton textiles, 1870–1914
Men and women in spinning division at Voortman mill based on
Scholliers (1996, 226–28).

ning in the mid 1880s, the gender gap narrowed. Women reaped the benefits
of globalization as Lindert and Williamson reasoned. Labor regulation magnified globalization's effects. The first pieces of major legislation were introduced in 1889. Labor costs increased by about 10 percent and women's hours
fell relative to men's. Throughout the 1890s, the firm hired more women to
operate ring-spinning machines and their pay rose, men moving out of the
industry. After limits on night work were introduced in 1909, wage and hour
ratios stabilized.[24]

The data from the Report gives a wider picture of regulation on gendered outcomes, revealing bandwagon or spillover effects of regulation across sectors of
activity.[25] Because the distribution of women in the Report is uneven across time
and space, table 5.3 compares outcomes for groups of countries before and after
legislation. The Old World is represented by Germany, France, and the Netherlands, states introducing major pieces of legislation after 1889. For women, the
new laws had modest effects on hours and wages. Men's hours dropped relatively
more. In the years after legislation, the gender wage gap was stable, and women
in fact worked slightly longer hours.

Table 5.3. Gender gap in Old and New Worlds

Region	Pre-legislation 1880–88	Post-legislation 1889–99	Pre-legislation 1880–88	Post-legislation 1889–99
Germany, France, Netherlands				
	Hours (var.) [n]	Hours (var.) [n]	Wages (var.) [n]	Wages (var) [n]
Women	64.7 (7.1) [48]	64.2 (3.5) [51]	.040 (.012) [48]	.047 (.012) [51]
Men	65.0 (6.6) [542]	63.2 (5.2) [292]	.078 (.040) [542]	.092 (.042) [292]
Australia, Canada				
	Hours (var.) [n]	Hours (var.) [n]	Wages (var.) [n]	Wages (var.) [n]
Women	60.2 (4.4) [85]	60.5 (3.8) [57]	.083 (.033) [100]	.081 (.033) [57]
Men	59.0 (5.6) [120]	58.0 (6.8) [304]	.218 (.088) [160]	.229 (.095) [348]

Source: U.S. Commissioner of Labor (1900).

Notes: Values in $/hr.

The absence of any significant movement merits discussion. Changes of this order may simply have resulted from the regular churning of the labor market. Still the direction of change is consistent with the assumptions that men and women were substitutes (slightly higher male wages) and work was coordinated (lower hours for men). Although the demand for women's work does not seem to have contracted, the variance in their hours fell considerably, implying a greater concentration of employment opportunities. But occupational specialization was well under way before the introduction of the factory acts. As for the long female hours, either the initial legislation was not binding, or women gave more labor time as wages per hour increased, or both. Bairoch's (1968) employment figures for manufacturing indicate that women held their own and were not pushed out of the labor market.[26]

The overall impression is that men gained relatively more, not necessarily at the expense of women, but because they successfully lobbied for better compensation and work schedules as they moved out of textiles into sectors with less competitive labor and product markets. The expansion of specialized export industries (which I will refer to in the next chapter) demanding skilled workers provided one such opportunity. While labor regulation did not exacerbate historical biases in the labor market, this does not imply that it had only a small effect on women's welfare either. The labor compact established a safety net where one had not previously existed.[27] Finally, the gains in wages understate improvements in well-being, because the additional leisure which was now at women's disposal is not accounted for.

In the New World, the story is mixed. Based on the Canadian census, women in cotton textiles saw negligible benefits from restrictions on young workers. The gender wage gap initially stood at about 0.52; after adoption, 0.47; both men and women had their hours fall from 60 to 58.[28] The evidence from the Report in table 5.3 confirms this pattern. The region is represented by Australia and Canada; while the former had implemented a broad range of limits on labor supply from an early date, the latter had only a minimum age law by 1885. In these regions of new settlement, women's hours were unchanged after legislation; their earnings actually fell slightly and the pay gap widened. The labor compact left a smaller footprint in the New World, and globalization seems to have run its course.

INEQUALITY IN LABOR-ABUNDANT REGIONS OF BRAZIL

When Bernardo Mascarenhas sought to establish a new cotton mill in Minas Gerais in the 1870s, he traveled to New England and Lancashire to select and purchase preparatory equipment and spinning and weaving machines.[29] He returned a year later with about 50 tons of equipment. After landing in Rio de Janeiro, the stock was transported first by rail, then in large barges, and finally in ox-carts. The machinery was not fitted to meet standards of Brazilian workers and local cotton supplies. Along with foreign machinery, Mascarenhas was then also dependent on foreign engineers and specialists. Millowners paid a steep premium for their services. According to an estimate, a British machinist earned five times the pay of his Brazilian counterpart at Mascarenhas's mill.

This account is certainly not apocryphal. In the current wave of globalization, inequality in labor-abundant countries ought to have narrowed, but evidence indicates otherwise. There is no shortage of hypotheses (Goldberg and Pavcnik 2007). One view is that labor market rigidities or imperfect product markets in emerging countries create obstacles to mobility and resource allocation, and wages adjust slowly, if at all. A related explanation of rise in inequality is that technological change is biased toward skilled workers in rich and poor countries alike (Acemoglu 2002). Inequality may be more pronounced in poor countries since imports of capital goods are highly complementary with skilled labor, and existing supplies of this type of worker are scarce.

In this section, I investigate the movement in relative wages in the labor-abundant manufacturing regions of Brazil. Inequality had deep historical roots in the country (Bértola et al. 2010). Because manufacturing was a small share of the economy, the wage floor was set in the primary exporting sector where earnings began to rise in the 1880s.[30] But as demand for primary products peaked, land rents rose faster than wages, and the distribution of income widened. In this section, I ask whether a bias in technological change aggravated inequality in the country's Southern Cone, or whether the accumulation of local human capital was a countervailing force. It is important to distinguish between these two outcomes since my main objective is to consider whether labor regulation had comparable effects on wages in labor-abundant regions of Old and New Worlds.

Some background on the Brazilian cotton textile industry is in order. The country had an ample supply of cotton and abundant cheap labor, but the industry was slow to emerge from the shadows of foreign competition in its home market. Originally situated in the countryside, producers drew on local labor supplies. By the 1880s, a modern urban industry was emerging. The labor forces in Rio de Janeiro and São Paulo, the hubs of the industry, were composed of workers from the coffee export sector and unskilled European immigrants. Both groups had limited experience of factory life and, it was believed, they were considerably less efficient than labor in rich countries.[31] At least initially, owners and workers clamored for protection, although this did not prevent imports of cheap and fine items.

Around the turn of the century, the fortunes of the industry changed. Initially, the industry had depended on ring-spinning technology, using long-stapled cottons from the northeast. There was much waste in the process—and many of the complaints about labor most likely stemmed from this. In fact, late into the century mules were actually more efficient at very low counts. By 1900, British machine builders started exporting ring-spinning machines that treated a variety of cotton grades.[32] The machines delivered to Brazil, which held fewer spindles than the typical ring frame Lancashire exported, could be more easily operated by women having little or no factory experience. The southern industry began exploiting local supplies of short-stapled fibers, much inferior to those of the north, and commenced producing cheaper grades of yarn that found a large domestic market (Clark 1910, 33).

There was a Brazilian side to this episode. Stanley Stein (1957, 52) reported that by 1890 domestically trained mechanics replaced foreigners. Not only did millowners order technology to meet the qualifications of local labor and raw materials, they also made adjustments to equipment, some engineers taking out patents on their adaptations (Von der Weid and Bastos 1986, 139, 144–46).

Communication between the 'field' and Lancashire was a pathway in the diffusion of tacit knowledge.[33] As technology adjusted to meet factor endowments, labor productivity was enhanced.[34] At one mill, employees were not granted promotion if they were illiterate; other mills experimented with personal policies inspired by visits to the U.S. (Von der Weid and Bastos 1986, 183).

If foreign technology helped establish the basis for long-term growth, local adaptation had untapped the "democratizing potential" of ring spinning (Saxonhouse and Wright 2010). The movement in the gender gap coincides with this interpretation. The earnings of women like those of men remained low, but as they accumulated experience the gender wage gap narrowed. In the São Paulo textile industry, the gap closed by about 25 percent for carders and spinners in the period from 1912 until 1920; only in the finishing processes did the wage gap widen. In all activities, women earned about one-half that of men before the war and about two-thirds after (Ribeiro 1988, 133–37). The supply of women in the industry kept up with demand; the percentage of female workers was about 65 percent in the interwar years, whereas it was only 50 percent ten years earlier. On the international scale, the participation of women in the industry rivaled that of Japan and Italy, and exceeded that of Belgium.[35]

As the labor market responded, textile production proceeded unabated. Protectionism, often invoked as a principal cause, was only part of the story. Although tariff levels remained high, they were specific and currency fluctuations eroded their effectiveness (Suzigan 1986, 379–83).[36] Inevitably, demands for greater protection ensued, but state authorities were wary of granting compensating increases, fearing lower custom revenues. Anyway, the extension of the rail network had created a large and integrated domestic market in which stiff competition prevailed (Summerhill 2003; Leff 1982, 176). An indigenous model of corporate governance protected and encouraged local and foreign investors (Mussachio 2009). With reliable access to credit, Brazilian companies constructed large, vertically integrated mills employing mainly women and children and powered by the newly installed electrical grid in southern states. The industry became cost competitive at coarse grades; the U.S. trade representative (Garry 1920, 35) estimated that domestic prices fell by 10 percent and dyed goods by 25 percent between 1900 and 1913 alone.[37] Since demand was price elastic, Brazilian producers captured the home market in a short time span. In the ten-year period after 1900, imports fell by more than 80 percent (Garry 1920, 41), leaving a small negative balance in trade (Stein 1957, 193). Even before the end of the war, Brazil had begun to sell goods in Montevideo and Buenos Aires (Redfield 1920, 59).

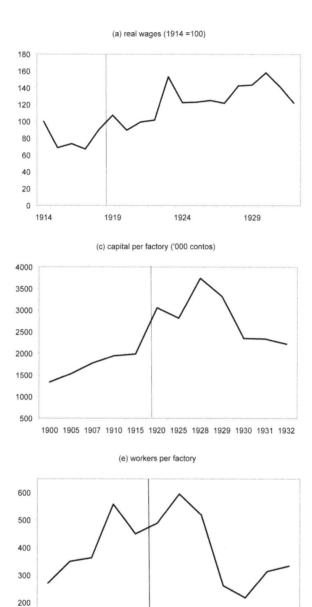

Figure 5.4. Regulation and adaptation in Brazil: Textiles
Wages in panel (a) are for São Paulo. Labor share in panel (b) is wages x employment
for the industry. Panels (c) to (e) for São Paulo. Capital in panel (c) is spindles and
looms. Data from Ribeiro (1988, 70) and Stein (1957, 191–93).

(b) labor share

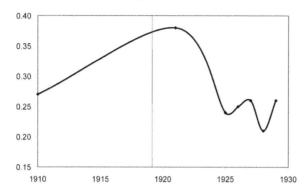

(d) spindles and looms per worker

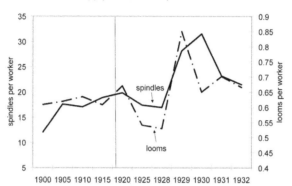

(f) exports and imports (kilos)

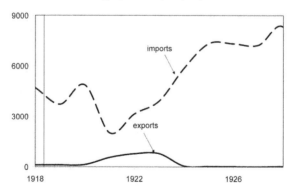

Employers did not foresee changes in the industrial relations environment in the 1920s (CIFTA 1919, 23; Ribeiro 1988, 78; Weinstein 1996, 56). Before the war, millowners made substantial fortunes that were not always passed on. In the Southern Cone, the steady inflows of unskilled Europeans and migrants from the northeast combined to sustain downward pressure on earnings. The sharp decline in real wages during the war was the prelude to a period of labor unrest. As elsewhere, the labor laws in the 1920s had both domestic and foreign origins. After a prolonged strike in Rio in 1919 and under pressure to conform to ILO recommendations, many factories adopted the *semana inglesa*, a compressed workday of eight hours, Monday through Friday, and half-day Saturdays (Von der Weid and Bastos 1986, 194); in total, hours per week fell from 60 before the war to 48 after (Garry 1920, 33; Pearse 1923, 33). In 1923, businesses' contributions to accident insurance increased; a 1925 law requiring paid vacations was followed by a 1926 provision restricting child labor (Ludwig 1985, 173–74; Ribeiro 1988, 159–61).[38] By this date, Brazilians and Belgians toiled the same number of hours per week.

A classic wage push was underway in textiles. Figure 5.4 tracks the effects of labor regulation for the Brazilian textile industry based on evidence taken from the censuses and industry surveys. Panel a presents the trend in real wages for textile workers in São Paulo. The fall in earnings after 1915 was a catalyst of the 1919 strike wave. Wages spiked upward after the imposition of regulation in 1919, rising again in the mid 1920s when more laws came on the books. Again capital was in the short run hostage to labor. The labor share of output (panel b) for the industry increased initially. As in Belgium, the rise in wages induced capital deepening (panel c), and the makeover of the workforce. In the absence of adjustment, foreign capital would seek better returns elsewhere. The number of spindles per worker was 50 percent greater in 1929 than 1921 (panel d) and larger factories (panel e) hired more women. I return to export performance in the next chapter.

The wage push of the 1920s had expected results on relative pay. Figure 5.5 presents trends in the ratio of unskilled to skilled wages for three sectors of activity in Rio de Janeiro over a long time horizon.[39] In the construction industry, the ratio first declined, but subsequently rose after 1910, consistent with claims of a steady accumulation of skill.[40] The adoption of labor laws in the 1920s compressed the wage distribution in production activities; in the unregulated service sector, the skill premium moved in the other direction.[41] At least in its implications for wages and capital investment, labor regulation in Brazil and Belgium shared much in common.

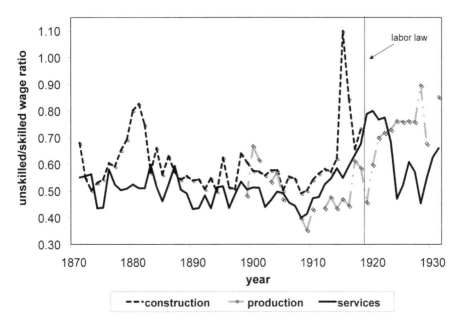

Figure 5.5. The skill premium in Brazil, 1870–1930
Wage ratios of unskilled to skilled workers in Rio de Janeiro. Skilled (sk) and
unskilled (unsk): *construction*—unsk: day laborer; sk: bricklayer, carpenter;
production—unsk: boiler operative, cooper, distillery operative, dock worker,
packing operative; sk: blacksmith, cartridge operator, electrician, machine
operator, overseer; *services*—unsk: barber, doorman, gardener; sk: cook, painter.
Data from Lobo (1978, 803–20).

CONCLUSION: FROM WAGE PUSH TO BIG PUSH

The contributions of labor regulation to between and within country inequality
were both complementary to and distinct from the effects of globalization on
the distribution of income. The wage-push model seems relevant to the Old
World, while in the New World regulation appears to have at best codified existing
practice. As a result, Europeans saw their well-being, broadly defined to include
leisure, encroach on levels found in the richer parts of the New World. Regarding
within country inequality, men captured some of the benefits of regulation,
but neither were women losers in the Old World. However, women and the
unskilled could not count on regulation to hold back globalization forces in the
New World. The European model did have a silver lining for North American
skilled workers: the improvement in well-being on the continent, probably

slowed down emigration, thereby moderating downward pressures on their earnings.

The wage push in Brazil paralleled developments in the Old World a generation earlier. Technical change was adapted to meet local factor prices. Labor inequality had deep historical roots, but regulation reduced the skill premium, and, again as in the Old World, the rise in the labor share was an incentive to invest in capital. The difference was that the Old World sold its new goods to expanding foreign markets, while Brazilians introduced regulation in a period of contracting trade. I take up this theme in the next chapter.

The response of the Old World to the labor compact goes some way to reconcile an old conundrum in economic history: how did continental latecomers catch up to richer and high-wage regions, like the U.K. and the U.S., exploiting more advanced and capital-intensive technologies. The conventional explanation, advanced by David Landes (1969), invokes the diffusion of new technologies. But the choice of technique does not square with the abundance of cheap labor on the continent. H. J. Habakkuk (1962) believed that labor-saving technologies were most appropriate in the labor-scarce U.S. The fertility decline in Europe may have altered factor prices, but before 1914 it was uneven across and within countries. How then did the Old World transform itself from a labor-abundant to a labor-scarce region?

My claim is that the labor compact was part of the story behind Europe's transformation. Regulation contributed to a "big push" (Rosenstein-Rodan 1943; Murphy, Shleifer, and Vishny 1989). In 1870, only a handful of businesses provided minor protection to workers; by 1914, European workers in key sectors had secured extensive safeguards, and bandwagon effects provided coverage in unregulated activities. The scope and breadth of regulations set in place a simultaneous and coordinated demand for more and better infrastructures—which meant investments in human and fixed capital. The labor compact as development policy, albeit unplanned and unintended, was a European-wide phenomenon. Countries exploited the innovations and blueprints of trading partners because they had adopted each other's labor laws. The rising tide of regulation promoted technological congruence in Europe and catch-up with industrial leaders.

6

DID LABOR STANDARDS HARM
OR BENEFIT TRADE?

How long are we going to sit here with our arms folded or else making things for no reason and for no one. In our situation I don't see what else we can do. Well, I'm of a different opinion. And what different opinion is that, what marvelous idea have you come up with? That we should make other things. If the Center is going to stop buying some things, it's highly unlikely that they're going to buy something else. They might and might not. The only thing I'm sure about is that we can't just sit around here waiting for the world to fall in on us.

—José Saramago, The Cave, *pages 54–55.*

The welfare state is simultaneously an arena for distributive struggles and a source of comparative advantage.

—Torben Iversen, Capitalism, Democracy and Welfare, *page 13.*

THE LABOR COMPACT AS A SOURCE OF
COMPARATIVE ADVANTAGE

In 1918, Brazilian manufacturers prided themselves on being captains of the seventh largest textile industry in the world (CIFTA 1919, 25). Conjuring up the Japanese path of development, they boasted the industry was on the cusp of a major breakthrough, the expansion of manufacturing decoupling economic growth from the curse of resources.[1] Even before the war, Brazil had made inroads in Southern Cone markets. In the expectation of continued growth, and as local workforces demonstrated more skill, producers began upgrading the quality of textiles manufactured. While the labor laws of the 1920s may have been unanticipated, Brazilian manufacturers had laid the groundwork to adapt successfully to the new industrial relations environment.

Brazil could certainly have drawn on Belgium's recipe of success. In debate on commercial and social policies, Émile Vandervelde claimed that workers responded positively to labor regulation.[2] As in an efficiency wage model, their effort rose with pay. But Vandervelde also demonstrated a keen grasp of the intensive and extensive margins of international trade. Labor regulation induced productivity improvements and lowered prices of old staples like cotton textiles and woolens, and prompted firms to develop new goods and new markets abroad. The labor compact made firms better exporters along both margins.

Belgium's timing could not have been better. The link from wages to labor productivity was stronger in the Old World than the New because adjustment to regulation occurred in an environment of expanding trade. A new international division of labor emerged in which the Old World sold higher value items worldwide, exploiting a budding supply of skilled workers. While new laws adopted in Brazil in the 1920s had also precipitated new investments in machinery, foreign markets were simultaneously closing down. For latecomers, the relation between wages and productivity was slack.

This chapter relates the different methods firms, workers, and states pursued to adjust to the labor compact. To begin, I ask whether the relation between regulation and trade differed across regions. The industrial core in the Old World had greater success in passing on or offsetting the costs of higher wages. For these countries, adjustment costs were not punitive because states had discretion in adopting labor laws to meet local requirements, while at the same time satisfying the demands of trading partners. Small countries, in particular, had leeway in their choice of regulations. Another explanation of the weak relation between labor standards and trade is that the type and nature of exports (and imports) had changed. The evolution of Belgian exports from low- to high-end manufactures was typical of the response induced by regulation. As prices increased, so did the terms of trade, and this meant consumers around the world paid for the Old World social model. The response of Brazil to labor regulation resembled Belgium's, even to the extent of raising the value of exports. But in the unfavorable trade environment of the interwar years, Brazil failed to reap the advantages of labor regulation.

INTERNATIONAL TRADE AND LABOR STANDARDS:
DIVERGENT EXPERIENCES

The first epoch of globalization is ideal to study the effects of regulation on trade.[3] States offered business no direct compensation to defray costs of adjustment. In France, despite a long history of dirigisme, "exporters were necessarily on their own" (Smith 1980, 222). While in the mid-to-late twentieth century, national authorities had the power to adjust exchange rates, the classical gold standard regime restricted devaluation and fiscal policy as means to make exports competitive. Firms certainly attempted to download costs directly on workers where the labor supply of adults was inelastic, but labor mobility put paid to this idea. Even in the unfettered U.S. labor market, Fishback and Kantor (1995) found modest evidence of wage offsets.[4] In all, if there was ever a short-term relation between standards and trade, it ought to have turned up one hundred years ago.

The effects of labor standards on producers varied with the type of trade. A new law imposed higher short-run marginal costs. At world prices, factories failing to adapt shut down, industry output and exports contracting. In imperfect competition, businesses had some flexibility. The price of goods increased and output fell. But even in the short run, firms tinkered with existing equipment and upgraded product lines, thereby passing on costs to consumers. Ultimately, in markets for differentiated goods, the immediate effect of regulation on exports depended on the degree of substitution between domestic and foreign goods. Over the medium-to-long term, structural change toward more specialized products or new production techniques restored, and perhaps improved competitiveness. While the primary sector avoided direct regulation, it faced higher input costs of intermediate goods that could not be offset at world prices. In countries with large resource sectors, the imposition of labor laws caused trade balances to worsen.

The model I (Huberman and Meissner 2007) use distinguishes between short-run effects and long-term consequences of labor regulation. I give full details of my research strategy and regression analysis in the appendix, but some features of the model ought to be highlighted up front. Because I do not have comparable series of exports for regulated industries only, like textiles, I am restricted in using the overall trade balance as my dependent variable. Although the proportion of manufacturing exports (see table 1.1) varied across countries, the increase in labor costs in regulated sectors had knock-on or spillover effects (Irwin 2007). Resource exporters had to absorb these costs as well. The independent variables consist of an indicator variable corresponding to the adoption of individual labor laws and macroeconomic controls. The regression

Table 6.1. Short-term effects of regulation on international trade, 1880–1914

Country	Negative	Positive
Australia	Min. age	–
Austria-Hungary	Women's hours; acc. ins.	–
Canada	Min. age; women's hours	–
Denmark	Min. age; factory inspection	Acc. ins.
Italy	Min. age; factory inspection	Acc. ins.
Norway	Women's hours; acc. ins.	–
Portugal	Factory inspection; acc. ins.	–
Spain	Factory inspection; acc. ins.	–
Netherlands	–	Women's hours
Switzerland	–	Min. age
United Kingdom	–	Min. age
No effect		
Belgium, France, Germany, Sweden		

Sources and notes: For methodology and regression results see appendix.

also includes lags in the year of adoption, allowing for the inevitable delay in application of new laws. Owing to small sample sizes, I limit my study to four pieces of legislation: factory inspection, minimum age restrictions on child labor, limits on women's night work, and accident insurance. The lack of correspondence in federal states between legislation, the jurisdiction of subnational units, and trade poses a different problem. Identifying the representative sub-national unit is most difficult for the U.S., which I drop from my analysis; there was less variation between Australian states and Canadian provinces in the adoption of labor legislation, and these countries are left in.

Table 6.1 summarizes the short-term effects of the labor compact on trade for 1880–1914. Two groups of countries emerge. Labor regulation was not a brake on net exports in Sweden and core countries that had long-established manufacturing sectors. But in the European periphery and the New World, the labor compact affected trade balances adversely, exports becoming more expensive and importing-competing sectors less viable. As for the type of legislation, limits on children's labor had the largest bite—it was significant in four countries—a not surprising result given the substantial wage gap between adolescents and adults. In all cases, the long-run effects of labor regulation were weak. The results mesh with the overarching argument I have proposed: the development of the labor compact was stronger in regions specializing in brand items.

The results cast light on the calendar of adoption at the country level. Bismarck was hesitant to improve factory regulations, fearing its impact on trade. The social entitlements introduced in the 1880s had small or no effect on trade because workers shouldered a substantial proportion of their cost.[5] Germany adopted limits on women's work only in 1892, by which date better-equipped firms could more easily meet the constraints of the new laws. These late measures seem to have had no effect on the trade balance, an outcome that may have convinced Wilhelminian policymakers to exchange market access for improved labor standards of trading partners.[6] In late Victorian and Edwardian Britain, contrary to claims of entrepreneurial lethargy, business adapted to legislation smoothly. Still, the British remained prudent. Minimum age legislation was adopted in the U.K. in 1902. By this late date, the U.K. had adjusted the type of its exports and had become more dependent on Empire markets. As a result, the new law had no effect on its trade balance.[7]

In other countries, regulation harmed trade. In Austria-Hungary, manufacturing goods comprised nearly 40 percent of exports in 1900. The adoption of accident compensation and limits on women's work cut into the trade balance. In the sprawling and fractious Dual Monarchy, labor regulation did not simply codify existing practice, but served the political objective of moderating demands for national autonomy. Hungarian authorities offered meager subsidies to defray the costs of improved working conditions (Eddie 1989, 874–78). In Switzerland, the textile industry survived on slight profit margins and had no leeway to adapt to the new laws. Factory owners shuttered mills and shifted investments toward machine making, chemicals, and the production of electrical equipment (Humair 2004, 615).[8] Exports of these sectors rebounded in the long run. Italy was a latecomer to legislation and, like Switzerland, had certain laws imposed on it by trading partners. In the wake of regulation, employment of children expanded in informal and resource sectors (Toniolo and Vecchi 2007); the reaction in Portugal was similar (Goulart and Bedi 2007). These outcomes paralleled the immediate effects of regulation in emerging economies today.[9]

While certain pieces of legislation had benign effects, still others impacted trade positively, even in the short run. In Denmark and Italy, the introduction of accident insurance improved trade balances. The same laws in the U.S., according to Fishback and Kantor (1995), met the needs of workers and firms. For both parties, regulation had discrete advantages over costly and seemingly arbitrary court decisions. More broadly, the positive coefficients corroborate a basic claim of social activists, like Vandervelde: The labor compact raised productivity, rewarding capital and workers alike.

DID STATES HAVE DISCRETION IN THE CHOICE OF
LABOR STANDARDS?

The mixed effects of regulation on trade pose a puzzle.[10] Countries coerced to adopt labor regulations of their trading rivals would be most susceptible to wage-push pressures. But the findings give only limited support to the hypothesis that the new laws harmed trade. For instance, small countries with large international exposures, Belgium, Netherlands, and Sweden, were most vulnerable to external pressures, but labor regulations do not appear to have caused any disadvantage in export markets. To reconcile this contradiction, I return to the event history analysis introduced in chapter 2 and examine the type of legislation adopted in country A in response to pressures from partner B.

Suppose that country A had the choice between high and low cost standards, defined by the relative incidence of legislation on firms' bottom line. On the domestic front, high cost standards gained politicians a large and loyal constituency, but were also perceived to do damage to the competitiveness of the economy. An alternative was to adopt policies having more symbolic than real effects. Now consider the 'open political economy' aspects of the decision. Country B might demand that A adopt a high cost standard like its own. Could A get away with regulation imposing lower costs? It might have, if it convinced its partner that adopting low cost standards, appropriate to its own level of development and size and wealth, was a prelude to tougher regulation in the near future. Certainly country B was not entirely satisfied, but had, at least, something to show its own constituents who targeted A in the first place. In this way, even piecemeal regulation acted as gateway standards. Rodrik (2007, 228; 2011, 69–76) proposed that a similar process was behind the general rise of labor regulations in the decades after 1945, when domestic concerns prevailed over international guidelines to harmonize labor standards.

The Berne meeting of the IALL in 1905 distinguished between types of labor standards.[11] Delegates considered limits on the working hours of women and children as high cost. According to one observer, 1.4 million women in Europe would be affected by a curb on night work, benefiting, on average, from a workday shorter by 2.5 hours.[12] Assuming that women comprised 60 percent of the labor force in textiles, and men's hours were unaffected, the potential reduction of labor input in the industry was about 10 percent.[13] Factory inspection laws were deemed low cost, as determined by the number of inspectors states had actually hired, and so was accident insurance whose burden was shared by workers, firms, and governments.[14]

I use a multinomial logit approach to study the possibility that the determinants of convergence varied with the type of labor standard adopted (table 6.2). I create three categories to capture country A's potential responses. Category 0 represents the outcome where there was no convergence between A and country B. Category 1 designates that A adopted limits on women's and children's work (restrictions on women's maximum hours and prohibition of night work, and minimum age laws for children) to emulate B's corresponding legislation. The third category (effectively category 2) indicates A's adoption of factory inspection or accident compensation when B had these policies in place.[15] The list of explanatory variables is identical to the short baseline in table 2.2, but I now include two indicators for lagged values of convergence. The first indicates the number of category 1 standards shared in the previous year; the other indicates the number of category 2 standards shared.

For high cost standards, category 1, the key determinants of policy convergence in column 1 are similar, but not identical, to previous results (chapter 2). Domestic forces trumped external pressures in the adoption of costly regulation. As its per capita GDP rose, country A was more likely to implement limits on women's and children's work and converge to country B. Size did not matter in the adoption of category 1 standards. Adoption was less likely the greater the degree of convergence already achieved. The lagged values of convergence in each category are consistent with the dynamic I proposed above. Countries may have acted sequentially, adopting one category of legislation before moving on to the other set as conditions became more opportune. Emulation was more likely the higher the level of convergence in the opposite group of standards.[16] Strikingly, and in contrast to my earlier results, the partial effect of trade integration for category 1 standards is not statistically significant. Trade exerted less pressure on these types of standards. And there was no difference between Old and New Worlds, domestic forces overwhelming external pressures everywhere in the adoption of costly regulation.[17]

All standards were not alike. I find opposite results for policies that were perceived to have imposed a smaller shock on an economy's cost structure. There are significant differences in the determinants of convergence between high and low cost standards. Country A's GDP per capita (an increase in GDP for a fixed population) has the opposite sign from that for high cost standards in column 1. Richer countries were *less* likely to emulate less costly standards. Alternatively, poorer countries were *more* prone to emulate less costly standards. Proportional rises in GDP and population (or size) had no effect on convergence. Turnout in country A is no longer statistically significant. Similar to the

Table 6.2. Determinants of convergence by type of labor regulation for country pairs

	(1) Convergence in women's night work, women's max. hours, minimum working age for children	(2) Convergence in accident compensation or factory inspection laws
International forces		
Trade Costs	0.00	−0.05
	(0.01)	(0.01)***
ln (GDP B)	0.01	−0.04
	(0.01)	(0.01)***
ln (Population B)	−0.01	0.04
	(0.01)**	(0.02)**
Turnout B	0.03	0.00
	(0.01)***	(0.02)
Domestic forces		
ln (GDP A)	0.03	−0.04
	(0.01)***	(0.01)***
ln (Population A)	−0.03	0.04
	(0.01)***	(0.02)**
New world A	−0.01	−0.19
	(0.01)**	(0.03)***
Turnout A	0.03	−0.02
	(0.01)***	(0.01)
New World A	0.03	0.29
x Turnout A	(0.03)	(0.05)***
Lagged level of similarity in	−0.01	0.02
column 1 labor standards	(0.00)*	(0.01)***
Lagged level of similarity in	0.02	−0.08
column 2 labor standards	(0.01)***	(0.01)***
Observations	2884	
Pseudo-R-Squared	0.10	

Sources: See table 2.2.

Notes: Standard errors in brackets clustered at the country pair level. I report average marginal effects. Estimation by maximum likelihood for a multinomial logit. The omitted category is no convergence. Quinquennial dummies are included but not reported. *significant at 10%; **significant at 5%; ***significant at 1%.

findings of chapter 2, emulation was slower in the New World, although higher voter turnout ratio accelerated the process.[18] Conspicuously, trade was a pathway in the diffusion of less costly labor standards.

States did not mimic blindly the policy agenda of neighbors or trading partners, but were selective in their implementation. Since domestic constraints and external forces were entangled, the outcome was a patchwork of labor laws across countries. Countries more exposed to trade were predisposed to emulate, but only on low cost standards. The adoption of factory inspection and accident insurance satisfied the demands of the domestic reform movement, and of trading partners and their constituents, because they were the first step to more stringent and comprehensive legislation. Still, while states appeared to have been more cautious in adopting costly standards in the face of international competition, there is no evidence of a downward spiral in social policy. If undercutting international competition mattered, the partial effect on the trade cost variable would be positive and statistically significant. Countries facing the stiffest international competition—where trade costs were low—would have been the least prone to emulate. However, greater integration did not render the transmission of labor standards less likely, and European countries, in particular, raised levels of labor regulation in line with key trading partners, while preserving some domestic independence in the sequence of policies adopted.

THE LABOR COMPACT AND THE INTERNATIONAL DIVISION OF LABOR

At first blush, whether or not the labor compact reduced trade appears to be dependent on the time horizon selected. The immediate incidence of regulation on trade dissipated over the long run. But this snapshot presents a partial view, obscuring the dynamic aspects triggered by labor regulation on productivity. Regulation was not a burden because it simply codified existing practices; rather it compelled firms to adjust, by altering capital-labor ratios, upgrading product mixes, or both. In the remainder of this chapter, I advance the hypothesis that Old World countries like Belgium successfully adapted to the new labor laws because markets were expanding before 1914 and terms of trade moved in their favor. In contrast, by the time New World countries like Brazil introduced labor legislation world markets had begun contracting. The divergent outcomes had enduring effects on the development of welfare states in the two regions.

To fix ideas, consider a model of heterogeneous firms integrating interindustry (comparative advantage) and intra-industry (product differentiation) trade

(Bernard, Jensen, Redding, and Schott 2007, 2009; Melitz 2003). These models start with the stylized fact that export firms are scarce because of the fixed costs of doing business abroad.[19] Exporters pay higher wages, and are bigger, and more capital and skill intensive than other firms. A fall in trade costs reduces the cutoff above which firms can export, increases profits to be earned in foreign markets, and induces new entrants into the sector. Low productivity firms in the import-competing sector exit. Exporters sell a greater variety of items abroad to more destinations; import variety increases as well. All together, the reallocation of resources raises average industry productivity and welfare.[20]

Now consider the adoption of labor regulation. In a standard trade model, regulation hurts exporters of labor-intensive goods. But in the wage-push model of chapter 5, regulation promotes new investments in plant and machinery, and businesses grow in size. As productivity improves, more firms make the cutoff of being viable exporters, even if trade costs remain the same. Because labor regulation cuts across sectors, the rising tide of productivity lifts exports broadly. To be clear, exports depend on comparative advantage and firm characteristics. Labor regulation imposes a penalty on inefficient firms, whether or not they benefit from comparative advantage. Again, the net result is more exports and imports and the reallocation of resources to productive activities.

The Belgian experience conforms to the hybrid model of heterogeneous firms confronting a wage push. Recall that in the aftermath of early factory legislation, capital was hostage to labor and its share of output was squeezed (see figure 5.1). The textile industry was unable to pass on increased costs in higher prices. In the medium term, new investments permitted more spindles per frame and faster turning speeds. In the urban sector, many of the newly constructed large mills integrated spinning and weaving processes, specializing in medium counts of yarn. Initially, the industry's productivity did not rise as expected (panel c), because a cluster of weaving sheds using rudimentary techniques were temporarily set up in the countryside to escape compliance or to fill orders that could not be met by the formal sector. But the modern sector achieved healthy profits based on expanding export markets and long production runs (Van Houtte 1949, 150). The bottom line is clear in the last panel (f). From the late 1890s, Belgian exports of coarse and medium quality items were competitive, taking market share in Europe at the expense of the British. Between 1900 and 1905, exports to Argentina increased fourfold, and those to Brazil and the U.K. threefold (Van Houtte 1949, 173).

Belgian export performance was along intensive (the average import or export value per firm product) and extensive margins (number of firms and trade products). Into the 1880s, the textile export trade was limited to a handful of

Ghent firms, mainly occupied in the finishing stages of Lancashire goods. From 1870 to 1889, growth of textile exports was slow, 2.2 percent per annum, the principal destinations being Belgium's close neighbors.[21] In contrast, exports surged from 1890 until the war, about 6.7 percent per annum. To established customers in the U.K., Belgium exported the same, but cheaper items (see figure 2.2). The extensive margin was the dynamic sector of activity, companies selling new high value goods and varieties to new outlets around the globe. By 1914, Belgium sold and purchased a broad range of unfinished and finished items to and from 54 countries, including 12 Latin American and 7 Asian outlets (Kertesz 1917, 333). The new long-distance trade is remarkable because Belgium's own trade costs were actually stable during the last decades before the war (Jacks, Meissner, and Novy 2010).

The Belgian response was typical of the tried-and-tested strategy forged in the heyday of the industrial revolution of substituting capital for labor (Allen 2009), except that the change in factor prices I have identified was policy induced. While labor as a whole became scarcer, some factors were saved more than others, millowners coming to prefer women and adolescents over men. As seen in chapter 5, the earnings of women rose, but into the 1900s their wages remained only 60 percent of men doing the same work. Primary school enrolment of children (5–14 years of age) in Belgium was about half of its continental neighbors, and, even as women's participation in the labor market fell, the employment of adolescents was unchanged (Van den Eeckhout 1993, 109; De Vries 2008, 220).[22] Men moved out of textiles into expanding sectors, mining and engineering (Buyst 2007).

Elsewhere on the continent, manufacturers opted to update existing machines rather than sending them to scrap. Ever loyal to the spinning mule, the French and German industries expanded the number of spindles and improved utilization speeds, at the same time spinning higher grades of yarn (Saxonhouse and Wright 2004, 131).[23] These industries became more skill intensive, a response to changes in demand for and supply of labor and institutional innovation. On the demand side, higher wages prompted the substitution of longer and better machines for unskilled workers. As for supply, limits on children's work and additional years of schooling had the effect of raising the qualifications of the average worker.[24] In Germany, legislation in 1897 establishing an apprenticeship program contributed to the supply of trained labor (Thelan 2004, 33).

In large countries in the European core, technological change in textiles was progressively biased toward skilled workers, a prelude to the trend that has held since the mid twentieth century (Goldin and Katz 2008). Globalization cannot be ruled out as a force behind the change in direction of technical change.

Since skills were more scarce in the world economy than in the Old World only, as trade opened up the relative price of skill-intensive goods rose. The change in product prices induced more innovations directed toward skilled workers (Acemoglu 2002, 2009). For certain countries in the European core, therefore, greater trade exposure entailed a permanent fall in demand for child labor. Figure 6.1 gives the divergent trends in number of spindles per mule and per ring frame in Old and New Worlds. A gap in capital intensity between the two regions had become evident by the late 1880s, exactly when countries in the European core began to extend the labor compact. A new pattern of global specialization had emerged.[25]

The spread of the labor compact opened the door to foreign markets. Recall that in the 1880s trade embargoes cast a shadow over continental European manufacturers, because they were dependent on a small handful of outlets for their manufactured goods. But by the turn of the century, cooperation had replaced coercion in assuring market access. As more countries adopted labor regulations, exporters succeeded in developing assorted markets on the continent and abroad for their specialized items. Table 6.3 presents a snapshot of trading networks in cotton and woolen textiles, and silk and lace manufacture, for several European countries on the eve of the war.[26] Column 12 gives the share of each country's exports of manufactured items sold in Europe. Intracontinental trade remained substantial, 65 percent of the total value of production having European outlets. But in contrast to 1880, all eight countries in the table exchanged goods with each other, certainly an underestimate of the actual number of their European partners.

The textile sector was unexceptional. The rise in world income was part of the story behind the expansion in international trade, but the scarcity of labor caused by the new labor laws induced a broad range of export industries in the core economies to upgrade merchandise, develop new products, and find new customers.[27] Again, the Belgian case is representative. Trade in metal and chemical products, mainly intermediate items, grew at the same pace as textile goods (Horlings 1997). As for product diversity, using a classification system akin to the three-digit level of the Standard International Trade Classification (SITC), the country imported and exported 77 items in 1870; 95 in 1890; 152 in 1900; and 189 in 1910.[28] A similar trend holds regarding destinations: Belgium had 36 trading partners in 1870; 55 in 1890; 107 in 1900; and 114 in 1910.

The conjunction of the labor compact and export-led growth was apparent in changes in business structure. On the one hand, regulation had more bite in large establishments because factory inspectors were more prone to monitor them. On the other, large firms were more productive and, hence, better ex-

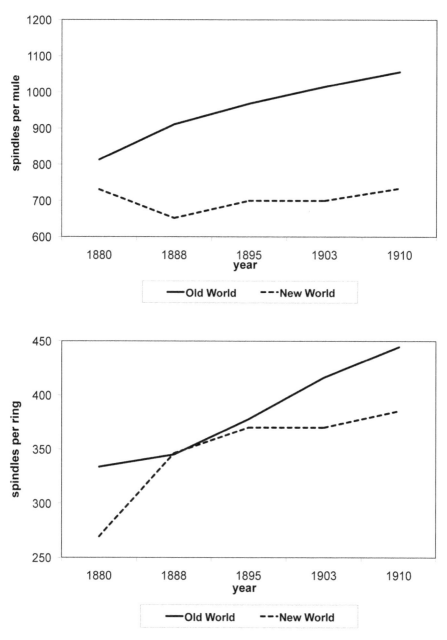

Figure 6.1. Spindles per mule and per ring frame
Data from Saxonhouse and Wright (2004, 144). Series of new investments. For mules,
Old World is Austria, Belgium, France, Germany, and the U.K.; New World is Brazil,
Canada, Mexico, India, and Japan. For rings, Old World as before, and Italy and
Spain; New World as before.

Table 6.3. Export and import markets for European manufacturers in 1913: Cotton textiles, silk, lace, and woolens

IMPORTER EXPORTER	A-H	Belgium	France	Germany	Great Britain	Italy	Nether- lands	Switzer- land	Other Europe	Americas	Asia	EXPORTS TO EUROPE as share of country exports (%)	EXPORTS TO EUROPE as share of all items exported in Europe (%)
Austria-Hungary		3.8	6.4	109.3	28.1	26.7	9.2	56.3	110.5	22.1	20.4	0.89	0.06
Belgium	16.9		186.8	256.9	141.7	25.6	38.7	3.2	68.6	40.7	10.9	0.93	0.13
France	12.0	330.5		166.2	462.4	91.7	11.5	122.2	58.4	312.3	64.8	0.77	0.21
Germany	197.3	45.8	64.2		275.3	56.3	90.7	100.5	138.7	266.7	83.2	0.73	0.17
Great Britain	24.7	153.7	209.4	503.8		32.1	124.7	64.0	467.7	1076.6	1329.3	0.40	0.27
Italy	30.2	4.0	59.0	94.6	63.6		0.5	106.6	95.8	150.3	44.7	0.70	0.08
Netherlands	0.0	73.2	1.0	44.2	45.3	0.0		0.0	9.3	10.6	76.2	0.67	0.03
Switzerland	25.8	8.2	24.0	101.8	109.1	16.7	3.6		28.4	117.1	14.0	0.71	0.05
Import share of all items imported in Europe (%)	0.06	0.11	0.10	0.21	0.20	0.04	0.05	0.07	0.16	=100%			=100%

Sources: Kertesz (1917).

Notes: All values in millions of German marks.

porters. In Belgium in 1910, companies in the tradable activities were about five times bigger than those in the domestic sector; capital-labor ratios of exporters were three times larger.[29] Challenged by imports, low-productivity firms exited, and output and employment reallocated toward high-productivity ends. By the eve of the war, 59 percent of workers were occupied in the international sector, 21 percent in the domestic, and 20 percent in other branches.

Across Europe, the shift in resources to the export sector realized gains in efficiency (Bernard, Jensen, Redding, and Schott 2007).[30] Contrary to expectations, the European social model did not lead to a perceptible rise in unemployment, because the labor compact delivered strong productivity effects in tradable and non-tradable sectors alike. The wage and employment evidence I reviewed in the previous chapter supports this conclusion. As export demand rose, so did wages of workers in the sector, many of whom were women. But workers in all activities benefited from the fall in import prices and the increase in variety, and business profited from lower costs and greater choice of intermediate goods. The general rise in wages confirms that scarce factors in the beleaguered import-competing sector shared in the gains of productivity as well, thus alleviating the decline in returns to endangered workers predicted in conventional models of trade.

TERMS OF TRADE EFFECTS: DID CANADA PAY FOR BELGIUM'S WELFARE STATE?

In Part I of this book, I claimed that at its origins the welfare state was a domestic and foreign affair. This section pursues the theme of interdependence. I investigate the consequences of the new international division of labor on trade between labor-abundant and labor-scarce regions. Consider the world trading order in 1900. The Old World had a comparative advantage in manufacturing and the New in resources. Suppose each country in the Old World produced a homogenous, labor-intensive good and was too small a producer to affect prices. When an individual country raised its labor standards, firms did not pass on the costs in higher prices. As markets contracted, companies cut wages, laid off workers, or shut down. But consider a scenario in which all states producing the same good simultaneously legislated a reduction in worktime.[31] Since the incidence of regulation fell on manufacture, labor input everywhere fell, and so did output, prices rising as a result. In an open economy setting, terms of trade for all countries whose comparative advantage was in the labor-intensive good improved. Harmonization shifted the costs of a labor standard from producer to consumer.

Putting aside welfare implications, the incentive in the Old World was to act like a cartel and adopt standards, thereby reducing output and raising prices.

The uncoordinated, but simultaneous rise of labor regulation beginning in the 1880s across countries raised prices in similar fashion, and it cannot be ruled out that the transnational reform movement had this effect, even if countries eventually decided to regulate according to their own agendas. Boutelle Ellsworth Lowe (1935, 77), an American chronicler of the IALL meetings, made explicit reference to the effects of a reduction in labor supply on output and prices. "Limitation of output by international agreement is an antidote for overproduction and the evils which reaction brings in its train." One delegate to the Berne conference asked disingenuously: "How is it possible to argue that the restriction of night work would not raise prices?"[32]

The obverse held in regions of the New World where labor was relatively scarce. In this type of model, it doesn't matter which country originated legislation. Any change in regulation affected prices of exporters of labor-intensive goods. Thus, if New World manufacturers raised standards, they effectively penalized themselves. They could not pass on costs to the resource sector whose prices were set on world markets.[33] New World countries relatively rich in capital could have retaliated and improved their terms of trade if they adopted capital-intensive legislation, but into the late twentieth century most regulation has remained biased toward labor.[34]

Developments in Canada fit this pattern. The extension of the labor compact around the globe harmed the international competitiveness of local industry, even as the number of laws actually adopted in Canada was modest. In textiles, tariff protection had been most effective for high-quality cotton goods—the average grade or count spun in Canada was about no. 70 before 1914 (Saxonhouse and Wright 2004)—but as European producers implemented new laws and upgraded export lines they began to challenge Canadian companies. After 1900, the value of production declined by 15 percent, the import share in domestic consumption increasing by a similar proportion (Taylor and Michell 1931, 10–34; Rouillard 1974, 16, 23). The incentive to replace capital with labor was weak, the manufacturing sector surviving on the steady supply of cheap labor that moderated wage pressures (Keay 2000). The country's overall trade balance worsened.

Figure 6.2 traces the terms of trade for Belgium and Canada. For Belgium, I use prices of cotton textile exports and grain imports; for Canada, prices of commodity exports and textile imports. Belgian export prices declined into the 1890s, but prices rose upward by about 15 percent from 1900, as more countries came to legislate limits on labor supply.[35] In Canada, the terms of trade declined after the first major piece of legislation was introduced in 1885 and stabilized shortly after. Manufacturing firms did not pass on the increase in costs to resource exporters. After the establishment of the IALL, the decline in the

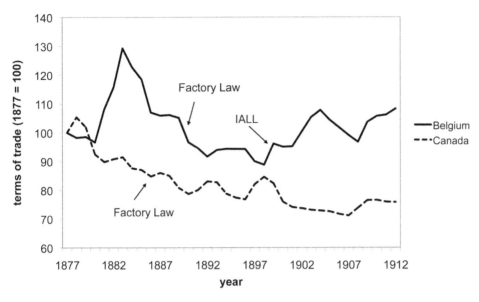

Figure 6.2. Terms of trade: Belgium and Canada, 1870–1914
Terms of trade = export prices/import prices. For Belgium, wheat import prices from
Blomme (1993, 171), and textile export prices from Van Houtte (1949, 269–71); for
Canada, commodity export and textile import prices from Urquhart and Buckley
(1983, 299–300).

terms of trade gathered momentum, as import prices rose faster than export
values. Canadian consumers, it would appear, footed the bill of the European
labor compact. Paolo Epifani and Gino Gancia (2009, 630) have observed the
same phenomenon in the last decades of the twentieth century. Europe has
passed on the welfare state in improved terms of trade. "If the price of a Nokia
phone partially reflects high domestic taxes, every unit sold to foreigners provides a subsidy to the Finnish welfare state."

Movements in terms of trade in Belgium and Canada recurred elsewhere in
Old and New Worlds. Nonetheless, it would be premature to conclude that
labor regulation was the prime mover of prices.[36] The literature has tended to
view the terms of trade from the optic of the New World (Lewis 1978). Aurora
Gómez-Galvarriato and Williamson (2008) described the trend in prices in
Latin America. After a long period of rising commodity prices, the terms of
trade turned back late in the nineteenth century, although there were some
country exceptions (Williamson 2006, 85). The reversal is attributed to rising
levels of productivity in key export industries, for instance Mexican mining,

oversupply in other products, like coffee, and increased demand for foreign machinery and capital equipment. Without minimizing these factors, the introduction of labor-intensive standards in the Old World moved prices in the same direction. Regardless of origin, the favorable direction in the terms of trade provided European exporters with a reprieve, even if for a short period, allowing them to absorb the adjustment costs they incurred in investing in new machinery, upgrading product quality, or developing new markets.

LABOR REGULATION IN BRAZIL IN THE INTERWAR PERIOD

Recall that by 1914 Brazil had made inroads in the Southern Cone. Undoubtedly, intracontinental trade was limited because neighbors had similar factor endowments, but the war years provide a natural experiment of what Brazilian trade might have been, certainly without "external interference," or intervention of major trading partners (Albert 1988, 93).[37] While the U.S. came to be a major destination for coffee, cocoa, and rubber, and had replaced the U.K. as the main supplier of industrial goods, Brazil established closer commercial ties with its nearest neighbors. Argentina had a relatively open economy until 1931; its manufacturing sector actually declined during the war (Diaz Alejandro 1970). In this market, Brazil competed head on with foreign rivals. Argentinean consumers were known to have had a preference for European goods, but they were also sensitive to price (Gravil 1975, 48). Figure 6.3 reports the part of Brazilian trade with Argentina. The war years were clearly exceptional as exports and import shares spiked at 18 and 23 percent.[38]

Why did the export expansion collapse in the 1920s? Did labor regulation cut into industry's competitiveness? Did Brazil ultimately fail to upgrade product lines? Some historians (Dean 1969, 88–104) have claimed the textile industry in particular was starved for capital and that existing plants and equipment tended to be run for longer hours.[39] But in São Paulo alone, between 1915 and 1920, the number of textile companies increased by 30 percent, workers and capital by 50 percent, spindles by 55 percent, and output doubled.[40] In the wake of labor regulation after 1919, businesses invested in new capital equipment and the average size of firms increased (see figure 5.4, panels c–e). The appreciation in the exchange rate in the early 1920s in the prelude to the return to gold was an additional incentive for local mill owners to purchase foreign machinery. This was also an invitation to foreign investment. A British trade delegate (Pearse 1923, 28) in the region imagined the new global trading order, one based on footloose capital and public technology that sought out sources of cheap labor and raw materials.

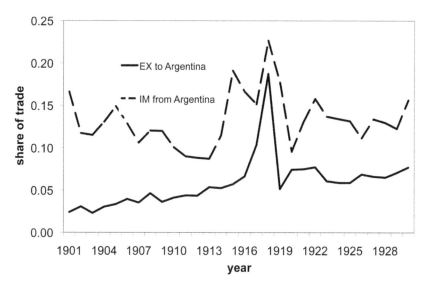

Figure 6.3. Share of Brazil trade with Argentina
Instituto Brasileiro de Geografia e Estatística (IBGE). Sector externo.

Those countries which have been exporting in the past to Brazil will have to reckon with the times when hardly any goods will be sent from Europe to this country, and if they wish to have a share in the Brazilian market, they will have to open their own mills in Brazil. Belgian and Dutch mill owners are largely interested in a Brazilian cotton mill and the profits are decidedly encouraging.

The rub was that engagement and expansion in high-income foreign markets demanded inventories of high-end goods. Again, Brazil met this condition. Figure 6.4 compares the quality of yarn manufactured in Belgium and Brazil based on purchase orders of new ring-spinning machines (Saxonhouse and Wright 2004).[41] In the 1890s, Brazil ordered machines spinning lower counts of yarn and compatible with labor and resource endowments. By 1914, the industry had begun purchasing equipment to spin finer grades, a tendency that peaked during the war years and after the passage of new labor laws. In Belgium, yarn counts actually declined in the immediate period after labor regulation in 1889, a change that may have reflected the hiring of women and adolescents. But by the early 1900s, the trend in counts was upward.[42] As legislated hours of work per week in the two countries converged, the challenge of labor regulation would seem to have been met by an improvement in product quality.

The point is that Brazil had the physical and human capabilities to expand in export markets, and sustained export expansion based on its war experience

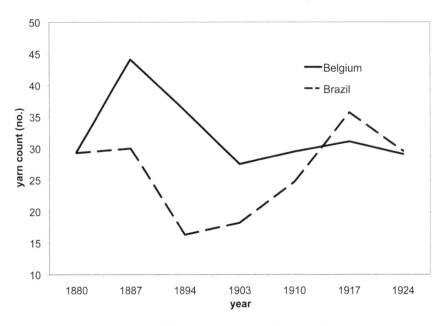

Figure 6.4. Quality of yarn spun in Belgium and Brazil
Data from Saxonhouse and Wright (2004, 144). Series of new investments
in ring frames.

was in its grasp. In this scenario, the new regulatory environment, as in Belgium, afforded an incentive to pursue the production of higher value goods. But despite resemblances to the Old World, developments unfolded differently in the country's Southern Cone. Brazilian textiles had made headway in its neighbors' markets in the early 1920s (figure 5.1, panel f), but by mid decade Argentina had become the object of a hemispheric Anglo-U.S. trade rivalry (Lewis 1975). As the world economy contracted, Lancashire began unloading goods at discounted prices, breaking its promise to assist Argentina in setting up its own textile industry, while granting Commonwealth preferences to its exports. British intervention in trade succeeded at Brazil's expense: while Lancashire's exports to the world contracted, those to Latin America remained stable in the decade before the depression. International political economy forces caused Brazil to lose the advantages of market size that contemporaneous Japanese firms had managed to access in South Asia.

In similar fashion, Brazilian producers lost ground in the domestic market. As the exchange rate improved in the mid 1920s, prices of foreign textiles fell, by nearly 40 percent between 1923 and 1926 alone (Versiani 1971, 54–55). Still, Brazilian manufacturers were able to meet the decline, and, beginning in 1927, relative prices began to shift in favor of domestic goods (Haber 1992, 357). But local producers could not contend with unfair trade practices, particularly the dumping of goods by the British.[43]

As export markets collapsed—trade costs had become prohibitive—the benefits of regulation that had accrued to Belgian firms vanished. Twenty years previously, Old World countries made the requisite adjustments to labor regulation in the context of expanding foreign markets, a luxury that was not available to Brazil. The allocation of resources did not materialize and the potential of productivity gains was nullified. Commenting on the failure to find markets for high-end goods, a United Nations field study (1951, 23) of the São Paulo textile industry, reported:

> All the mills manufacture a limited number of yarns and are outstanding for the high quality of their management. The productivity of mills nos. 3 and 5 should be higher since conditions of manufacturing and supervision there are excellent. However, they were designed to make very fine yarns and, at the time of the investigation, market conditions obliged them to manufacture yarns of a much lower count. As a result, their processes were thrown off balance, causing a reduction of productivity.

Plagued by low demand, industry sought higher tariffs (1929) and an embargo on the import of foreign machinery (1931). In 1943, Getúlio Vargas assembled existing laws on regulation and social entitlements in the Consolidation of Labor Act, proclaimed—by its architect at least—as the world's most progressive legislation.[44] But labor policy was imposed in a top-down and corporatist fashion whose objective was to secure social control (French 2004, 15–19; Colistete 2007, 99–100; Rudra 2008, 179), and embedded in a larger import substitution initiative. Ultimately the Brazilian welfare state satisfied a restricted population of urban clients (Haggard and Kaufman 2008, 62–63). The synergy between exports and productivity, critical in the expansion of the European labor compact, was not part of the equation.

CONCLUSION: THE WELFARE STATE WAS A DOMESTIC AND FOREIGN AFFAIR REVISITED

A standard history of the rise of the welfare state in Brazil goes something like this: Labor regulation was initiated during the macroeconomic dislocation caused by World War I (French 2004; Musacchio 2009). In the wake of inflation and exchange rate fluctuations, the state sought the support of selected groups of labor and business. On the one hand, the state acquiesced to labor's demands for improved working conditions, and, on the other, it granted manufacturers increased tariff protection. Regulation is cast as one pillar of the inward-looking regime that dictated Brazilian economic policy for much of the twentieth century (Haber 1997). Domestic forces trumped external constraints.

This chapter has put forward a complementary explanation. The inward response was as much a consequence of the contracting interwar trade environment as it was the result of domestic political forces. Without external access, labor regulation was not the lever of growth it had proven to be in Belgium. Institutional failure may not have been the smoking gun of Brazilian development; de-globalization was the culprit.

All the advantages seem to have favored the Old World before 1914. Countries partially escaped the burden on costs of duplicating labor policy of trading partners. States had some leeway in placating foreign rivals and domestic interests. Where regulation had some bite, business substituted capital for labor and moved up the product ladder. Finally, in more competitive sectors, the rising tide of legislation on labor-intensive manufacturing contracted industry output and raised prices, providing firms a reprieve to adjust to new investments, product lines, and customers. To be sure, there were other sources of productivity growth in the periods studied. In the case of Belgium, however, it is difficult to ascribe the transition from a labor-abundant to labor-scarce economy to the fertility transition or emigration. And while regulation in a closed economy also promotes new capital investments, my claim, in the spirit of new trade models, is that the allocation of resources in an open economy has larger aggregate productivity and income effects.

Timing was not everything in building the welfare state, but it helped. In Europe, workers came to support globalization and employers labor regulation. Without forsaking the gains of trade, the welfare state in Europe expanded. In Latin America, under the fog of tariff protection, the development of the welfare state was stunted. These choices had long-term consequences. While the recent wave of globalization has challenged, but not substantially weakened, the European welfare state (Lindert 2006), the obverse has held in poorer countries. Brazil began to open its economy in the 1980s, but without historical precedent and memory, it opted not to extend the safety net to those who most suffered from dislocation caused by trade. As in many parts of the developing New World, greater trade exposure has meant the undoing of social entitlements and employment protection for clusters of workers who had enjoyed its limited benefits (Rudra 2008). I return to the divergence in social policies between rich and poor countries in the conclusion.

THE LABOR COMPACT IN THE LONG TWENTIETH CENTURY

The standard of expenditure that guides our efforts is not the average, ordinary expenditure already achieved; it is an ideal of consumption that lies just beyond our reach, or to reach which requires some strain. The motive is emulation—the stimulus of an invidious comparison which prompts us to outdo those with whom we are in the habit of classing ourselves.

—*Thorstein Veblen*, Theory of the Leisure Class, *page 81.*

ECONOMISTS IN HISTORICAL PERSPECTIVE

The ever-growing divide between leisure-bent Europe and much of the rest of the world has become a vexed concern of economists and political scientists.[1] Explanations of recent worktime differences across OECD countries are as many as they are diverse. Linda Bell and Richard Freeman (1995, 2001) attributed longer hours in the U.S. to rising wage inequality; Edward Prescott (2004) claimed that excessive Old World tax regimes have curtailed the incentive to supply labor time; others have credited labor unions (Alesina, Glaeser, and Sacerdote 2005) and partisan politics (Burgoon and Baxandall 2004) for Europe's long vacation periods; lastly, and more fundamentally, Olivier Blanchard (2004) pinned the divergence on different preferences toward leisure. Although their points of departure differ, these views share the claim that the divergence was recent in origin. "The gap [U.S. vs Germany] is not a longstanding historical pattern" (Bell and Freeman 2001, 104).

The attention to current developments has its shortcomings. Using contemporary data it is difficult to sort out empirically the roles of incentives and policy, and to separate these factors from culture and other fixed factors. Consider Bell and Freeman's incentive-based argument that those who work longer move up in the wage distribution, the gains for doing so being greater the more unequal the wage distribution. The incentive structure and wage distribution in the contemporary U.S. could well be the product of recent polices, like those impeding unionization (DiNardo, Fortin, and Lemieux 1996), but the origins of today's rules and behavior can be traced to earlier industrial relations and legal regimes, and perhaps a deeper work ethic based on the drive to emulate some better-off reference group (Bowles and Park 2005). There is no simple way to disentangle the chain of causality and, while certain econometric specifications improve the quality of the estimates, the pitfalls of omitted and endogenous variables remain.

In this chapter, I bring a historical perspective to these issues. I ask whether today's patterns in worktimes can be found in the first wave of globalization. I answer in the affirmative. The decline in worktimes was greater in the Old World than in the New, a pattern repeated in the decades after 1950. Inequality was as much a catalyst of long hours in the New World before 1914 as it is today. My claim is that globalization and the labor compact were both cause and effect of the decline in hours. While regulation, the offspring of international trade, in Europe shortened the workweek and compressed wage distributions, greater egalitarianism in turn reinforced demands for more leisure time. In light of previous discussion, workers in both tradable and non-tradable sectors took some of the benefits of increased productivity in shorter hours. In the New World, the safety net was porous, the workweek long, and dispersion of wages large; as inequality rose, so did the incentive for individuals to give long hours. In a related study, Lindert (2004, 15) referred to this outcome as the Robin-Hood paradox: redistribution from rich to poor is least likely where it seems most needed. The great wave of globalization, it would appear, has had enduring consequences.

That said, the rise in inequality does not fully explain the divergence in worktimes between Old and New Worlds. Location effects, broadly defined to include cultural values, mattered too. Immigrants to the New World adopted the attitudes toward effort they encountered in their new environments. The inference is that the labor compact was coupled to values which globalization reinforced and perpetuated.

WORKHOURS AND WORKDAYS, 1870–2000

This section introduces basic trends in the different components or dimensions of worktime, hours of work per week (or per day), days of work per year (or weeks of work), and hours of work per year, from 1870 to 2000. My aim is not to write a history of worktimes, but to compare and contrast developments in the period before 1914, the interwar years, and the decades after 1950. While the interwar years are exceptional, there are certain similarities between the early period and the decades after 1950, the key years in the current debate about international differences in work patterns The resemblance is striking despite changes in the institutional environment over the last 130 years, and it underlies the claim that a historical perspective can deepen our understanding of contemporary movements in worktimes.

HOURS OF WORK PER WEEK

Table 7.1 collects evidence on the length of the workweek since 1870 for a sample of countries. The appendix gives full detail on sources and methodology. The unit of measurement is weekly hours of full-time production workers (male and female) in non-agricultural activities.[2] These values control for days of work. There are sources of measurement error in the table, not least because national authorities may have differed in what they recorded, some reporting standard or legal hours, others actual hours. I consider the series best approximates usual or normal hours that workers would have been engaged for during the year.

The underlying series do not show the peaks and valleys we would expect to find if workers supplied overtime or faced downtimes because of temporary plant closures. Part-time work in the period before 1914 and into the interwar years was minimal. Only in the 1970s did a sizeable proportion of the labor force in certain countries begin to work less than full-time (OECD 1998, 2004).[3] Women's hours tended to be close to those of men in the early years. The gap between men's and women's hours in many countries widened with the rise in female labor force participation in the 1960s. The table reports male and female work hours in 2000. By this date, European men and women worked less than their counterparts elsewhere. Of course, changes in labor supply and the rise in the number of part-timers have affected total hours worked, and I control for this in constructing an annual hours of work series below. That said, since my objective is to compare national work patterns, table 7.1 is a reasonable starting point to examine long-term patterns.

The contraction in hours was as universal as it was regular. The decline before 1914 (0.30 percent per year) was comparable to that after 1950 (0.35 percent). The long-run decline is generally attributed to the combined effects of the rise in income and fall in the relative cost of leisure (Greenwood and Vandenbroucke 2005), although economic growth and the diffusion of time-using leisure goods were certainly not contemporaneous across and within countries. Notwithstanding the common downward trend, national and regional patterns emerge.

Table 7.1. Hours of work per week, 1870–2000

	1870	1880	1890	1900	1913	1929	1938	1950	1960	1970	1980	1990	2000 (M)	2000 (F)
Belgium	72.2	69.3	66.5	64.2	59.5	48.2	48.0		42.5	39.9	38.5	36.6	37.3	36.5
Denmark	69.9	64.6	59.9	56.0	55.8	48.5	47.6	46.0	44.4	39.0	37.5	35.0	39.3	37.7
France	66.1	66.0	65.9	65.9	62.0	48.0	39.0	44.8	45.9	44.8	40.7	39.9	36.9	34.6
Germany	67.6	66.3	65.1	64.0	57.0	46.0	48.5	48.2	45.6	43.8	41.6	39.0	40.8	39.0
Ireland	63.8	62.0	60.2	58.6	56.4	46.6	48.2	45.0		42.7	41.1	42.1	40.7	38.0
Italy	63.3	63.4	63.6	63.8	62.4	48.8	48.5	47.8	42.4	42.9	42.5	39.6	41.4	35.4
Netherlands	65.0	63.4	61.9	60.5	58.6	48.1	48.5	49.2		45.1	40.8	34.0	37.6	30.1
Spain	64.7	62.7	60.8	59.1	56.7	48.5	47.0				40.0	38.9	36.9	34.0
Sweden	69.6	64.6	59.9	56.0	56.0	48.0	46.3	46.8	43.4		37.7	38.2	39.1	36.3
Switzerland	65.4	63.1	60.9	59.0	56.3	48.5	46.3	47.5	46.1		43.8	41.6		
U.K.	56.9	56.6	56.3	56.0	56.0	47.0	48.6	45.7	44.7	42.0	40.0	42.4	42.0	38.9
Australia	56.2	53.3	50.5	48.1	44.7	45.5	45.0	39.6	39.6	39.6	39.2	40.1	42.6	38.5
Canada	57.2	59.0	60.9	62.6	57.9	49.0	47.2	42.3	40.7	39.7	38.5	38.0	42.8	36.0
U.S.	62.0	61.0	60.0	59.1	58.3	48.0	37.3	42.4	40.2	38.8	39.1	39.7	43.3	37.2

Argentina							45.5	25.3		42.8	46.8	43.8	47.1	40.3
Brazil							48.0	47.6	49.9		46.0	43.0	44.3	42.4
Mexico							45.2		46.3	44.5	47.0	44.8	44.9	42.3
Old World	65.9 (4.08)	63.8 (3.16)	61.9 (3.08)	60.3 (3.66)	57.9 (2.44)	47.8 (0.90)	47.0 (2.78)	46.8 (1.51)	44.4 (1.48)	42.5 (2.18)	40.4 (1.94)	38.7 (2.76)	39.2 (1.95)	36.1 (2.70)
New World	58.5 (3.10)	57.8 (4.00)	57.1 (5.76)	56.6 (7.56)	53.6 (7.74)	47.5 (1.80)	43.2 (5.19)	41.4 (1.58)	40.2 (0.55)	39.4 (0.49)	38.9 (0.38)	39.4 (1.12)	42.9 (0.36)	37.2 (1.25)
Old World (weighted)	64.4	63.5	62.6	61.8	58.6	47.5	46.7	46.9	44.6	43.3	40.9	39.5	39.7	36.4
New World (weighted)	61.4	60.5	59.6	58.8	57.7	48.0	38.4	42.3	40.2	38.9	39.1	39.6	43.2	37.2
World	64.3 (4.92)	62.5 (4.10)	60.9 (4.08)	59.5 (4.63)	57.0 (4.13)	47.8 (1.07)	46.1 (3.56)	45.4 (2.82)	43.2 (2.33)	41.7 (2.35)	40.1 (1.82)	38.9 (2.47)	40.1 (2.35)	36.3 (2.45)

Sources: See appendix.

Notes: Hours of work per week of full-time production workers. Old and New World (weighted) are population-weighted averages. New World is North America and Australia. Standard deviations in parentheses.

In 1870, Australia had the shortest workweek, followed closely by the U.K. All other European countries had initially longer hours than their offshoots. But the decline in hours from 1870 to 1914 was slightly greater in the Old (0.3 percent per year) than in the New World (0.2 percent). This pattern was not too different from that found in the period after 1950.[4] By 1914 the length of the workweek was about the same for all countries in our sample except for Australia, France, and Italy. These comparisons are evident in the bottom lines of table 7.1, where I give Old and New World average hours weighted by population. This procedure, which amounts to a comparison between the U.S. and an average of Germany, France, Italy, and the U.K., suggests that the so-called reversal was well under way by 1914. The trends may have reversed in the 1930s and immediately after the war, but these were due to exceptional circumstances. The Latin American figures are not included in New World averages, because before 1960 data are fragmentary. Still, their pattern does not appear to be unlike that of other countries in the region. In 1900, Brazilian hours per week were slightly less than those in Belgium and Canada; in the interwar year, they were about the same as Belgium's and slightly lower than Canada's; in 2000, Brazilian men worked about 20 percent longer than Belgians, and 5 percent more than Canadians.

In long-run perspective, the interwar years were atypical. After the Great War, political and social pressures exerted downward pressure on the length of the workday and the dispersion of hours narrowed rapidly across and within regions. At its founding conference in 1919, the ILO exhorted countries to adopt a common standard, the Washington Hours Convention. Recall that Brazil's labor laws were modeled on recommendations of the ILO. The period of harmonization was shortlived. The U.S. and the U.K. failed to ratify the eight-hour resolution adopted by the ILO, and by the mid 1920s national authorities like Switzerland and Belgium had loosened their commitments to the common standard. In the wake of the depression, France and the U.S. led the way in worktime cuts, but the likeness is misleading. In France and Italy, the state legislated reductions in hours (Matessini and Quintieri 2006); in the U.S., the executive branch used its powers of moral suasion to encourage worksharing. Australia and Canada provide examples of a third way: job sharing and hour cutbacks were relatively unimportant (Gregory, Ho, McDermott, and Hagan 1988; Green and MacKinnon 1988). By 1929, Canadians had the longest hours in the world and Australians came to accept a 45-hour work week.

The divergence of worksharing practices during the thirties was typical of the labor-market regimes that had been established in Old and New Worlds. Europeans had a long tradition of reduced worktime during periods of falling output—still another mechanism to contain the costs of labor regulation. The predisposition toward worksharing was codified in the revamped and enlarged unemployment insurance schemes adopted in the 1920s that subsidized time loss at work (Huberman 1997). Into the late twentieth century, worksharing has remained an integral component of the European model of industrial relations. In contrast, the U.S.'s experiment with job sharing in the 1930s was bittersweet. Although some jobs may have been saved, many held that managers used the policy arbitrarily, turning one group of workers against another (Moriguchi 2005). At Bethlehem Steel available work during the depression was shared only among "efficient and loyal workers" (Jacoby 1985, 212). After the war, U.S. labor contracts avoided worksharing clauses, with layoffs determined by seniority.

In the immediate postwar years, Europeans toiled long hours, surpassing North and South Americans, but this was to be expected. During a period of rapid catch-up, hours worked tend to be longer because capital is in short supply. Thereafter, age-old patterns reasserted themselves. From 1950 on, as in the early period, the steepness of decline was greater in Europe (0.4 vs 0.2 percent per year). While European unions pressed responsive governments to cut the length of the workday, organized labor in the U.S. forsook cuts in hours as workers joined the drive to stock up on consumer goods (Hunnicutt 1988), a phenomenon reinforced by growing inequality. Regardless of the causes, when Europeans began to work fewer hours per week (unweighted) than in the New World in the 1980s, it was the culmination of a century-long trend.

DAYS OF WORK

Table 7.2 gives the number of days off (vacations and national holidays) over the long twentieth century for the sample of countries. At the outset, days off were rooted in traditional religious and social calendars, and work patterns across the oceans converged.[5] Immigrants to the U.S. practiced certain Old World customs and rituals (Gutman 1973), while Europeans adopted May Day, a U.S. creation. But by 1900 the New World had made a break with Old World habits. Firms with large investments in fixed capital were under pressure to work as many days as possible.[6] In Catholic Europe, many of the religious festivals had been transformed into secular holidays and, although in certain northern European countries the work year was long, the Old World had on average twice the number of days off that their offshoots enjoyed. Although paid holidays and vacations were rare before 1914, the parallels with the late twentieth century are evident: Europeans had more weeks off than the rest of the world.

From the end of hostilities until the 1930s the drive for more days off gathered momentum. Internal and external forces mattered in the Old World. Before 1914, the average worker had limited savings for vacations, but in the interwar

Table 7.2. Vacation and holidays, 1870–2000

	1870	1900	1938	1950	1980	1990	2000
Belgium	18	21	30	28	34	34	33
Denmark	13	14	27	27	30	35	37
France	19	23	33	28	30	36	36
Germany	13	18	31	29	29	35	42.5
Ireland	14	20	33	20	28	28	30
Italy	23	24	37	24	35	40	41.5
Netherlands	4	5	21	24	33	35	37.5
Spain	31	31	44		30	35	36
Sweden	11	13	28	29	30	37	38
Switzerland	13	18	33	25	28	28	33
United Kingdom	14	20	30	24	28	30	32.5
Australia	8	9	22	22	32	32	32
Canada	8	9	22	22	25	25	24
United States	4	5	17	18	22	23	20
Argentina					26	26	26
Brazil				42	43	43	43
Mexico					23	23	23
Old World	16	19	32	26	30	34	36
	(7.00)	(6.71)	(5.84)	(2.90)	(2.46)	(3.75)	(3.82)
New World	7	8	20	21	26	27	25
	(2.31)	(2.31)	(2.89)	(2.31)	(5.13)	(4.73)	(6.11)
World	13.8	16.4	29.1	24.6	29.6	32.4	33.4
	(7.31)	(7.61)	(7.09)	(3.50)	(3.44)	(4.88)	(6.16)

Sources: See appendix.

Notes: Days off work. New World is North America and Australia. Standard deviations in parentheses.

years, due to the insistence of unions and the backing of the ILO, European states and employers began converting days off into paid vacation days (Cross 1988; Furlogh 1998). The Soviet Union and Eastern European countries first introduced paid vacations in the early 1920s, and faced by growing labor power most western and northern European states emulated their programs (ILO 1939). From the 1930s on, the dispersion in days off across Europe narrowed steadily. The evolution of the attitudes of British unions was typical (Graves and Hodge 1940). Initially, organized labor had demanded a shorter and standard workday, but in the interwar years, when eight hours per day Monday through Friday plus half-day Saturday was the norm, unions campaigned successfully for more days off which took the form of a compressed workweek and more paid holidays. By the mid 1930s, unions were able to translate the new workweek of five days into ten days of vacation time, comprising two weekends, one bank holiday, and five paid days off.

In North America, legislation was not imminent and the story unfolded differently. Employers who had instituted paid vacations as a part of a larger plan to win over workers from unions in the 1920s appear to have dropped them in the 1930s (Jacoby 1985). Some firms attempted to replace longer holidays with four-day weeks, but workers rejected these programs, preferring the customary five and a half days of work. A National Industrial Conference Board study for the U.S. found that more than half of the 300 establishments surveyed had either suspended or discontinued their paid vacation plans after the depression.[7] All told, the average North American production worker had about one week of paid vacation in the 1930s, about half that of a European worker, and considerably fewer public holidays.

After 1950 historical patterns persisted. In Europe, state legislation mandated further increases in paid vacation time, and though Canadian workers were able to negotiate similar benefits, in the U.S. and Australia there is still no statutory minimum paid leave (ILO 1995). The Latin American experience is mixed. While Brazilians have had exceptionally long vacations—the figures include two days for *carnaval*—workers in Argentina and Mexico had fewer days off than the richer countries of the New World. Europeans' preference for more and continuous vacation time today may be the outcome of a "social multiplier," the joint decision of families, neighbors, and communities to synchronize time off (Alesina, Glaeser, and Sacerdote 2005). But the European desire for leisure is not a recent phenomenon, the coordination problem having been solved at an earlier date and well before the rise in female labor force participation. Although the decline in days worked was slow, about two days per decade over the twentieth century, the cumulative effect was large. By 2000, using figures for days of work from table 7.2, the greater number of vacation days in Germany compared to the U.S. explained almost half the gap in annual worktimes between the two countries.[8]

Did New World employees have short careers to compensate for long work days and brief vacation periods? This is unlikely, evidence of intertemporal substitution being scarce (Costa 2000). Careers were long everywhere before 1914, and retirement patterns in the early and late periods were also similar across countries. The average American supplied relatively more labor effort than a European across time as well over the life cycle.[9]

ANNUAL HOURS OF WORK

Table 7.3 presents hours of work per year for the sample of countries from 1870 until today. The New World labored fewer hours than the Old for most of the nineteenth century, but after weighting by population there was little difference between the two regions before 1914. Figure 7.1 calls attention to the greater contraction in European worktimes during two sub-periods, 1870–1914 and 1950–2000. Old and New Worlds reversed positions in the mid 1970s, and, thereafter, the gap slowly widened. Latin America followed the patterns of other regions of new settlement. From a historical perspective of one hundred years and more, claims that divergence in hours of work is a recent phenomenon appear to be greatly exaggerated.

The long-run perspective exposes fundamental differences between Old and New World work patterns, despite distinctive national histories. Consider the cases of Australia and the U.K., the pair with the shortest work years in 1870. Australia with its early labor regulation was an outlier in the New World. Into the interwar periods, hours of work fell steadily, but the trend in hours has remained flat since 1950. Ian McLean (2007) claimed that the low level of labor input was not sustainable as the economy became increasingly dependent on natural resources. In Britain before 1914, time on the job hardly fell, a sharp contrast to its continental neighbors. By the mid 1970s, it had converged to European levels—and well ahead of EU directives. Although their respective journeys were distinct, by the end of the century Australia and the U.K. had evolved into typical New and Old World countries.

INEQUALITY AND WORKTIMES IN THE LONG RUN

In the U.S., the 1970s marked an end to the labor-market regime that had its origins in the immigration restrictions of the 1920s (Wright 2006). Sustained by pro-labor legislation of the 1930s, and the spillover effects of pattern bargaining embedded in the Treaty of Detroit in the 1950s, U.S. wage disparities in these decades narrowed, sometimes rapidly. Beginning in the 1980s, the fall in minimum wages and de-unionization campaigns widened the dispersion in earnings, although other factors also operated, chiefly the skill bias of technological change which raised wage premiums at the upper end (Lemieux 2008). In the 1990s, outsourcing contributed to the widening of inequality.

The surge in inequality in the U.S. is a forceful explanation of the divergence in hours of work between Americans and Europeans. To Bell and Freeman (2001), individuals' labor supply decisions are embedded in the wage

	1870	1880	1890	1900	1913	1929	1938	1950	1960	1973	1980	1990	2000
Belgium	3483	3344	3177	3064	2841	2229	2196	2404	2289	1851	1736	1699	1547
Denmark	3434	3172	2933	2742	2731	2301	2203	2071	1929	1871	1693	1492	1473
France	3168	3165	3119	3115	2933	2198	1760	2045	2025	1849	1696	1558	1443
Germany	3284	3223	3108	3056	2723	2128	2187	2372	2144	1808	1696	1541	1463
Ireland	3108	3017	2869	2795	2690	2182	2171	2437	2320	2103	1954	1992	1686
Italy	3000	3008	3006	3014	2953	2153	2162	1951	2012	1825	1724	1674	1612
Netherlands	3274	3194	3105	3037	2942	2233	2281	2156	2002	1709	1667	1414	1352
Spain	2968	2876	2787	2710	2601	2342	2030	2052	2042	2124	1968	1832	1815
Sweden	3436	3187	2937	2745	2745	2152	2131	2009	1902	1683	1523	1550	1645
Switzerland	3195	3083	2925	2834	2704	2281	2085	2092	1952	1835	1721	1617	1597
U.K.	2755	2740	2669	2656	2656	2257	2200	2112	2134	1919	1758	1698	1653
Australia	2792	2647	2501	2385	2214	2186	2109	2023	1945	1837	1815	1806	1797
Canada	2845	2934	3017	3102	2868	2354	2212	2111	2014	1874	1825	1830	1825
U.S.	3096	3044	2983	2938	2900	2316	1756	2008	2033	1942	1853	1840	1878
Argentina								2034	2073	1996	1974	1850	1872
Brazil								2042	2134	2096	1985	1879	1841
Mexico								2157	2153	2064	2054	2063	2155
Old World	3191	3092	2967	2888	2774	2223	2128	2155	2068	1871	1740	1642	1572
	(224.4)	(171.8)	(155.7)	(169.6)	(122.9)	(68.0)	(138.6)	(169.4)	(138.9)	(137.8)	(125.4)	(163.4)	(131.7)
New World	2911	2875	2834	2808	2661	2285	2026	2047	1997	1884	1831	1825	1833
	(162.4)	(205.0)	(288.6)	(375.7)	(387.2)	(88.10)	(239.2)	(55.6)	(46.3)	(53.3)	(19.7)	(17.5)	(41.4)
Old World (weighted)	3094	3051	2971	2934	2781	2200	2102	2144	2078	1869	1755	1631	1564
New World (weighted)	3063	3020	2964	2924	2868	2313	1807	2017	2027	1930	1848	1837	1868
World	3131	3045	2938	2871	2750	2230	2133	2132	2053	1874	1759	1682	1627
	(238.8)	(194.1)	(186.1)	(212.2)	(192.4)	(73.0)	(128.8)	(157.0)	(126.8)	(122.8)	(116.9)	(163.2)	(161.2)

Sources: See appendix.

Notes: Old and New World (weighted) are population-weighted averages. New World is North America and Australia. Standard deviations in parentheses.

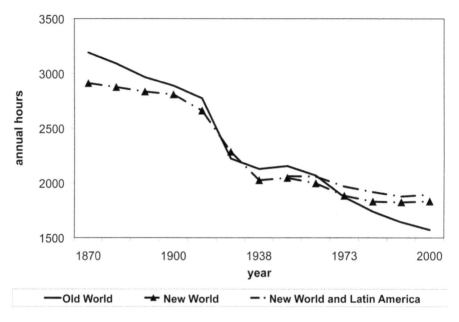

Figure 7.1. Annual hours of work in Old and New Worlds, 1870–2000
Data from table 7.3. Adapted from Huberman and Minns (2007).

structure of the firm and sector of activity: the greater the dispersion of wages, the larger the rewards of supplying extra labor time. While their model may be best suited to professionals whose pay is directly related to their effort, like lawyers, Samuel Bowles and Yongjin Park (2005) provide a more general framework to study the link between inequality and hours. Invoking Thorstein Veblen, they posit that hours of work increase in the degree of inequality because of social emulation, or the craving to adopt the consumption standards of the rich.[10]

My claim is that similar pressures operated in the nineteenth-century New World. Globalization forces in the absence of regulation contributed to rising inequality, intensifying the propensity toward emulation, or of keeping up with the Joneses. In the U.S., Clayne Pope (2000, 139) wrote, "new participants entered, relocated, changed occupations, and took risks to capture the opportunities before them." The norm of mobility gave American workers the occasion to realize their goals. Across occupations, individual workers did not forsake long hours and firms accommodated them (Long and Ferrie 2007).[11] Social pressures of this type were certainly present in the Old World, but regulation was an effective counterweight and even before 1914 the incentive to work longer was weak. Individuals who supplied extra labor time had no guarantees of exceptional rewards or upward mobility (Eichengreen 2007, 385).

In this section, I exploit data from the Report for 1870–1900 to advance the hypothesis that the relation between inequality and hours of work has deep historical roots. My research strategy proceeds in three stages: first, I ask whether the relation between wages and hours was different between regions using data exclusively from the Report, what I call the baseline or 'micro' model.[12] Second, I add 'macro' controls to the baseline regression. The objective is to reduce differences between Old and New Worlds. Next, I add measures of inequality and labor power. If the gap between regions persists, I cannot reject the hypothesis that other factors, like culture, partially explained divergence in worktimes.

Table 7.4 reports regression results of weekly hours of work on wages and control variables for sex, occupation, country, year, and region. Column 1 gives the baseline results.[13] For males, a 10 percent increase in the hourly wage led to a shorter workweek of 1.2 percent, about 40 minutes based on the figure for 1900 from table 7.1. Regional differences were stark.[14] The coefficient on the New World dummy indicates that, conditioning on wage levels, the workweek was about 10 percent longer in the New World.[15] The inclusion of occupational and year dummies have little impact on this result (column 2). Because the sample from the Report is unbalanced, in the next two columns I have weighted the observations by the relative size of each country in the sample. Although the New World dummy is smaller, it remains significantly different. The baseline results hold when the sample is restricted to manufacturing (column 5).

Across all specifications, the estimated wage coefficient remains stable and slightly greater than estimates reported for the period after 1950, but this is to be expected.[16] The "demand for leisure," to use Fogel's (2000, 186) phrase, varied across regions. The coefficient of the interaction term, New World x wage, is significant in column 6, indicating that the responsiveness of hours to wages was smaller in the European offshoots. The New World dummy in this specification is twice as large compared to column 1. Although it would be premature to conclude that preferences were different across the oceans, it would appear that labor market outcomes did indeed diverge before 1914.

Table 7.5 gives estimates of coefficients for a regression of hours on micro variables from the Report, including a New World indicator, and typical macro variables, the proportion of workers in agriculture, average age, capital per worker, and a business cycle indicator. The divergence between New and Old World is of the same order of magnitude as in the baseline regression. In column 1 of table 7.5, the variables have the expected sign, except for capital intensity. A drawback of the capital measure is its level of aggregation. Assuming that capital intensity at

Table 7.4. Micro determinants of hours of work, 1870–1900

	(1)	(2)	(3) (WEIGHTED)	(4) (WEIGHTED)	(5) MANUFACTURING	(6)	(7) RICH COUNTRIES
ln (wage)	−0.12	−0.13	−0.12	−0.13	−0.11	−0.16	−0.13
	(−88.15)	(−109.41)	(−27.40)	(−31.75)	(−29.56)	(−73.62)	(−24.39)
Female	−0.08	−0.10	−0.07	−0.08	−0.09	−0.09	−0.09
	(−37.30)	(−47.69)	(−13.82)	(−15.57)	(−17.54)	(−47.06)	(−41.39)
New World	0.10	0.103	0.05	0.06	0.07	0.18	0.04
	(58.57)	(66.94)	(13.47)	(14.76)	(15.21)	(32.29)	(2.80)
New World x ln (wage)						.034	0.00
						(−14.33)	(−0.05)
Year dummies	Yes	No	Yes	No	No	No	No
Occupation dummies	Yes	No	Yes	No	No	No	No
Constant	3.84	3.76	3.91	3.81	3.82	3.70	3.84
	(673.78)	(1221.66)	(218.72)	(372.70)	(409.16)	(694.25)	(267.58)
R-square	0.42	0.37	0.42	0.35	0.22	0.38	0.38
F-test	410	4122	77	504	314	3173	2603
N	20890	20890	20890	20890	3267	20890	16816

Sources: All data from U.S. Commissioner of Labor (1900).

Notes: The dependent variable is log hours of work per week. OLS estimates. t statistics in parentheses. Rich countries are Australia, Belgium, Denmark, Germany, the Netherlands, U.K., and U.S. Columns 3 and 4 are estimated by weighted least squares with observations weighted to approximate the relative population size of each country in the sample.

	(1)	(2)	(3) MANUFACTURING	(4) US and UK	(5) RICH COUNTRIES
In (wage)	-0.106	-0.120	-0.069	-0.123	-0.122
	(-75.54)	(-95.79)	(-16.92)	(-94.93)	(-91.58)
Female	-0.068	-0.082	-0.069	-0.085	-0.082
	(-34.04)	(-41.91)	(-13.22)	(-41.51)	(-38.75)
New World	0.052	0.072	0.032	0.108	0.002
	(13.36)	(19.19)	(3.65)	(8.16)	(0.27)
Average age	0.019	0.02	0.01	0.007	0.006
	(17.63)	(19.03)	(6.00)	(3.04)	(1.64)
Proportion agriculture	0.170	0.156	0.181	0.102	0.299
	(15.86)	(14.69)	(7.52)	(2.99)	(13.37)
In (K per worker)	-0.022	-0.030	-0.05	-0.024	.014
	(-6.07)	(-8.90)	(-6.27)	(-3.02)	(1.84)
Deviation from GDP trend	-0.102	0.007	0.052	0.023	-0.008
	(-5.25)	(0.61)	(1.79)	(1.89)	(-0.61)
Year dummies	Yes	No	No	No	No
Occupation dummies	Yes	No	No	No	No
Constant	3.49	3.44	3.80	3.71	3.46
	(82.20)	(118.40)	(52.06)	(55.54)	(51.68)
R-square	0.48	0.43	0.28	0.42	0.39
F-test	452	2161	179	1912	1509
N	20356	20356	3154	18710	16659

Sources: Age is average of population from Baier, Dwyer, and Tamura (2006); proportion of labor in agriculture from Mitchell (1981) and Lindert (2004); capital per worker from Baier, Dwyer, and Tamura (2006); GDP from Maddison (1995, 2001). See table 7.4 and appendix for other details.

Notes: The dependent variable is log hours of work per week. OLS estimates. t statistics in parentheses. In column 4, U.S. = New World. Rich countries are Australia, Belgium, Denmark, Germany, the Netherlands, U.K., and the U.S. Sample size is reduced from table 7.4 because of missing observations for average age and capital per worker.

the macro level does track establishment levels, there may have been a limit to how long firms could have extended the length of the workday without doing harm to their workers and capital stock. This was the case in manufacturing in column 3.[17] In column 4, I consider whether there was an Anglo-American model of the workweek and restrict the sample to the U.K. and the U.S. I reject this view. The last column reports a positive coefficient for capital intensity at the 10 percent level when the sample is restricted to the richest countries. Advanced technology in this group of countries may have led to long hours because it had less harmful effects on workers' productivity. Only in this specification with a reduced sample size is the New World dummy eliminated.

In the next stage, I add two competing explanations: labor power and inequality. Of course, these factors are not entirely mutually exclusive and my historical account has suggested their interdependence. But explanations of the recent divergence in hours have treated them as separate, and for the sake of comparison I will do likewise. I use voter turnout to pick up any effect of labor power on hours, as this seems the best available indicator as to whether the median voter was likely to have any interest in the issues facing the industrial worker of the day. Recall that I have found that voter turnout had stronger effects on policy adoption in the New than in the Old World, where external forces also mattered. Because of data limitations, I cannot test directly either Bell and Freeman's hypothesis (1995, 2001), which requires firm level evidence, or Bowles and Park's (2005), which requires aggregate measures of inequality. I do have a sufficient number of wage observations in the sample at the occupational level from which I can construct the difference between maximum and minimum wages for each year.[18] This provides a measure of wage dispersion within categories, but the occupations are broadly defined to get some indicator of the ratio of skilled to unskilled wages.

Table 7.6 reports the effect of inequality and labor power on hours, taking into account other macro variables. To get a better idea of the different dynamics I separate Old and New Worlds. In line with previous findings (chapter 2) on the relative importance of domestic factors in policy adoption, labor power is significant in the New World only, but in the Old, more votes, by itself, did not necessarily translate into reduced hours. Domestic factors were entangled with external factors in the region. Anyway, the labor movement needed to form bridges with other groups to get reform passed, since governments, not unions, legislated hours. Inequality seems to have operated as anticipated. In the New World, wage dispersion prompted longer hours, a result that is stronger when Australia is omitted. Consistent with the historical account, Australia stands apart from other settler countries and biases the results against finding a difference between regions (columns 1 and 2). In the Old World, inequality had the

Table 7.6. Macro determinants of hours of work, 1870–1900: Inequality and labor power

	(1) NEW WORLD	(2) NEW WORLD no Australia	(3) OLD WORLD	(4) OLD WORLD 1890–1900
ln (wage)	−0.123	−0.125	−0.112	−0.097
	(−92.06)	(−93.05)	(−32.38)	(−4.80)
Female	−0.083	−0.082	−0.073	−0.056
	(−39.28)	(−39.20)	(−14.31)	(−6.96)
Average age	0.012	0.006	0.017	0.045
	(5.70)	(2.86)	(9.71)	(9.58)
Proportion agriculture	0.310	0.166	0.139	0.044
	(10.61)	(4.79)	(8.59)	(1.32)
ln (K per worker)	−0.002	−0.028	−0.040	−0.076
	(−0.37)	(−3.99)	(−7.20)	(−5.36)
Voter turnout	0.140	0.087	0.012	−0.099
	(7.32)	(4.51)	(1.17)	(−4.80)
Inequality	0.015	0.022	−0.002	−0.002
	(10.82)	(13.12)	(−2.57)	(−1.59)
Year dummies	No	No	No	No
Occupation dummies	No	No	No	No
Constant	3.33	3.87	3.42	3.07
	(47.74)	(46.53)	(117.85)	(30.32)
R-square	0.38	0.38	0.56	0.63
F-test	1425	1398	1398	313
N	16391	16299	3980	1298

Sources and notes: The dependent variable is log hours of work per week. OLS estimates. t statistics in parentheses. Inequality is calculated as the difference between maximum and minimum wages for each year. For other variables, see tables 7.4 and 7.5, and appendix.

opposite sign. In consensual Europe, the relation between egalitarianism and shorter hours has deep historical roots.

LOCATION, LOCATION, LOCATION: CULTURE AND EFFORT

So far, I have claimed that the interdependence of trade and labor regulation made for greater egalitarianism and shorter work years in Europe. These forces were weaker in the New World. But it is also clear that I have not explained fully the gap between Old and New World hours, even after including controls for fixed and time-varying factors. From an early date there was something different in the dynamics between work and pay in Old and New Worlds. In this section, I investigate the role of culture in the choices across regions to give more or less effort. To be clear, my claim is not that values operated independently of trade or as a brake on the labor compact, but that local effects, a product of history and geography, were entangled with policy outcomes in the Old and New Worlds.

The literature on why New World workers gave—and continue to give—long hours independent of their levels of income is crowded, but religious affiliation and a work ethic are at the top of the list. These interdependent factors are central to the popular, if not dominant, narrative of comparative economic history, in which workers in the New World were inclined to give greater labor effort, pushing outward the frontier and creating legal, social, and economic institutions that secured the rewards for working hard. Did globalization promote the sorting of populations between two locations: stayers in Old World who had a taste for social policy and leavers to the New World who had a dominant streak of individual initiative?

Religious affiliation has been a salient factor in New World economic history. Landes (1999, 175) evoked the Puritan mantra of the seventeenth century, 'Time is short and the work is long,' and Rodgers (1978, 9) observed that Puritans "threw out the irregular carnival of saints' days, and replac[ed] it with the clocklike rhythm of the weekly Sabbath." Undoubtedly, religious beliefs of the nineteenth century did not have the theological trappings of earlier versions, but "the ascetic injunctions of the Protestant ethic [were] retained and multiplied their force (Rodgers 1978, 11)." There was variability in religious affiliation across the sample of countries. The U.S., Germany, and the Netherlands exhibited a high degree of pluralism in 1870. In that year, 52 percent of the Old World was Protestant; the figure in the New World was 62 percent.[19]

A related view is that a work ethic was embodied in a wide body of institutions and not restricted to religious attendance. I follow recent studies (Tabellini 2005) and use educational attainment, in my case primary school enrolment in 1870, as an indicator of cultural attitudes. The idea here is that education instills and transmits cultural traits. From an economics perspective individuals who have increased their earning power through education are expressing their commitment to market work, which is consonant with historians' claim that greater levels of schooling are associated with a stronger attachment to the culture of self-improvement.[20] Here the emphasis is on preferences that get passed on from one generation to another.[21] If education was a cultural trait, it would be expected

Table 7.7. Culture and hours of work, 1870–1900

	(1)	(2)	(3)
In (wage)	−0.120	−0.120	−0.120
	(−95.72)	(−95.74)	(−95.86)
Female	−0.082	−0.082	−0.082
	(−41.87)	(−41.85)	(−42.04)
New World	0.071	0.065	0.042
	(19.17)	(12.31)	(6.86)
Average age	0.018	0.018	0.014
	(19.02)	(18.83)	(12.83)
Proportion agriculture	0.157	0.173	0.190
	(14.85)	(12.46)	(13.53)
In (K per worker)	−0.030	−0.028	−0.018
	(−8.84)	(−7.72)	(−4.86)
Primary enrolment 1870 / 1000			0.086
			(7.33)
Protestant 1870		0.008	0.005
		(1.76)	(1.17)
Year dummies	No	No	No
Occupation dummies	No	No	No
Constant	3.45	3.41	3.40
	(128.41)	(94.88)	(94.81)
R-square	0.43	0.43	0.43
F-test	2530	2169	1910
N	20377	20377	20377

Sources: Religion and enrolment from Lindert (2004) and Mitchell (1981). For other variables, see tables 7.4 and 7.5, and appendix.

Notes: The dependent variable is log hours of work per week. OLS estimates. t statistics in parentheses. These values are rescaled. Protestant is a dummy variable =1 where the majority of the population was Protestant in the late nineteenth century.

that countries with initially high levels of enrolment would put in place incentives that perpetuated the relation between schooling and work.

My objective is to see whether or not sorting based on culture unlocks the puzzle as to why the New World labored longer than the Old. I use a binary variable to measure religious affiliation in 1870 (1 where more than 50 percent of the population was Protestant; 0 otherwise); I use primary school enrolment rates in 1870 to represent cultural preferences. Column 1 in table 7.7 reproduces the main result of table 7.4, a positive New World coefficient after controlling for micro and macro variables. In the next columns, I evaluate the contribution of the culture. Protestantism did lead to longer hours, but the coefficient is significant only at the 10 percent level (p = .08).[22] The effect of schooling on lengthening the workday was more pronounced. Combined, religion and schooling reduce the size of the New World coefficient by less than a half—they do not eliminate it.

My research strategy based on elimination has its pitfalls, but it appears that the values I have identified were not the entire story behind long hours in the New World. Other and unknown location effects immigrants encountered mattered. If in Rome, do as the Romans do—and in the New World this meant long hours of work. But while initial conditions and values may partially explain the divergences in Old and New World worktimes, it does not follow that geography locked in social policy at an early date. After controlling for location, the time-varying factors of income and inequality retain their importance in explaining the long-term trends in hours.

CONCLUSION: PLUS ÇA CHANGE, PLUS C'EST LA MÊME CHOSE

Debates on worktimes in OECD countries have focused exclusively on the period after 1970, if not later. Historians can contribute to the conversation. I have found strong parallels in worktimes in the years before 1914 and after 1950. In both periods, the Old World had more days off and hours per week declined faster than in the New World. There is no fundamental break between early and late stages of globalization. Egalitarianism, the outcome of trade and the labor compact, contributed to the contraction of worktimes in the Old World in the late nineteenth century as it does today.

If history does matter, policy proposals to transform the Old World into the New, or vice versa, by changing tax schedules or consumption patterns in one direction or another, need to be reconsidered. Thus, Prescott's (*Wall Street Journal*, October 21, 2004) prescription of "freeing European workers from their tax bondage" is hard to reconcile with the long-term pattern in hours of work. Over the twentieth century, institutions have had the effect of codifying past behavior, thereby promoting ever-growing divergences in outcomes. Owing to this feedback mechanism, it is problematic to claim that policy is transferable and will have similar effects everywhere. We cannot be certain that workers of the world today are intrinsically alike and will respond similarly to the same incentives. Over generations, the distinction between nurture and nature has become blurred.

It would be premature to conclude, however, that the labor compact is strictly a Western European phenomenon, the outcome of a unique confluence of economic, political, and social forces that have stayed the course of time. In the concluding chapter, I argue that, for poor and rich countries alike, the relation between trade and the labor compact is as relevant today as it was in the past.

VANDERVELDE'S GIFT

To shut small nations out from the great markets of the world through customs barriers would condemn them to a cramped and narrow life which would check the development of their industry in every branch, and stifle progress towards the attainment of labour reforms and the high standard of living for workers which . . . is the object of the International Labor Organization.

—*Émile Vandervelde, "Labour Reforms in Belgium," page 130.*

THE IMPORTANCE OF BEING UNIMPORTANT

How can we reconcile the growth of international trade and the expansion of the labor compact? My answer is that the relation between trade and labor standards was double sided. Labor regulation, which preceded the welfare state, was not a mere rejection of markets, but a response to the volatility and uncertainty of the new world order. Trade and redistribution were compatible, and certainly desirable. Even as individual countries adopted regulation, trade was a pathway in the diffusion of labor standards. The welfare state was not built in any one country. From its origins it was a transnational movement. And there was a flip side: the labor compact hastened the growth in trade and changed its nature as well. The new laws compressed wage inequality, inducing business to enhance labor productivity. Firms became better exporters and importers as a result. Labor standards and international trade have been inextricably linked since the 1870s, an odd couple perhaps, but a marriage nonetheless promoting growth and egalitarianism simultaneously.

International trade created a wedge between Old and New World social models. While countries of new settlement were in fact richer, had a larger proportion of voters, and experienced greater volatility in terms of trade, labor standards developed more slowly in the region. The labor-scarce New World inclined toward protectionism, but workers' attempts to seek coalition partners on tariffs and the labor compact failed. Instead, labor and its partners turned their attention to immigration quotas. The labor-abundant Old World had a stronger predisposition to support free trade. Nonetheless, labor's endorsement of trade in the region was conditional on a new deal in employment conditions and social entitlements that distributed the gains of globalization to women and men alike. Over time, labor in Europe became attached to free trade, as capital was to regulation.

This was not the complete story of the Old and New World divide. As long as the international regulatory environment was uneven and capital and labor mobile, social policy at the country level was vulnerable. But here, too, the Old World was favored. Initially, countries depended on narrow markets for their exports of manufactured items. These markets were fickle. At any time, trading partners could block access, forcing producers to unload goods at bargain prices. Who could possibly take Swiss cheese besides the French? By means of coercion and collaboration, trading partners came to have similar, although not always identical, labor standards. The spread of regulation deepened markets for brand items. These forces were weaker in the New World, which exported mainly natural resources in competitive markets. By 1914, two different models of the delivery of social and commercial policy had emerged: In the Old World, free trade was coupled with the labor compact; in the New World, tariff protection was paired with immigration quotas.

It may be argued that I have put too much weight on labor standards both as a potential brake on trade and as a possible source of growth. By 1914, different labor-market regimes had evolved in Old and New Worlds, each with distinct sets of formal and informal institutions and rules, of which the labor compact was a component. These regimes were unified in the sense that the various dimensions of the labor market were self-reinforcing.[1] The norm in the U.S. was short job attachments, long hours of work, and matching wage premiums (Ferrie 2005). Individual initiative was sovereign, and unions bargained more over wages than for collective goods like hours of work. Immigration reinforced these tendencies. This type of regime supported and was supported by a permissive labor compact. In Europe, the representative worker was relatively less mobile and had a preference for egalitarianism. The labor compact reinforced and was reinforced by these outcomes. Regulation promoted investments in human capital, thereby establishing bonds between workers and firms (Long and Ferrie 2007). Europeans wanting irregular or long hours found employment in the informal sector, in the countryside, or across the Atlantic. I do not deny the significance of unified regimes with strong feedback mechanisms. Rather, my intention is to be faithful to contemporary observers. The salient debate before 1914 concerned the effects of labor standards on trade and appropriate policy responses. Contemporary observers identified only indirect implications of the uneven playing field in labor laws for the larger discussion of labor-market regimes.

A related shortcoming is that the ramifications of individual pieces of labor regulation on costs were trivial. My rebuttal is twofold. First, perceptions of labor standards mattered, if only because the new laws were as likely to be imposed by hardnosed foreign states as to be the product of malleable domestic interests collected under a big tent. The fear that labor regulation was a slippery slope had resonance because legislation was perceived to pose a challenge to established elites. Second, even if individual laws were ineffectual, they were collectively important. The adoption of limits on women's work followed, and in short order, limits on children's employment. The same process was repeated across countries. Riding the waves of trade, the labor compact blanketed Europe's rich and poor countries, and democratic and authoritarian regimes alike, by the eve of the war. The implication is that the adoption of a minor and seemingly unimportant change in labor law in one country had ripple effects on labor costs everywhere.

THE LABOR COMPACT IN THE INTERWAR PERIOD

Émile Vandervelde and social reformers behind the IALL held decisive roles in the early years of the ILO and defined its policy direction. With historically grounded premonition, Vandervelde (1920) warned that in the aftermath of the war and the redrawing of European boundaries, old and new states would face strong pressures to resort to protectionism, even as free trade was enshrined in Wilson's Fourteen Points. In the epigraph to this chapter written in 1919, Vandervelde was concerned that the ILO's foundational convention of an eight-hour day, and subsequent labor standards, would be jeopardized if market access were restricted.

Vandervelde's (1920) intervention prefigured the main lines of this book. He briefly summarized Belgian experience: Employers had been initially reluctant to support labor regulation because they feared lost competitiveness abroad and more imports at home. Because of domestic and foreign pressures, the state was compelled to accommodate emerging interest groups coalescing around the demands for labor regulation and free trade. The new laws had immediate repercussions on balance sheets, but over time businesses made necessary adjustments. Citing the success of the textile industry, Vandervelde saluted the increase in firm size and productivity, and trumpeted the new export items sold to new destinations. Labor regulation may have been the response to the dislocation caused by the new global order, but social protection had contributed equally to the extension of the market.

To Vandervelde, the labor compact and globalization were inseparable. Commenting on the U.S., he ascribed the porous welfare state to its isolationist policy. Vandervelde lamented that newly emerging countries in Latin America would follow the same roadmap, forsaking the opportunities Europe had benefited from before the war. And he was preoccupied that as more countries opted out of the international trading order, working conditions around the world would suffer. This was the historical lesson he (Vandervelde 1920, 119, 130) drew for labor standards in the 1920s:

> Although the eight-hour day will on the one hand certainly result in an initial diminution of output, it will on the other hand necessitate considerable mechanical improvements calculated to increase output. Belgium will stand equipped with modern plants for the large-scale production which characterizes the new era of commercial development. For small countries like Belgium, the policy of making social legislation international in scope carries with it as an *essential condition* [my emphasis] of success the policy of bringing the markets of the world within reach of their industries.

In its first decade, the ILO drew successfully on the lessons of the pre-1914 period. Several of the early ILO conventions had separate provisions for China, India, and Japan. For instance, Convention 1 on hours of work specified a general limit of 48 hours per week, but 57 hours for Japan and 60 for India (Rodgers 2011, 48). Delegates at the 1905 IALL convention in Berne had agreed to a similar two-tier framework for countries in the European periphery in their resolutions on night work for women and age limits for children. As for safeguarding their early achievements, prominent ILO policymakers (Fontaine 1920) invoked the France-Italy labor accord of 1904 (see chapter 4) as a template to relieve pressures of interwar population movements on existing social policy. Nevertheless, the early gains were undone. In the end, the record on the adoption of the foundational convention on working time was mixed: Belgium ratified in 1926; Canada in 1935; and Brazil has never signed. States resisted extending the scope of international agreements on working time. For instance, the Netherlands and Switzerland opposed the Forty-Hour Week Convention. An ILO official (cited in Rodgers et al. 2009, 112) characterized the episode "either as a melancholy chronicle of repeated failure or as an inspiring saga of sustained refusal to accept defeat."

In the lens of the first wave of globalization, the collapse in international trade during the 1930s lay behind the failure to harmonize labor standards. It may have appeared that employment conditions had converged—France and the U.S. had comparable worktimes in 1938—, but this was mere coincidence. In the absence of pressures emanating from international trade, states went their own way, implementing policies to reflect domestic concerns. The labor compact and international trade were effectively decoupled. In the isolationist 1930s, immigration ceased and Canada was prepared to make concessions on employment conditions and social entitlements. Along Bismarckian lines, the New Deal was established behind tariff walls.

Polanyi's (1944, 244, 248) interpretation of these events was that "history was in the gear of social change." While the final outcome was, at the time of his writing, uncertain, the "emerging regimes" in Germany and the Soviet Union, and the U.S., and to a lesser extent the U.K., had discarded laissez-faire principles. This was the curse of slavish adherence to the market in the previous century. The collapse of the international system in the interwar years "let loose the energies of history—the rails set by the tendencies inherent in a market society."

Vandervelde's reading was different. While the adoption of the New Deal in the U.S. and progressive legislation in Canada gave comfort to reformers, he rejected the 'welfare state in one country' prescription. Vandervelde foresaw that the North American social model would remain porous and spillover effects modest in the absence of expanding foreign trade. Rejecting the rigid determinism of his contemporaries, he affirmed that the market is the lever of growth. The challenge was to design policy to assure that workers shared in its benefits. In particular, improvement of working conditions at home and abroad was dependent on the political will of states to remain open to trade, balancing the demands of commercial partners and those of domestic interests. In the immediate postwar years, Europe would choose Vandervelde's roadmap.

THE LABOR COMPACT AFTER 1945

In 1955, the ILO mandated a commission, chaired by Bertil Ohlin, to report on the "social aspects of problems of European economic co-operation." The commission (ILO 1956, 1) interpreted its terms of reference to investigate whether or not "international differences in labor costs and especially in social charges" constituted an obstacle to economic integration; whether "a freer international market" called for a "greater degree of international consultation and co-operation than at present"; and, lastly, whether the "free international movement of labor" would claw back existing labor standards and entitlements.

The responses of the commission combined theoretical insights and historical observation.[2] To begin with, disparity in labor standards is bound to persist even as trade increases, because of differences in productivity, itself a result of increased trade between countries. Still, "it may be found desirable to harmonize to some extent action for the improvement in workers' living standards," where wages in any one sector are lower than the economy average, owing perhaps to workers' poor bargaining position. International pressure is required to bring these sectors up to an acceptable norm. "Such measures for harmonization should not be regarded as a prerequisite to the liberalization of trade, but should be undertaken during the period of transition." Low-standard countries have an incentive to improve their labor laws when they have commitments of market access, an essential condition of the first wave of globalization. International labor mobility does not pose a threat to social policy. "Countries will come to adopt a more flexible attitude towards the question of admitting foreign workers and we would consider this to be a desirable concomitant to free international trade." Again, these types of arrangements had been in place before 1914.

By the mid 1950s, Europeans had already put in place many of Ohlin's recommendations, developing a new version of the labor compact which drew on its historical legacy of "powerful collectivist predispositions" (Eichengreen 2007, 45). Globalization was part of the equation. While the adoption of labor regulation in the first wave launched a wage push, after 1945 unions demonstrated wage moderation. The strategy was favored because the reallocation of agricultural labor to industry that had begun before 1914 was postponed until the 1950s (Temin 1997). With business, workers exchanged wage restraint for reinvestment of profits in enhanced technologies; with the state, workers committed themselves to social peace because they did not want to jeopardize the extension of unemployment insurance, and health and retirement benefits, and promises of more vacation time. As part of the social pact, all parties agreed to greater international exposure that also operated as a disciplinary device. Workers did not demand excessive wages for fear of overpricing themselves, firms upgraded their plant and equipment to fend off stiff import competition, and states guaranteed market access for trading partners to get the benefits of membership in political and commercial unions.

To be sure, the bonding mechanisms often showed strains, but domestic and international institutions like centralized bargaining and the European Payments Union monitored and enforced compliance. In this regard, the postwar consensus had made improvements on the informal network that existed before 1914.

The macroeconomic environment had also changed. Under the rules of Bretton Woods, states had more room to adjust exchange rates, within bounds, than had prevailed under the gold standard regime, thereby offsetting some of the increased costs of labor regulation. Still, Vandervelde and his associates would not have been uncomfortable at the bargaining table when Belgian labor and capital agreed in the late 1960s to an ambitious cooperative compact that reinforced their commitment to trade openness, an agreement that coincided with the government's decision to expand the welfare state (Eichengreen 1996, 49).

Since the macroeconomic shocks of the 1970s, the labor compact has been under stress. While the history of this period is beyond my purview, Europe's commitment to social protections appears to be less endangered than elsewhere (Lindert 2006). The relation between regulation and globalization is as strong as ever. In figure 8.1, I compare the reduction in worktimes and degrees of openness for my sample of countries for 1870–1914 and 1973–2000. The stability of the relation is unremarkable since the underlying dynamic was the same. In both periods, labor regulation was a response to greater external exposure, but the causality also ran from higher wages to greater productivity, and to expanding export markets. The end result was a strong relation between falling worktimes and trade. Small open and regulated economies, like Belgium and Switzerland, exhibited large contractions in annual hours in both periods.

In the Americas, the relation between trade and the labor compact has been historically weak. Five New World countries are above the line in the bottom panel of the figure. In Canada, worktimes actually increased in the first wave of globalization when tariffs were high, and declined slowly in the second when trade barriers came down. The welfare state has proved to be the least resilient in Latin America, where it had developed in a closed economy environment. In 2008, Brazilians worked longer hours than Canadians.

LESSONS FROM THE HISTORY OF LABOR STANDARDS

In the first wave of globalization, countries traded ideas and goods. Bilateral labor treaties having their origins in the complex commercial networks and political alliances between states specified benchmarks on limits of work for women and children and for other types of labor regulation. In the absence of a centralized authority, individual states had some discretion in the choice of policy, with the result that international labor law of the period is best described as pluralist by design. The costs of defection were large since countries could lose market access for their brand goods. Comparable pressures may be weaker today. Since trade based on comparative labor endowments is on the rise (Krugman 2008), low-wage

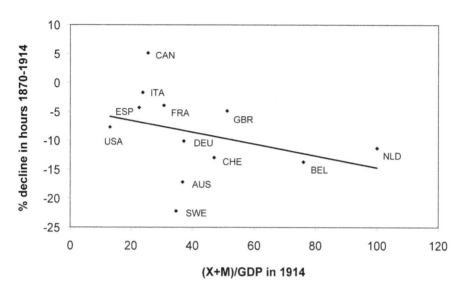

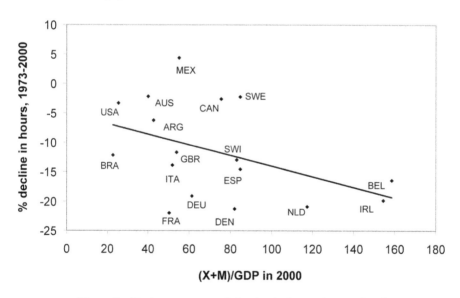

Figure 8.1. Trade openness and the the decline in hours of work
Trade from table 1.1 and Penn World tables 6.3; annual hours of work from table 7.3.

countries do not have the same incentive as in the past to upgrade labor conditions. The growth in outsourcing has weakened attempts to identify and shun laggards to the reform movement, since business moves easily between locations. There may be some enlightened governments willing to exploit international pressure to get around domestic resistance to reform. This was the case of Italy in 1905. Other authorities may adopt labor standards as a signal to attract foreign investment, as did Russia before 1914 and Brazil in the 1920s. But other countries may not be moved by ideas of a social norm against child labor and night work for women, say, if the costs of non-compliance are small. Social clauses in trade agreements like NAFTA are loosely enforced and penalties small (Hiscox and Smyth 2008). What pressures can be brought upon low-wage countries manufacturing undifferentiated goods or harboring outsourcing of production to improve their regulatory environments?

In the remaining sections of this chapter, I take the risk of extrapolating from the book's major findings to revaluate labor standards in the global economy today. I begin with challenges at the individual level, before moving on to national and international responses.

CONSUMERS AND LABOR STANDARDS

Consumers, along the lines suggested by Elliott and Freeman (2003), can buy better working conditions abroad.[3] In effect, they are exchanging ideas for higher priced goods. A similar outcome occurred in the first epoch of globalization The wave of regulation of labor-intensive manufacture that had swept across the Old World contracted output, and prices rose as a result. Beginning in 1900, the reversal in terms of trade shifted the burden of new laws onto consumers of manufactured goods around the world, although the incidence was relatively greater on countries exporting resources. To be sure, consumers' roles before 1914 and today are not identical. In the first wave of globalization, consumers did not choose to label goods as 'fair trade' because they had met some labor-standard norm. In fact, this choice was out of their hands. Today consumers have more discretion, although Rodrik (2011, 277) questions whether they "have enough information to make the right choices," and is not optimistic that consumers will limit their purchases over the long run. But can consumers by themselves really make a difference? The historical episodes I have studied have drawn attention to the success of cross-class and cross-border coalitions in the spread of the labor compact. All social actors have responsibility in improving working conditions. If successful, consumer embargoes on goods that fail to meet an international norm of production will increase prices of close substitutes. The rise in prices will change incentives faced by businesses and states previously hostile to adopting labor laws. In this scenario, social activists can find foreign coalition partners more disposed to push for better working conditions.

My depiction of the labor compact as a catalyst of new investments conflicts with the mantra that regulation handcuffs business seeking to benefit from declining trade costs. The gains from trade derive from the seamless relocation of resources between and within industries, and domestic policies curtailing mobility increase levels of unemployment (Freund and Bolaky 2008; Helpman and Itskhoki 2008). In particular, employment protection laws have been a drag on firms' abilities to respond to the challenges of globalization (Bertola, Boeri, and Nicoletti 2001).[4] This view seems to have inverted Polanyi's dictum of markets vs states. While the older view believes there was not enough state intervention, the newer claim is that there is too much.

My response is that not all labor standards are alike in their effects on growth. Before the inception of the labor compact, paternalist employers unilaterally imposed working conditions. These entitlements were limited and non-transferable. State regulation was a response to the failure of markets to deliver decent conditions and social entitlements, and in this sense brought markets to operate closer to their ideal. The labor compact standardized employment conditions inside and outside the factory, fostering labor mobility within and across borders. Human capital accumulated as a result, let alone because of the additional years of schooling as children were restricted from working. These regulations were not a drag on growth.

Even in its early phase, the labor compact was not static. Initially, states provided factory inspection and regulated the supply of women and children. But as international exposure increased displacing workers from less competitive sectors, the demand for social entitlements intensified. It may well be that the incidence of the labor laws was modest because omniscient states did not replicate exactly those of their trading partners and adopted policies having the least harm to their comparative advantages. But regulation in the open economy before 1914 promoted shifting of resources to export industries at the expense of the import-competing sector, and aggregate productivity improved as a result. The low levels of unemployment in the European core before 1914 was the reassuring outcome of the flexible structure of regulated economies. Lastly, egalitarianism advanced growth because it favored higher savings and investment rates (Alesina and Rodrik 1994).

The adoption of employment protection laws is the exception that proves the rule. The history of these laws has little in common with the original labor compact, having been adopted by a group of countries in the European periphery, Spain and Portugal, and in Latin America, whose autocratic rulers sought to buy labor peace beginning in the 1920s. Similar types of laws are weaker, if not non-existent, in contemporary western and northern Europe. In these regions, the labor compact has been modified without sacrificing its achievements. In Belgium, France, and Germany, long vacation times are an extension of earlier demands for a shorter workday, and during slack periods unemployment insurance has been used to supplement time loss, a policy that had its origins in the pre-1914 period (Huberman 1997). There is little evidence that the shorter work year has been a check on labor productivity (Blanchard 2004). In the Nordic countries, centralized bargaining has provided for wage flexibility to insure international competitiveness while preserving social entitlements.

PREFERENTIAL TRADE ZONES, IMMIGRATION, AND LABOR STANDARDS

The North American Free Trade Agreement has renewed concerns of globalization's effects on working conditions in the region. I have argued that countries take on the labor standards of trading partners. To a Canadian eye, the concern is that the U.S. and Mexico have considerably inferior regulatory environments. Although exports from Mexico have surged across the borders, wage increases in the country have been restricted to export zones situated along its northern frontier, and working conditions have seen little improvement (De la Garza Toledo 2003; Zepeda, Wise, and Gallagher 2009). A more balanced view is that the U.S. has not imported Mexican rules because jurisdictions in the U.S south had weak labor regulations well before NAFTA. Any improvement in employment conditions will prove difficult to obtain in the region.

Reports of the harmful effects on Canadian social policy of the opening up of markets seem to be greatly exaggerated. The dispersion of labor regulations and social provisions across provinces is as wide as ever (Huberman 2005). The Canadian experience confirms that, as in the past, domestic forces prevail over external constraints in the development and makeup of social policy in the New World. It is unlikely that Canadian trade by itself will be sufficient to exert upward movement in the labor standards of its NAFTA partners. Given the history of regulation in North America, the large differences in factor endowments, and the type of exports, other pressures will need to be brought to bear on partners in order to improve working conditions in the region.

The delivery of social policy in the European Union is faced by other problems. With the adoption of a single currency, states have forsaken the ability to adjust exchange rates to accommodate the costs of labor regulations. Looking forward, the aging of the population poses a challenge to the European social model. While immigration is intended to offset declines in the labor force, the inclusionary rights provided by the EU have acted as a "welfare magnate" (Sinn 2007). The fear is that inflows of foreign workers will gradually undermine states' abilities to provide universal benefits.

The differences from the first wave of globalization are striking. In the New World, high tariffs encouraged population inflows and diluted demands for the labor compact; inevitably, labor turned toward immigration quotas to provide income and employment security. In the Old World, the free flows of labor and goods were complements. All social actors expressed real concerns about the viability of the labor compact, since resident workers initially received preferential benefits. In response to threats to the labor compact, governments resolved to give all workers the same entitlements, under the condition that home countries of foreigners reciprocate and raise labor standards. The pledge of market access was the cornerstone of these negotiations. Countries, mainly in the European periphery, agreed to adopt costlier laws as long as they had guarantees of markets for their exports. This required that economies in the European core made concessions on their tariffs. As trade increased, the challenge foreign workers posed to the labor compact diminished. Tito Boeri's (2009) proposal that the EU make concerted efforts to improve welfare states in poor regions as a counterweight to immigration echoes earlier experiences.

WHAT ROLE FOR INTERNATIONAL LABOR STANDARDS AND SOCIAL CLAUSES?

In rich countries, labor and business have demanded that social clauses imposing tougher labor standards on poorer partners be appended to WTO and preferential trade agreements. The burden of this book has been to demonstrate that, in the absence of international governance, decentralized market forces in the early epoch of globalization succeeded in harmonizing the regulatory environment. Without forsaking domestic concerns, countries had an incentive to adopt comparable labor standards to those of trading partners because they wanted to protect market access. But states also came to recognize that improved standards because of their salutary effects on the development of new product lines and export destinations deepened economic integration, enabling further improvements in well-being.

It would be rash to conclude that international governance has no role to play in equalizing the rules of the game. The gap in working conditions between rich and poor countries is large, as is the difference in wages. The combination of coercive measures and conciliation—trade wars and reciprocal labor accords—enforcing labor regulation in the early wave of globalization may be ineffective in the second wave. Yet in today's trading order, the poor world has legitimate concerns that the imposition of labor standards, without corresponding reduction in barriers for its exports, serves only to empower protectionist interests of advanced economies. Such measures harm the very workers who are intended to benefit from an international code of labor standards. Before 1914, states made credible commitments to open markets. If guarantees to market access by international institutions today are weak or fleeting, better working conditions at home and abroad will prove difficult to attain. Inevitably, workers will have no option but to turn their backs on globalization. Émile Vandervelde's 'essential condition' of coupling the labor compact and trade is as relevant as ever.

APPENDIX

Table 1.2 gives the dates countries adopted legislation. Wherever possible, I selected dates of introduction or amendments to laws that came close to meeting standards of the Final Protocol of the International Conference on Labour in Factories and Mines held in Berlin in 1890. The Berlin meeting outlined a model labor code intended to be the basis of a late nineteenth-century European social charter. The final Protocol recommended that children under 12 years of age be prohibited from factory work; the elimination of night work for young women; and a working day for women of 11 hours. In an attempt to be consistent, I relied on dates in the proceedings of the International Association of Labour Legislation (1907, 1911). The IALL distinguished between dates of adoption and dates when the legislation came into effect.[1] Where the IALL did not make the distinction, I relied on official publications; when official reports gave conflicting years, I assumed that change occurred mid-way between the last two dates identified. The list at the end of this section gives sources consulted for tables 1.2 and 1.3. To avoid duplication, other sources consulted in preparation of the tables and cited in the text and footnotes appear in the full list of references to this book.

In the Old World, I assume that legislation was standardized within national borders.[2] For Switzerland, I take federal legislation; for Australia, the date the first state passed legislation meeting the Berlin standard; for Canada, when Quebec and Ontario achieved this level; for the U.S., I give two values: first, when ten states passed legislation, and, the second, when the ten most populated states adopted the law. In the case of Mexico, new labor laws were passed in the wake of the revolution; I have followed labor historians (Bortz 2000, 674–83; Gómez-Galvarriato 1999) and record adoption in 1913.

Other laws governing women's and children's work and factory conditions could be included in table 1.2. The correlation between these measures and the years of adoption in the table is strong.[3] Certain details of these measures (for instance, night work of children) varied greatly across countries. I selected laws that had less dispersion in various dimensions, although heterogeneity across countries cannot be ruled out (table 1.3).

The choice of dates for the U.S. merits discussion because of different histories of regulation at the state level. Despite its federal structure, Fishback (2007, 302) claimed the "geography of adoption showed that neighboring states were likely to adopt legislation with similar features within the same time frame." Twenty-two states adopted workers' compensation between 1911 and 1914 alone (Fishback and Kantor 2000, 58). For other regulations, legislation was most common in industrial northern states with the largest share of workers in manufacturing and import-competing activities—key sectors in my analysis. As for dates of introduction, years recorded in table 1.2 approximate those reported by Commons and Andrews (1936, 97–102). For women's hours, they gave 1908, the year when the Oregon ten-hour law for women was upheld, to mark the beginning of "enforceable hour limitation laws for women." On the basis of my procedure, I estimate that night work of women was introduced in 1913.

With regard to social entitlements, the dates do not presume universal standards for social expenditure, because of the variability in these measures and in program funding. For Europe, dates refer to national programs. In the case of accident insurance, I took dates from the comprehensive international Report prepared by the U.S. Commissioner of Labor (1911). I have followed the Report and record that Russia adopted accident insurance in 1903. The Poor Law is not included. In Western Europe, relief expenditures as a share of national product were declining from 1850 on—by 1880 they represented as little as 0.5 to 1.0 percent of GNP (Lindert 2004, 39–66).

In table 1.3, factory inspectors and numbers of workers are taken from the ILO (1923a, 1923b); Mitchell (1981); Price (1923); Silvestre (2008). The U.S. employment figure is for Pennsylvania reported by the U.S. Department of Commerce (1989, 130). Information on night rest for women, age restrictions for women, and minimum age are for New South Wales (Australia) and Ontario (Canada). For these countries sources are listed below. Figures for U.S. are modal values for the closest years to 1900, 1910, and 1919, based on Fishback, Holmes, and Allen (2009, 58–62); Engerman (2003, 52–54); Goldin (1990, 76–77); Moehling (1999). All other countries from Brooke (1898); Engerman (2003, 12–22, 52–54); Follows (1951); Keeling (1914). Employer costs for accident insurance as share of wage bill are averages of available years from adoption until 1910 reported by the U.S. Commissioner of Labor (1911); figure for U.S. is mean value for the first 10 states that adopted compulsory accident insurance after 1911 in Fishback and Kantor (2000, 58).

OLD WORLD

Bellom, M. 1897. *État actuel de la question des accidents du travail dans les différents pays.* Congrès International des Accidents du Travail, Rapports. Brussels: P. Weissenbruch.

Brooke, Emma. 1898. *Factory Laws of European Countries.* London: Grant Richards.

Droz, Numa. 1889. *État de la question des accidents du travail.* Congrès International des Accidents du Travail, Rapports, vol. 1. Paris.

Fraser, Derek. 1984. *The Evolution of the British Welfare State.* Second edition. London: Macmillan.

International Labour Office (ILO). 1923a. *Factory Inspection: Historical Development and Present Organisation in Certain Countries*. Geneva: ILO.

ILO. 1923b. "Some Problems of Factory Inspection." *International Labor Review* 8: 789–810.

Keeling, Frederick. 1914. *Child Labour in the United Kingdom*. London: P. S. King & Son.

Rimlinger, Gaston. V. 1971. *Welfare Policy and Industrialization in Europe, America and Russia*. New York: Wiley.

Silvestre, Javier. 2008. "Workplace Accidents and Early Safety Policies in Spain, 1900–32." *Social History of Medicine* 21: 67–86.

United Kingdom. *Parliamentary Papers*. 1905. Vol. LXXIII. "International Conference on Labour."

Villard, Harold G. 1913. *Workmen's Accident Compensation and Insurance in Belgium, Norway, Sweden, Denmark and Italy*. New York.

NEW WORLD

Argentina

Bonaudo, Marta, and Elida Sonzogni. 1999. "To Populate and to Discipline: Labor Market Construction in the Province of Sante Fe, Argentina 1859–1890." *Latin America Perspectives* 26: 65–91.

Guy, Donna J. 1981. "Women, Peonage, and Industrialization: Argentina 1810–1914." *Latin America Research Review* 16: 65–89.

Pichetto, Juan Raul. 1942. "The Present State of Social Legislation in the Argentine Republic." *International Labour Review* 46: 385–99.

Australia

Castles, Francis G. 1989. *The Comparative History of Public Policy*. New York: Oxford University Press.

Clark, Victor. 1907. *The Labour Movement in Australasia: A Study in Social Democracy*. London: A. Constable.

Jones, Michael. 1980. *The Australian Welfare State: Evaluating Social Policy*. Sydney: Allen & Unwin.

Kewley, Thomas H. 1969. *Australia's Welfare State: The Development of Social Security Benefits*. Melbourne: Macmillan.

Platt, Desmond C. 1989. *Social Welfare, 1850–1950: Australia, Argentina, and Canada Compared*. Basingstoke, Hampshire: Macmillan.

Smith, Yvonne. 1988. *Taking Time: A Women's Historical Data Kit*. Melbourne: Union of Australian Women. http://home.vicnet.net.au/~wmnstime/1834to1899.htm.

Canada

Government of Canada, Department of Labour. 1918. *Labour Legislation in Canada*. Ottawa.

MacDowell, Laurel Sefton, and Ian Radforth, editors. 1992. *Canadian Working Class History: Selected Readings*. Toronto: Canadian Scholars Press.

United States

Abbott, Edith. 1910. *Women in Industry: A Study in American Economic History*. New York: D. Appleton.

Baker, Elizabeth Faulkner. 1925. *Protective Labour Legislation*. New York: Longmans, Green.

Commons, John R. 1935. *History of Labor in the United States*. New York: Macmillan.

Commons, John R., and John B. Andrews. 1936. *Principles of Labor Legislation*. Fourth edition. New York: Harper and Brothers.

Jones, Ethel B. 1975. "State Legislation and Hours of Work in Manufacturing." *Southern Economic Journal* 41: 602–12.

DIRECTED DYAD YEAR MODEL

The directed dyad approach improves on country-year event history analysis because it includes information on interaction effects between neighbors or trading partners and common features of the country pairs. In event history models, external factors are usually weighted averages of arbitrarily defined 'neighbors,' or other countries comprising the reference group. The model I use permits countries to be leaders and followers over different policies and in different country pairs. To be sure, some degree of sample selection is unavoidable because B appears only when it has adopted at least one of the five pieces of legislation. For sample selection to force a change in the sign of a marginal effect, A's "error term" would have to be strongly correlated with B's. The selection problem increases in severity as the correlation between the included explanatory variables and B's error term becomes greater. These problems turn out to have a small effect on the coefficients.[4]

Some comment is in order about the dependent variable. A pair of countries can be present up to two times in each year since the order of adoption for each country may not have been the same across labor laws. Over 50 percent of the 'emulations' in the data are associated with convergence to a standard previously adopted by five or fewer countries. The number of leaders in the sample period is restricted by definition, and as a result most countries were followers in the diffusion process. To be clear, my approach explains only partially why country B was in fact the first mover. My primary interest is the transmission of policy between trade partners.

As for the determinants of policy convergence, the trade cost measure is related to the (geometric average of) bilateral trade shares of GDP (Jacks, Meissner, and Novy 2008, 2010). The tariff equivalent is obtained by inverting the trade shares. In effect, the term measures the wedge between observed bilateral trade and that predicted by size alone, which would be the key driver in a world without barriers to trade. The variable is strongly related to observable proxies for barriers to trade including tariffs, transportation networks, exchange rate variability, and language differences. The measure for year t is calculated as

$$\tau_{ABt} = \left(\frac{x_{AAt} x_{BBt}}{x_{ABt} x_{BAt}} \right)^{\frac{1}{2(\sigma-1)}} - 1$$

The variables x_{AA} and x_{BB} are proxies for intra-national trade, or domestic absorption, and x_{AB} and x_{BA} represent total exports from country A to country B and exports from B to A. The parameter σ is the elasticity of substitution between all goods, domestic and foreign (and foreign vs foreign), and is assumed to be equal to 11. The term can be interpreted as the extent to which foreign trade is more costly than domestic trade; it falls as countries trade more together.

The sample in the baseline regression consists of information on the adoption of five standards in 17 countries, across a maximum of 16 partners, and for the 33 years from 1881 to 1913. The exact number of observations per country depends on the length of time required to converge on a partner's law, and the number of standards and dates of adoption of each partner. Countries in the baseline sample (and occasions they initially appear as a follower/leader) are: Argentina (14/0), Australia (5/6), Austria (5/12), Belgium (14/13), Canada (12/10), Denmark (11/9), France (6/15), Germany (2/15), Italy (10/8), the Netherlands (10/14), Norway (13/14), Portugal (15/2), Spain (15/7), Sweden (11/11), Switzerland (10/10), United Kingdom (11/16), and the United States (14/14).

TRADE BALANCES AND THE LABOR COMPACT

I (Huberman and Meissner 2007) follow the empirical growth literature to study short- and long-run impacts of labor standards on trade. The specification is comparable to that of Luis Catão and Solomos Solomou (2005), who examined the relation between the trade balance and the real effective exchange rate. I augment a version of their trade balance model with controls for labor standards.

The baseline specification consists of a dynamic fixed effects model. This approach may produce biased coefficients because of a short time frame. With over thirty years of data, the bias is expected to be small. An advantage of the auto-regressive distributed lag specification is that stationarity testing is not necessary and consistent estimates are provided whether or not the variables included are stationary. I estimate for the dynamic fixed effects model

$$\Delta \ln\left(\frac{EX_{it}}{IM_{it}}\right) = \beta_1'[STNDS_{it-1}] + \left[\sum_{k=0}^{1}\beta_{2k}' \Delta\ STNDS_{it-k}\right] + \beta_3 \ln\left(\frac{EX_{it-1}}{IM_{it-1}}\right)$$

$$+\beta_4\Delta\ \ln\left(\frac{EX_{it-1}}{IM_{it-1}}\right) + \beta_5 \ln(RER_{it-1}) + \beta_6\Delta\ \ln(RER_{it}) + \beta_7 \ln(GDPCAP_{it-1})$$

$$+\beta_8\Delta\ \ln(GDPCAP_{it}) + \mu_i + \varepsilon_{it}$$

where i subscripts countries, t years, k time lags, and Δ is the first difference operator. The dependent variable is the first difference of the logarithm of the ratio of exports to imports (EX/IM).[5] *STNDS* is a vector of indicator variables equal to one when a country has implemented one of four labor standards: accident insurance, factory inspections, maximum work hours for women, and minimum age for child labor. These standards were selected because of data availability. The first lag of the change in these indicators is also included, and so are the lagged level of the dependent variable, the lagged first difference of the dependent variable, the lagged level and first difference of the real exchange rate (*RER*), the lagged level and first difference of the change in the logarithm of GDP per capita (*GDPCAP*), a country fixed effect (μ_j), and an error term (ε_{it}).

The model captures short- and long-run associations between labor standards and the trade balance. The coefficients collected in the vector β_{2k} are the short-run effects of changes in standards. To calculate long-term effects, divide the coefficients of the variables in lagged levels by the coefficient on the lagged level of the dependent variable and multiply by negative one. Typically, information criteria likelihood tests were undertaken to determine the optimal lag length; to conserve degrees of freedom I use a maximum of one lag of first differenced variables. The results are robust, however, to inclusion of a further lag term for all first differenced variables. I first experimented with panel estimation. Table A.1 reports regression results at the country level. I have identified significant coefficients having (expected) negative signs.

WAGES AND WORKTIMES, 1870–2000

Comments on the Fifteenth Annual Report of the U.S. Commissioner of Labor

The Report compiled observations by occupation at the establishment level; for instance, it gave the average wage and hours of work of male cotton-textile spinners in one mill in Lancashire in 1891. I have coded occupations into five categories: mining and construction, iron and steel, textile, manufacturing, and service. All together, I have coded 18,000 observations on wages and about 10,000 on hours for the period 1870 to 1900. The wage and hours data are uneven by coverage and occupation, but wherever possible imbalances have been corrected using regression techniques. Occupations were then weighted by employment shares to derive national estimates. Huberman (2004) gives further information on occupations, employment weights, and regression methods.

There are flaws in the underlying sources used by the authors of the Report, many of which are based on census returns or surveys ignoring smaller firms. The bias would be toward finding shorter workdays, because very small establishments like workshops tended to have longer worktimes. The data for the U.S. poses another set of problems. The coverage consisted of all the surveys of the federal and state departments of labor. The introduction to the Report affirmed unequivocally that the "compilation may be considered exhaustive for the United States and nearly so for foreign countries." The surveys are based on retrospective information of a cross-section of firms in operation continuously throughout the period, and concerns have been raised about their regional and industrial representation because of the different survival rates of firms across space and time. The direction of the bias is ambiguous, but some comfort can be taken from the research of Atack and Bateman (1992) who found little evidence of regional differences in worktime; overall, the early surveys used by the Department of Labor are in line with the more comprehensive estimates they culled from a representative sample of the 1880 Census of Manufacturing.[6]

I have deflated hourly wages (which the Report recorded by the day) using the price indexes cited by Williamson (1995). Table A.2 gives the pertinent descriptive statistics from the Report and the 'macro' variables used in chapter 7.

Table A.1. Trade balances and labor standards: Country results

	Australia	A-H	Canada	Denmark	Italy	Norway	Portugal	Spain	Switz.
First year of accident insurance	—	-0.12 (0.029)***	—	-0.06 (-0.088)	-0.04 (-0.072)	-0.07 (0.029)**	-0.11 (0.048)**	0.06 (-0.216)	0.04 (0.017)**
Second year of accident insurance	—	0.04 (-0.058)	—	0.36 (0.059)***	0.12 (0.066)*	-0.01 (-0.044)	—	-0.28 (0.098)**	-0.11 (0.017)**
First year of limits on women's hours	—	-0.16 (0.056)**	-0.09 (-0.032)**	—	—	—	—	—	—
Second year of limits on women's hours	—	-0.07 (-0.082)	-0.13 (-0.151)	—	—	—	—	—	—
First year of minimum age requirements	-0.06 (-0.111)	0.03 (-0.045)	-0.04 (-0.127)	-0.40 (0.091)***	-0.07 (-0.199)	0.00 (-0.055)	—	—	—
Second year of minimum age requirements	-0.26 (0.097)**	—	-0.17 (0.095)*	-0.16 (0.067)**	(0.057)***	—	—	—	—
First year of factory inspections	—	-0.01 (-0.022)	-0.11 (-0.069)	-0.19 (0.045)***	-0.13 (0.035)***	—	-0.31 (0.120)**	-0.23 (0.116)*	—
Second year of factory inspections	—	—	-0.04 (-0.093)	0.05 (-0.065)	—	—	0.36 (0.112)**	-0.21 (0.053)***	—
Accident insurance lagged level	—	-0.02 (-0.061)	—	-0.33 (0.101)***	-0.08 (-0.084)	-0.06 (-0.043)	—	-0.04 (-0.179)	0.10 (0.024)**
Limits on women's hours lagged level	—	0.02 (-0.045)	0.10 (-0.166)	—	—	—	—	—	—

(continued)

Table A.1. *continued*

	Australia	A-H	Canada	Denmark	Italy	Norway	Portugal	Spain	Switz.
Minimum age requirements lagged level	0.25	0.15	0.14	0.35	—	—	—	—	—
	(−0.149)	(0.022)**	(0.080)*	(0.073)***					
Factory inspections lagged level	—	−0.11	0.07	−0.13	−0.20	−0.01	−0.01	0.28	—
		(0.039)**	(−0.08)	(0.063)*	(0.098)*	(−0.068)	(−0.177)	(0.136)*	
Lagged level of EX/IM	−0.35	−0.56	−0.61	−1.09	−0.29	−0.40	−0.77	−1.08	−0.74
	(−0.224)	(−0.36)	(0.282)**	(0.300)***	(−0.225)	(−0.325)	(0.231)**	(0.286)**	(0.211)**
Lagged first difference of EX/IM	−0.21	−0.28	0.24	0.33	−0.40	0.57	0.18 −0.15	0.49	0.49
	(−0.227)	(−0.195)	(−0.343)	(0.182)*	(0.180)**	(0.274)*		(0.223)**	(0.226)**
Constant	−0.41	4.18	0.13	1.32	−3.24	−0.96	1.52	4.49	−0.22
	(−1.089)	(−2.728)	(−0.895)	(−3.548)	(−6.157)	(−4.534)	(−2.466)	(−6.261)	(−0.600)
Observations	32.	32.	32.	32.	32.	32.	32.	32.	27.
R-squared	0.42	0.66	0.61	0.73	0.66	0.41	0.68	0.59	0.55

Sources: Trade data from Mitchell (1981); exchange rates from Obstfeld and Taylor (2004); GDP per capita from Maddison (1995; 2001).

Notes: Sample is from 1882 to 1913. Dependent variable in each column is the change in the log of the export/import ratio. Regression included lagged first difference of real exchange rate, and lagged and first difference of log of real GDP. These variables were insignificant. Robust standard errors in brackets. A "—" symbol means the coefficient could not be estimated due to insufficient data. * significant at 10%; ** significant at 5%; *** significant at 1%.

Table A.2. Hours and wages: Descriptive statistics

	FULL SAMPLE	OLD WORLD	NEW WORLD
Hours per week (establishment)	60.00	59.50	60.20
	(6.1)	(7.5)	(5.6)
Average wage (establishment)	0.17	0.10	0.19
	(0.092)	(0.047)	(0.092)
Maximum wage (establishment)	0.22	0.12	0.25
	(0.075)	(0.038)	(0.059)
Minimum wage (establishment)	0.15	0.09	0.17
	(0.057)	(0.037)	(0.048)
Log average wage (establishment)	−1.90	−2.42	−1.76
	(0.600)	(0.554)	(0.526)
Male (%)	0.88	0.89	0.87
Services (%)	0.10	0.06	0.12
Average hour	64.40	66.20	64.20
	(8.5)	(9.9)	(8.3)
Average wage	0.15	0.07	0.16
	(0.072)	(0.037)	(0.069)
Textiles (%)	0.21	0.21	0.22
Average hour	62.10	61.40	62.30
	(4.9)	(6.7)	(4.2)
Average wage	0.10	0.07	0.11
	(0.068)	(0.04)	(0.071)
Iron and steel (%)	0.27	0.26	0.27
Average hour	60.50	60.50	60.70
	(0.065)	(7.600)	(4.300)
Average wage	0.19	0.11	0.21
	(0.065)	(0.043)	(0.054)
Mining and construction (%)	0.26	0.30	0.25
Average hour	56.90	56.20	57.10
	(5.1)	(6.1)	(4.6)
Average wage	0.23	0.13	0.27
	(0.106)	(0.040)	(0.097)
Manufacturing (%)	0.16	0.17	0.15
Average hour	58.40	59.40	58.10
	(5.3)	(6.8)	(4.7)
Average wage	0.18	0.10	0.20
	(0.075)	(0.045)	(0.067)

(continued)

Table A.2. *continued*

	FULL SAMPLE	OLD WORLD	NEW WORLD
GDP per capita	3218	3192	3226
	(554)	(859)	(435)
Average age	32.40	31.80	32.50
	(0.782)	(1.310)	(0.484)
Proportion in agriculture (%)	0.41	0.29	0.45
Voter turnout (%)	0.62	0.39	0.68
Capital per worker	9.10	8.60	9.20
	(0.362)	(0.432)	(0.235)
Primary enrolment/1000	736	569	781
	(104)	(121)	(12)
Protestant in 1870 (%)	0.56	0.52	0.57

Sources and notes: Old and New World countries from table 7.1. Mean hours and wages, proportion male, and occupational breakdown of 'micro' sample for 1870–1900 from U.S. Commissioner of Labor (1900). Standard errors in parentheses. For other variables, sample size varies because of missing observations for some countries and years. Reported means (unweighted) for 1870–1900, unless indicated otherwise. Wages are in U.S.$ per hour. Age is average of population from Baier, Dwyer, and Tamura (2006); proportion of population in agriculture and voter turnout from Lindert (2004); capital per worker from Baier, Dwyer, and Tamura (2006); primary enrolment from Mitchell (1981) and Lindert (2004).

Hours of Work per Week

The list at the end of this section gives sources consulted for tables 7.1 to 7.3. To avoid duplication, other sources consulted in preparation of the tables and cited in the text and footnotes appear in the full list of references to this book. Estimates for 1870–1900 are from the Report as calculated in Huberman (2004). Values for 1913 are from various independent sources; where these were not available, hours are predicted based on trends until 1900. From 1929 to 2000, I have taken estimates from the ILO, except for Canada (Ostry and Zaidi 1972), U.S. (Jones 1963; Owen 1988), and Australia (Butlin 1977); the values for Spain in 1938 are for 1936. From 1950 to 1980, figures are from the ILO Yearbook (1950–1980), except for U.S. (McGratten and Rogerson 2004), and Australia (Butlin 1977). From 1980 to 2000, figures from the ILO (2005), except for U.S. (McGratten and Rogerson 2004), Canada (Heisz and LaRochelle-Côté 2003), and Denmark (Eurostat, various years).[7] For these later years, I have tried to find the best fit with the pre-1914 series, taking into account the methodology used by the ILO after WWI which is skewed toward manufacturing.[8] The U.S. series approximates the levels and trends found in the Current Population Survey (Sundstrom 2006). For Latin America, I rely on ILO estimates. After 1870, Buenos Aires represents Argentina; São Paulo, Brazil.

Hours per week and per day are interchangeable. I prefer hours per week because this was the common method of recording worktimes in the past. Hours per work per day can be inferred from table 7.1. I assume full-time work consisted of six days from 1870 to 1913; five and a half from 1929 to 1950; and five from 1960 to 2000. Undoubtedly, there were differences between countries, but there were also important sectoral variations making national patterns difficult to identify.

Days of Work

Figures for 1870 and 1900 are from Huberman (2004); those for 1938 to 1990 from studies of vacations and holidays conducted by the ILO (1939, 1995), U.S. Department of Labor (Monthly Labor Review 1955), and Green and Potepan (1988); values for 2000 are from a variety of sources, including EIRO (2003), OECD (2001, 2004), and official websites. There has been little change in the number of vacation days in the sample of countries since 1990. There are discrepancies between the figures in Table 7.2 and those reported elsewhere, owing to different measures used by the ILO, EIRO, and the OECD. Alesina, Glaeser, and Sacerdote (2005) found a similar problem with French data. For Latin America, figures are from ILO (1995); days off in Brazil refer to municipal workers in São Paulo. I assume two days off for *carnaval*. The Consolidacao das Leis do Trabalho of 1943, and amendments until 1995, legislated days off in Brazil; Federal Labour Act of 1969 in Mexico; Decree 290/1976 in Argentina.

Annual Hours of Work

Values for 1870 to 1913 (Huberman 2004) are based on estimates of the number of weeks worked (adjusted for days absent) and hours per week. The interwar observations have been calculated from tables 7.1 and 7.2 using the same method. From 1950 on, I have used figures contained in the University of Groningen Total Economy Database (2010). These are estimates of total work hours divided by the number of workers. I have spliced datasets because of the increase in women's labor force participation (and the fact that full-time women tend to work a shorter week than men), and because of the rise of part-time work in the second half of the century. Despite these adjustments, the trend in annual work hours moves in line with that of hours per week, giving support to the assumptions underlying table 7.1. For further detail on method, see Huberman and Minns (2007).

Butlin, Noel. 1977. "A Preliminary Annual Database 1900/01 to 1973/74." Reserve Bank of Australia, working paper 7701.

EIRO. 2003. "Working Time Developments." http://www.eiro.eurofund.ie/2004.

Eurostat. 1995. "Le temps dans L'Union européenne: estimation de la durée effective annuelle (1983–1993)." Statistiques en bref, no. 4. Luxembourg.

Eurostat. *Labour Force Survey*. Various years.

Green, Francis, and Michael J. Potepan. 1988. "Vacation Time and Unionism in the U.S. and Europe." *Industrial Relations* 27: 180–94.

Heisz, Andrew, and Sebastien LaRochelle-Côté. 2003. "Working Hours in Canada and the United States." Statistics Canada, Business and Labour Market Analysis Division, working paper 209.

ILO. 1934–1938, 1950–1980. *Yearbook of Labour Statistics*. Geneva: ILO.

ILO. 1939. "Facilities for the Use of Workers' Leisure During Holidays." Studies and Reports, Series G (Housing and Welfare), no. 5. Geneva: ILO.

ILO. 1995. *Conditions of Work Digest: Working Time Around the World.* Geneva: ILO.

ILO. 2005. "Labour Establishment Surveys." LABORTSTA, http://laborsta.ilo.org.

Jones, Ethel B. 1963. "New Estimates of Work per Week and Hourly Earnings, 1900–1957." *Review of Economics and Statistics* 45: 374–85.

McGratten, Ellen R., and Richard Rogerson. 2004. "Changes in Hours Worked, 1950–2000." *Federal Bank of Minneapolis Quarterly Review* 28: 14–33.

Monthly Labor Review. 1955. "Paid Vacations for Workers in Western Europe." 78: 88–89.

OECD. 2001. "Trends in Working Hours in OECD Countries." Labour Market and Social Policy, occasional papers 45.

OECD. 2004. *Employment Outlook.* Paris: OECD.

Ostry, Sylvia, and Mahmood A. Zaidi, 1972. *Labor Economics in Canada.* Second edition. Toronto: Macmillan.

Owen, John. 1988. "Work-time Reduction in the U.S. and Western Europe." *Monthly Labor Review* 111: 51–54.

Sundstrom, William A. 2006. "Hours and Working Conditions." In *Historical Statistics of the United States: Millennial Edition, Vol. 2,* edited by Susan Carter et al. New York: Cambridge University Press. Pp. 301–35.

NOTES

CHAPTER 1. THE VIRTUOUS CIRCLE OF TRADE AND THE LABOR COMPACT

1. For sources on the left and free trade, see Bairoch (1989), and section 4 of this chapter. Polasky (1995) is Vandervelde's biographer.
2. The term 'labor compact' is from Kreuger (2000).
3. Many studies (Garrett 1998; Iversen and Cusack 2000; Burgoon 2001) of international trade and the welfare state are restricted to OECD countries after 1970. Exceptionally, Rudra (2008) examines the developing world, and Harrington (1998) trade and social spending in the first wave of globalization.
4. Typical is Kemp's (1989, 733) history of French social policy. A "peasant economy does not make great demands on the state; the family, the local community, and the church take care of many of those afflicted by misfortune. Even in the towns, hospitals, asylums, old people's homes, care of orphans, the blind, the deaf, and the lame fell largely in the province of private and religious charity with some support from local authorities on an ad hoc basis."
5. A new generation of historians has begun to challenge the home bias of welfare-state narratives. Conrad (2008) refers to the standard approach as an "internalist paradigm."
6. Between 1870 and 1914, the decline in international trade costs was on the order of 20 percent (Jacks, Meissner, and Novy 2008).
7. According to O'Rourke and Williamson (2002), beginning in 1850 open market forces trumped local factor endowments in determining wages and land rents.
8. This statement foreshadows Freeman (1995). Minutes of the 1928 Congress of the International Federation of Textile Workers' Associations (IFTWA).
9. See, for example, Pierson (1996), and Clayton and Pontusson (1998) on a race to the bottom in social policy.
10. Williamson (2006, 148) comments on the relation among trade, the extension of the vote, and the welfare state.
11. "If Cobden had spoken Yiddish, and with a stammer, and if Peel had been a narrow, stupid man, England would have moved towards free trade in grain as its agricultural

classes declined and its manufacturing and commercial classes grew (Stigler 1982, 63–64)."

12. The end of the Corn Laws was not synonymous with the beginning of free trade (Nye 2007, 90–98).

13. The late Marx (1981, 922) was less sanguine on the benefits of free trade. "Ideas on free trade have long since lost any and every theoretical interest, even if they may be still be of some practical interest to some state or another."

14. Hagemann (2001), Kaufman (2004), and Steenson (1991, 92–94) relate the history of German socialists and free trade.

15. The Fabians supported free trade until 1903 (McBriar 1962, 131–34; Trentmann 1997). On the Webbs' changing attitudes, see Clarke (1978, 87–89).

16. See Fletcher (1983, 1984) for a complete list of Bernstein's publications.

17. At their Gotha congress in 1876, German socialists declared themselves "étrangers à la lutte entre la protection et le libre-échange," but in Stuttgart their view had dramatically changed: "La politique protectionniste est inconciliable avec les intérêts du prolétariat, des consommateurs, de l'évolution économique et politique et la démocratie" (cited in Milhaud 1899, 41).

18. Harris (2002, 428–29) relates the influence of the Belgian social insurance model on the U.K.

19. The New World was also an innovator. Henry George's single land tax proposal appealed to European social democrats, since it relaxed states' dependence on custom duties to finance redistributive programs. I describe George's influence on Vandervelde in chapter 3.

20. The first post-Civil War income tax sponsored by William Jennings Bryan was voted in 1893 (later overturned by the Supreme Court) as part of a tariff reform bill. The income tax enacted in 1914 was part of a package of reform measures including tariff reductions (Sanders 1999). I thank Gerald Friedman for this reference.

21. There has been a revival of interest in Bernstein, but neither Berman (2006) nor Jousse (2007) comments on his pro-globalization stance. Following Lenin, Hobsbawm (1982, 338) condemned Bernstein as an "arch revisionist," relegating social democrats' positioning on free trade to a historical footnote.

22. I discuss the Berlin Conference in chapter 4. The pre-1870 figures for Germany are for Prussia. Finland was a duchy of Russia before 1914, and Norway was in a political union with Sweden until 1905. Both had wide autonomy in social and labor policy before independence.

23. For seven countries in table 1.2, factory inspection and accident insurance were put in place in the same decade. In France, compulsory accident insurance was adopted as an alternative to factory inspection; in Spain and Italy, factory inspection was introduced after accident insurance.

24. There were good reasons for employers to comply with the new legislation, if they had initiated the reforms in the first place (Fishback 2007). Before the advent of workmen's compensation in Washington state, employers supported factory inspection because workplaces certified as safe lowered liability claims (Fishback and Kantor

2000, 97). In Sweden, employers' associations monitored working conditions to guard investments in workers (Swenson 2002, 103).

CHAPTER 2. CHALLENGE AND RESPONSE

1. This section is based on Huberman and Meissner (2010).
2. For the pieces of legislation in table 1.2, the null hypothesis of zero rank correlation cannot be rejected.
3. To be clear, this chapter studies adoption. I examine the effects of legislation and adaptation in the second half of the book.
4. Summarizing the "emerging paradigm" of open economy politics, Lake (2009, 238) wrote: "[I]nternational institutions may actually create an important endogenous dynamic with important effects on [domestic] politics."
5. See Farnie and Jeremy (2004) for a world history of the cotton textile industry. This paragraph relies on the chapter by Saxonhouse and Wright (2004). The quality of yarn spun is measured by count or number which rises with fineness.
6. Until 1900 or so, mules were better suited than rings at very low counts.
7. British textile wages were about 25 percent higher than Belgian wages in 1900 (Williamson 1995).
8. Three year moving averages. British prices are for no. 32; Belgium, no. 20.
9. As international trade expanded in Canada beginning in the 1960s, Abowd and Lemieux (1991) found that during recessions the decline in wages was larger for unionized than non-unionized workers.
10. The re-export trade was well established by the 1870s. This paragraph draws on the accounts of the British consular reports (UK PP 1870, 26–48).
11. Slaughter (2001) speculates that volatility was greater in the first wave of globalization than in the second, because the volume of trade in primary products was more important, and because manufacturing imports and exports were more interchangeable than today. Demand is more elastic in an open than closed economy, even where imports and exports are not perfect substitutes.
12. Alesina and Glaeser (2004, 70–71) report the variability in the terms of trade between 1970 and 1990 was greater in the U.S. than Europe.
13. Chapter 6 compares the effects of deep factors, like culture and religion, and time-varying factors, such as income and trade, on the labor compact in Old and New Worlds.
14. Migration within Europe did not appear to have had the same effects on wages as in the New World. Inflows of unskilled labor mapped onto existing factor supplies, and the region's comparative advantage in labor-intensive items was unaltered. I contrast responses of Old and New Worlds to immigration pressures in chapter 4.
15. Capital flows were about 4 to 5 percent of national income before 1914. From a twenty-first-century perspective, Obstfeld and Taylor (2004, 60–61) concluded: "The size of flows is still smaller than a century ago." The general picture is the same whether a price or quantity yardstick is used.

16. Workers had mixed views on capital exports. Jean Jaurès endorsed his country's for-
    eign investments because of benefits accruing to workers in the export sector (Berger
    2003, 53–62).
17. Alsatian firms after 1871 did profit from higher German tariffs (Silverman 1971). Fig-
    ures in this paragraph are from Clark (1987). My calculation understates the costs of
    legislation because it assumes that wages remain the same after legislation. Across
    countries, the actual rise in wages depended on labor supply and demand. In chapter
    5, I report that limits on hours of work of children and women increased wages by
    about 5 percent. This rise may not have been trivial because of the narrow profit
    margins in textiles, and because the wage bill comprised two-thirds of the cost of
    converting raw materials into finished products. My estimate of profit loss corre-
    sponds to De Long's (1986) calculations of the costs of 'Senior's last hour.'
18. I develop a model of this type in chapter 5.
19. Interestingly, Mares's case studies were protectionist states, France and Germany.
20. In the absence of perfect capital markets, the representative worker is willing to ex-
    change lower expected earnings for a wage structure offering insurance against un-
    certainty. Unions can negotiate this type of protection, but government intervention
    is preferred, delivering the same amount of protection with smaller amounts of un-
    employment (Agell 1999, 2002).
21. Even factory inspection provided income smoothing, because it was paid out of rev-
    enues deviating from the benefit taxation criterion, thereby making the rich the net
    contributors and the poor the net receivers of economic resources.
22. The next two paragraphs update Huberman and Lewchuk (2003).
23. In separate (unreported) regressions, GDP per capita had no significant effect on
    adoption.
24. Trade variables are lagged decadal values to get around problems of endogeneity.
    Burgoon (2001) found a similar relation between the components of the welfare state
    and international competition between 1970 and 1995.
25. Danish farmers were reluctant to make insurance contributions since they could not
    pass on increased costs in world markets. In Sweden, a progressive income tax was
    first introduced in 1902 and amended in 1910 (Schön 2010,182). In the U.K., progres-
    sive taxation was the Liberal response to the Conservative proposal of tariff reform
    (Daunton 2010, 41). In the Netherlands, the principle of redistribution was widely ac-
    cepted, but agreement on the financial contributions of central and municipal
    authorities was more difficult to achieve (Van Zanden and Van Riel 2010, 79).
26. The next two sections summarize and extend Huberman and Meissner (2010).
27. I thank Thomas David for recommending sources on the Swiss textile industry. For
    evidence of employers' resistance to legislation and estimates of production values,
    see Humair (2004, 364–69). On import and export values, see Dudzik, (1987, 313–19);
    on wages, machinery speed, and coal prices, see Gruner (1998, 434), and Besso (1910,
    3–21, 89–92).
28. Brown (2001) summarizes the model.
29. Chapter 4 describes the transition in trade policy from confrontation to conciliation.

30. By the late 1890s, Von Laue (1960, 348) wrote, "Russia had a set of laws more enlightened than those of France or the United States." Cambodia improved labor standards in 2001 to attract foreign investment (Elliot and Freeman 2003, 11).

31. On intra-industry trade in Germany, see Brown (1995); in France, Messerlin and Becuwe (1986).

32. Conybeare (1987, 179–203); Humair (2004, 595–618); Smith, (1980, 222–23).

33. In 1891, France took 18.6 percent of all Swiss exports; Switzerland received 6.0 percent of French exports. Between 1892 and 1894, French total exports fell by 6.9 percent. Trade data from Mitchell (1981, 545, 595) and Conybeare (1987, 191).

34. On the Canada-Germany trade war, see Trentmann (2008, 137–40), Conybeare (1987, 182), and Saul (1960, 185). The U.K. feared losing market access in countries having MFN agreements with Germany.

35. The labor standards are: factory inspection, minimum age, night work of women, eleven-hour working day for women, and accident insurance. There are no cases where countries adopt and then abandon a particular standard, although they may have made modifications.

36. I report average marginal effects. Standard errors are clustered at the country pair level (regardless of whether a country is located in position A or B) to correct for any bias in errors arising from arbitrary serial correlation over time.

37. The logarithm of GDP per capita (entered as a single variable in a separate unreported specification) has a positive, but statistically insignificant marginal effect.

38. Eichengreen (1992) observes that, until the adoption of universal suffrage across Europe after the war, mass politics exercised negligible influence.

CHAPTER 3. MARKETS AND STATES IN OLD AND NEW WORLDS

Epigraph: Lines from a Belgian worker song in support of free trade (BAP 1894–5, 1576).

1. Gourevitch (1986), O'Rourke and Williamson (1999), and Rogowski (1989) have applied the Heckscher-Ohlin model to the political economy of trade policy. Trentmann and Daunton (2004) expose the assumptions underlying this approach.

2. Portions of the next three sections draw on Huberman (2008).

3. For a history of commercial relations, see Kossmann (1978, 232), and Degrève (1982, 34–36).

4. Table 1.1 gives degrees of openness. Average tariff revenues mask sectoral differences. Belgium escaped the rise in grain duties gripping its large continental neighbors, but the livestock sector received increased protection after 1870. The commercial history of textiles is more complex (Scholliers 2001). The weaving side had its level of protection rolled back in 1882, as did the yarn sector in 1895, an episode to which I will return to later.

5. The theory assumes technologies are similar across all trading partners and specialization is incomplete—both textiles and grain are produced in the Old World. Under these conditions, trade acts as a substitute for (and replicates) the mobility of factors, thereby assuring global factor price equalization. Models with three or more factors of production and goods are less straightforward. I follow Rogowski (1989) and assume

that pre-1914 the labor-land ratio pinned down attitudes of workers regarding commercial policy.

6. Between 1870 and 1913, unskilled wages rose by 2.63 percent per annum in Denmark, 2.73 percent in Sweden, and 0.92 percent in Belgium. The contrast with Denmark, whose transformation is cited by O'Rourke and Williamson (1999) as the classic open-economy response to the grain invasion, was stark. Imports from the New World affected domestic grain prices and production by the same order of magnitude in the two countries. The responses were hardly similar. The key variable in the O'Rourke and Williamson model is the wage-rental ratio. In Belgium, overcrowding in the countryside supported higher rents; in Denmark, the profitable dairy sector sustained land prices. Lastly, relative to Belgium, Danish migration overseas was substantial. While the wage-rental ratio hardly changed in Belgium, it nearly doubled in Denmark.

7. Mayda, O'Rourke, and Sinnott (2007) find that attitudes to trade in the late twentieth century corresponded to Stolper-Samuelson predictions.

8. The classic statement on the agrarian question and European socialists remains Gerschenkron (1943). The reconciliation of urban and rural Belgium was a central concern of Vandervelde (1889, 1897, 1910).

9. My translation.

10. On the effects of train transport on grain prices in international and domestic markets, see Daudin, Morys, and O'Rourke (2010).

11. Cited in Vandervelde (1889, 4).

12. In Acemoglu and Robinson (2006), the relation between inequality and democracy has an inverse U-shape. In extremely egalitarian societies, the demand for redistribution and, hence, democracy is low; in extremely unequal polities, reforms impose high costs on elites and democracy is scarce.

13. On the double-sided relation between democracy and trade, see López-Córdova and Meissner (2008).

14. The debate was prolonged, extending from March to June 1895, and covering more than 600 pages in BAP 1894–5. Unless otherwise cited, references in this section are from pages 878, 880, 1571, 1575, 1856, 1879, 1895, and 1912.

15. In the fault-line model of Witte, Craeybeckx, and Meynen (2000, 13) class was the predominant fissure before 1914: "Recent Belgian political history is dominated by three intertwining problems—the socio-economic, the religious philosophical and the language dispute. The labor vs. capital conflict came to a head around the mid-19th century."

16. The aim, as one parliamentary representative put it, was to: "S'aventurer à concilier l'interventionnisme en matière de travail et de salaire avec la proscription de toute protection douanière" (BAP 1894–5, 1685). The British Liberal Party made a similar argument a decade later during debate on the People's Budget (Murray 1980, 49–50).

17. Vandervelde's words were direct: "Il est inutile de rappeler que, dans un pays comme la Belgique, qui ne produit pas la moitié de ce qui est nécessaire à sa subsistance, les droits protecteurs constituent un impôt direct, payé au profit de quelques-uns, par la grande

masse des consommateurs" (BAP 1894–5, 879); "[Le protectionnisme est] un système dans lequel le grand capitaliste de Gand, et les agrariens de Flandres se mettent d'accord pour savoir ce que les ouvriers individuels devront payer non pas en faveur des ouvriers agricoles, mais en faveur des capitalistes et des propriétaires" (BAP 1894–5, 1891).

18. George's classic work, *Protection or Free Trade* (1886), was published in French in 1888, numerous editions of which can be found in Vandervelde's personal library (Institute Émile Vandervelde Bibliothèque et archives, Brussels). I thank Robert C. Allen for referring me to the influence of George on European socialists.

19. Commercial treaties from the Pahre dataset. See chapter 4.

20. Vandervelde's exact words were: "Nous ne demandons pas de protection pour aucune industrie" (BAP 1894–5, 1675).

21. Strikwerda (1997) gives examples of coalition building in municipal politics.

22. The liberal's strategy paid off, winning more seats than the socialists between 1904 and 1914 (Kossmann 1978, 477).

23. Proportional representation can result in coalitions exploiting state budgets to solicit and maintain the support of partners. Persson and Tabellini (2004) report that since the 1980s PR systems have larger than average budget deficits; in the first half of the century, PR had weaker effects on social spending (Aidt, Dutta, and Loukoianova 2006), Finland being the only other European country to have adopted PR before the war. There is a commercial side to PR. Rogowski (1987) observes that PR polities having large voting districts, as in Belgium, tend to support free trade, because elected representatives can insulate themselves from regional and sectoral pressures.

24. Benefits were distributed in two ways. The Ghent system directed benefits to individual members of union administered funds; the Liège system subsidized unions. The objective was to ensure the most effective means of delivery; support of unions was secondary (Vanthemesche 1990, 353). The number of Ghent programs expanded rapidly, increasing from 310 in 1909 to 634 by 1913 (Goossens, Peeters, and Pepermans 1988, 292–94; Harrington 1998, 221–28).

25. Even if the primary function of the tariff was revenue collection, secondary effects on industry were often considerable. Green (2000, 211) concludes that Canadian secondary manufacturers had effective protection.

26. O'Rourke and Taylor (2007) contrast coalition formation in Old and New Worlds.

27. Canada, *Fielding Tariff Inquiry Commission, 1905–06*. References in this paragraph are from vol. 3, page 438, and vol. 4, pages 681 and 683. For a summary of labor's representation, see Craven and Traves (1979, 24–25).

28. Goldin (2000, 613–14) identifies the same policy outcome in the U.S. "By restricting the flow of less-skilled immigrant labor, [quotas] were the single most important piece of legislation in the twentieth century."

29. The wage series is for transport workers in Toronto (MacKinnon 1996).

30. Fudge and Tucker (2000) and Webber (1995) relate the early history of Canadian labor legislation.

31. On similarities in Canadian and Brazilian immigration policies, see Sánchez-Alonso (2006, 395–406). Brazil began subsidizing immigration in 1888.

32. In Ontario after the war, labor and farmers formed a coalition government more accommodating to social legislation such as a minimum wage for women.

33. The trade union movement pressured the government to pass the Alien Act of 1897, making it illegal to assist or encourage the importation or immigration of any alien or foreigner into Canada under contract.

34. In Canada, 15 percent of the labor force was organized; in Belgium, 5 percent. From 1902 until the war, Canada had on average 120 strikes per year; Belgium, 60. In the same period, 60 percent of Canadian strikes ended in gains for workers; in Belgium, 40 percent (Huberman and Young 1999; Neuville 1979, 217). A small number of Canadian strikes, mostly unsuccessful, opposed foreign workers (Avery 1972). Friedman (1998) finds a parallel distinction in strike dimensions for the U.S. and France.

35. Wise (1892, 150–51) acknowledged the influence of Richard Ely and Henry George.

CHAPTER 4. INTERNATIONAL LABOR STANDARDS: IDEAS OR TRADE BASED?

1. Frieden (2006) discusses extensively the inherent conflict between domestic politics and global markets.

2. The results go through in a model of intra-industry trade in which products are differentiated by country of origin (Brown, Deardorff, and Stern 1996).

3. At issue in many studies is the relevant dependent and independent variables. Using the fraction of textiles and clothing exports in total exports, Rodrik (1996) finds a weak effect of labor standards on trade, except for statutory hours of work. Mah (1997), analyzing the effects of ILO conventions on export performance, reports that ratifications led to lower exports. Flanagan (2003) overturns these results. Using gravity model specifications, Maskus (2004) observes that labor standards had negligible effects on trade, though Van Beers (1998) concludes otherwise for a smaller sample of OECD countries.

4. For divisions on the left between reformers and militants, see Haupt (1986); on the origins of international liberalism, see Zacher and Matthew (1995) and Mandelbaum (2002).

5. International Federation of Textile Workers' Associations (IFTWA). Minutes of the Annual Congress, 1900. Fowler (2003, 99–107) gives a brief history of the movement.

6. In 1900, 22.7 percent of textile workers in the U.K. were under 14 years of age (Boot and Maindonald 2008); in Portugal and Italy, the figure was about 10 percent (Goulart and Bedi 2007, 24; Toniolo and Vecchi 2007, 20); only Belgium, at 25 percent, was close to the British proportion (De Herdt 2001, 27). For a comparative history of child labor, see Cunningham and Viazzo (2001).

7. Labor delegates at the IALL meetings were almost exclusively British.

8. IALL activists and observers (Fontaine 1920; Francke 1909; Potter 1910) compiled the first histories; more detached, the second generation of historians (Delevingne 1934; Follows 1951; Shotwell 1934) cast the pre-1914 movement as a prelude to the ILO. Recent scholarship is divided. Engerman (2003) raises doubts of the movement's success; Van Daele (2005) interprets the IALL as a transnational epistemic community.

9. Brentano (cited in Follows 1951, 82–83) wrote: "The Germans by opposing such [international labor] treaties and encouraging long hours for women and minors hinder the universal acceptance of free trade principles. In America, particularly, the establishment of a high tariff wall is a rebuke to the long working hours of women and young people of Europe."

10. Core standards are basic rights of workers, including the right to organize, and the elimination of slave contracts and exploitation of children. These types of rules concern the organization of the labor market; other standards, like the restriction of the length of the workday, specify particular market outcomes.

11. Eight countries attended the Basle conference of 1901; Berne 1905, 14; Zurich and Berne 1913, 16. Attendance from Follows (1951). Denmark, Italy, the Netherlands, Portugal, and Spain were underrepresented in the IALL. For membership statistics, see Métin (1908, 43).

12. British delegates influenced Lancashire workers and firms to negotiate an agreement on women's and children's labor to avoid conflict with the IALL.

13. Full details in Huberman and Meissner (2010). Since French was the predominant language at the international meetings, the IALL dummy can be considered a proxy for shared cultural values.

14. See Hall (1997) for a comparison of interest- and idea-based approaches to political economy.

15. According to Follows (1951, 143), the Berlin conference influenced the Danish and Austrian governments' decisions to forbid Sunday work.

16. Cited in Follows (1951, 91).

17. Bertocchi and Strozzi (2004) claim that from the early twentieth century on discrimination in the provision of benefits did not deter immigration.

18. Initially, British trade unions were hostile toward immigration, but their attitudes changed markedly by the mid-1890s. In 1903, Keir Hardie denied that immigration caused unemployment and focused his attention instead on programs to alleviate the hazards of job loss. The British Alien Act of 1906 was a "minor victory" for the protectionist lobby (Hunt 1985, 186).

19. Europe's commitment to rights of inclusion was undone in the interwar period, and subsequently reinstated under the authority of the European Union.

20. On citizenship in pre-modern nation states, see Van Zanden and Prak (2006). Obligations and entitlements varied across and within countries. For instance, Jenson (1989) relates how the U.S. and French welfare states incorporated different representations of women's market and household work.

21. Typically, Esping-Anderson (2001, 136) asserts that Bismarck's social insurance made Germans.

22. Conrad (2008) discusses the Kaiserreich's treatment of German communities abroad. Nugent (1995, 35) gives figures on return migration.

23. There were variants to the basic approach. Belgian authorities claimed that its 1897 accord with France on workers' savings strengthened commercial relations and preempted retaliatory trade practices (Métin 1908, 25–36).

24. Cited in Métin (1908, 152–53). My translation.
25. I am grateful to Robert Pahre for allowing me access to his commercial treaty data set. Many of the accords were unconditional MFNs (Pahre 2007, 157–76). Irwin (1993, 454) refers to MFN agreements as "progressive bilateralism," because they promoted multi-party accords without diverting trade. The clustering of bilateral labor accords after 1904 conforms to this model.
26. High-tariff countries, like France and Germany, most often sought out bilateral agreements (Pahre 2007, 204–46). In the Cobden-Chevalier era, Lampe (2009) finds that states having high tariffs were more likely to cooperate than those with low tariffs.
27. For histories of the France-Italy labor accord, see Follows (1951, 170); Fontaine (1920); Lowe (1935); Métin (1908, 49–59). The complete text is reprinted in Chatelain (1908, 176–92).
28. In the ten-year period after 1887, Italian exports to France fell by 57 percent, and French exports to Italy contracted by 21 percent. Italian exports to France comprised 40 percent of its total exports in 1887; French exports to Italy, less than 6 percent of its total exports (Conybeare 1987, 185).
29. Earlier in the decade, the Italian (liberal) Prime Minister Giovanni Giolitti had invited socialists into his cabinet. In the years before the accord, the minimum working age was raised and employment of women on night shifts was controlled (as opposed to banned), but Giolitti guarded against making further improvements because workers were underrepresented in Parliament, universal suffrage being granted only in 1911 (Baudoin 1905; Zamagni 1993, 117).
30. Trade statistics from France, *Annuaire statistique*, various years.
31. U.S. Commissioner of Labor (1911, 24–27); Lowe (1935, 195, 200); Chatelain (1908, 194–200, 213–15).
32. OLS regression; robust standard errors clustered at the country pair level are in parentheses; * indicates significance at the 5 percent level; ** significance at the 1 percent level. Tariffs and distance between capitals are positive and significant; common border and year dummies are negative and significant. Variables defined in tables 2.1 and 2.2.
33. Calculated as $(1-\rho)\{ln(1+0.91\tau^0)^2 - ln(1+\tau^0)^2\}$, where τ^0, the average trade cost in the sample in the year before a trade treaty was signed, equals 0.52 , and ρ , the elasticity of substitution, equals 11. The expression is derived from a gravity model of trade. See Jacks, Meissner, and Novy (2008, 2010).
34. These are the same five laws in table 2.2.

CHAPTER 5. DID THE LABOR COMPACT REDUCE INEQUALITY?

1. Exceptionally, Kreuger (2007) claims that labor and product regulations in the second wave of globalization have had positive effects on trade.
2. Casella (2005) proposes a model along these lines.
3. For variants of the wage-push model, see Acemoglu (2002); Alesina and Zeira (2006); Blanchard (1997).

4. The assumption here is that the elasticity of substitution between new capital and labor is greater than one. In their model of the French economy, Caballero and Hammour (1998) assume an elasticity of six.

5. In line with the model, French workers' compensation per hour improved in the 1970s, but as unemployment subsequently increased, labor's share of output returned to its initial level.

6. The 1889 law made it illegal for children under 12 years of age to be employed in industry, and for boys aged 12–16, and for girls 12–21 to work more than six days a week, or more than 12 hours a day. Night work was prohibited for boys under 16 and for girls under 21 (De Herdt 2001, 36).

7. I thank Eugene White for pointing out to me the relevance of nominal wages under the gold standard.

8. The real exchange rate appreciated by 2 percent in 1889, and another 3 percent in 1890 (López-Córdova and Meissner 2003). For statements on eroding competitiveness, see BAP (1894–5, 1531).

9. Scholliers (1996, 87–90) finds evidence of an increase in female textile employment. As capital replaced labor, unemployment temporarily rose, putting downward pressure on wages—nominal values actually fell by 5 percent from 1900 to 1910 (panel a)—exactly as the Caballero-Hammour model predicts.

10. Smaller territories, such as the Mediterranean Islands and parts of the Caribbean, have been grouped.

11. The method of conversion does not appear to bias results. Changes in wages in table 5–1 match those in O'Rourke and Williamson (1999), who use a different sample and international exchange rates. Taking their index of unskilled workers, real wages in the European core rose by about 70 percent between 1870 and 1900. See also Betrán and Pons (2004).

12. The Old World is Belgium, France, Germany, and the Netherlands; New World, Australia and Canada. The U.S. is excluded since the timing in the adoption of labor laws varied across states.

13. In the Old World, for manufacturing, textiles, and iron and steel, the variance in wages and hours declined after 1885. See table A.2.

14. Within country inequality accounted for about 60 percent of overall inequality.

15. I have followed the procedure set out in Crafts (1997). Voth (2000) gives estimates for the period before 1850; Bell and Freeman (1995) for the period since 1945.

16. This may be an overestimate, since hours per person increased in the United States and Canada.

17. Emigration was not substantial for these countries.

18. On the relation between the skill premium and the poverty gap, see Goldberg and Pavcnik (2007).

19. Based on the Report, a rough estimate of the contribution of regulation to narrowing the skill premium can be made. I calculated the difference between maximum and minimum wages at the occupational level for each year. This gives a measure of wage dispersion for the five categories of activity (see the appendix). In the Old World textile

industry, wage dispersion fell 20 percent from 1870 to 1900, but by 15 percent between 1885 and 1900, around the time regulation became more widespread and would have taken effect. Assuming that trade was the only source of egalitarianism before 1885, this meant that regulation, if its effect was independent of globalization, was responsible for a third of the contraction in inequality from 1885. In the New World, inequality was always greater and the trend in wage dispersion was flat.

20. On the close relation across countries between wage inequality and the gender gap, see Blau and Kahn (1996).

21. Fuchs (2005) and De Vries (2008) review debates on gender and labor regulation.

22. On the possible outcomes, see Goldin (1990, 192–204).

23. Values and figures in this paragraph are based on Scholliers (1996).

24. A similar dynamic unfolded in the Lancashire textile industry (Boot and Maindonald 2008). In Lancashire, as in Ghent, men moved out of the industry.

25. Jay (1910) reported a bandwagon effect in France following the adoption of protective labor laws of the 1890s. According to a comprehensive 1910 survey of the Ministry of Labor, 73 percent of industrial enterprises had implemented a ten-hour workday for both female and male workers (Fuchs 2005, 631).

26. In all sectors of activity, labor participation declined (Bairoch 1968), but these figures include women whose husbands earned high wages. The emergence of the male breadwinner–female homemaker household was a complex process that integrated decisions on various dimensions, including family size, schooling, and consumption (De Vries 2008, 186–237).

27. Women's political gains were less assured. To firm up its coalition for social legislation, the POB forsook its traditional demand of extending the franchise to women (Hilden 1993, 301).

28. Before legislation, children under 16 comprised 26 percent of the workforce; the figure in 1890 was 11 percent. The proportion of women employed was stable at about 52 percent over the period. Employment shares of children and women from the Census of Canada (1881, Vol. III, 485: 1891, Vol. III, 120–21). Similarly, in the U.S., legislation did not curtail female employment in manufacturing (Goldin 1990, 197).

29. This paragraph is based on Mascarenhas (1972). Stein (1957, 34–39) and Birchal (1999, 128–83) give portraits of Brazilian entrepreneurs.

30. After 1880 nominal wages stabilized, but real wages rose as prices of consumption goods fell. Immediately after the war, real earnings collapsed. Own-wages (wages divided by the prices of manufacture) tracked the pattern of real wages (Gómez-Galvarriato and Williamson 2008). On the long-term changes in the distribution of income, see Frankema (2009).

31. Clark (1987, 166) reports that Brazilian workers were one third less efficient than their British, Canadian, and U.S. counterparts.

32. During this interval, the quality of yarn fell from number 30 to 25 (Saxonhouse and Wright 2004). For commentaries on the shift to coarse yarns, see Centro Industrial do Brasil (1917, 333). Saxonhouse and Wright (2010) attribute advances in fiber control to the opening of world trade.

33. Lancashire machine makers began publishing manuals in Portuguese around the turn of the century (Platt-Saco-Lowell DDPSL/3/16/2). On personal communication and technology diffusion, see Gong and Keller (2003).

34. This account differs from that of Clark (1987, 2007), who claims that the developing world was plagued by inefficient labor. His argument follows from the assumption that capital and labor were used in fixed proportions, set by best practice in the U.S. or the U.K. In his model, the hiring of additional labor was superfluous. For a critique, see Allen (2008).

35. Figures on female labor force participation are from the ILO (1937, 223). On female employment opportunities, see Hahner (1977, 92).

36. The tariff was a main source of government revenue (Versiani 1971, 53). Bulmer-Thomas (2003, 143) advises against overemphasizing the effectiveness of the tariff. "Changes in the rate of protection were almost arbitrary and difficult to anticipate. A rate of protection of 20 percent in the United States was qualitatively different from a similar rate in Latin America." Anyway, inflation in the early 1890s reduced the degree of protection; while the subsequent depreciation of the currency restored actual protection levels, between 1898 and 1905 the exchange rate appreciated as Brazil sought to join the gold standard (Haber 2006, 550). Brazil was on the gold standard from 1906 to 1914, and 1926 to 1930.

37. The Centro Industrial do Fiação (1917, 324–27) provided evidence of the fall in local prices, after controlling for exchange rate fluctuations and inflation.

38. Rio de Janeiro manufacturers petitioned the government to raise tariffs in 1919, because the "law of work accidents and granting of the 48 hour workweek, adopted by the owners in accordance with the spirit of the times, increased our costs" (CIFTA 1919, 35).

39. The breakdown of skilled (sk) and unskilled (unsk) are: *construction*—unsk: day laborer; sk: bricklayer, carpenter; *production*—unsk: boiler operative, cooper, distillery operative, dock worker, packing operative; sk: blacksmith, cartridge operator, electrician, machine operator, overseer; *services*—unsk: barber, doorman, gardener; sk: cook, painter. Source: Lobo (1978, 803–20.). Immigration was a countervailing force, turning restrictive after 1928 (Sánchez-Alonso 2006, 403). Overall, the movement in wages in figure 5.5 is consistent with Frankema's accounting of changes in the distribution of income (2009, 147–76).

40. Based on the U.S. Department of Labor Report (1900), earnings of Brazilian textile workers at the 25th and 50th percentiles increased proportionately before 1900.

41. The wage push had a regional dimension. From 1920 to 1929, the increase in wages in the regulated south was twice as rapid as in the unregulated northeast (Gómez-Galvarriato and Williamson 2008).

CHAPTER 6. DID LABOR STANDARDS HARM OR BENEFIT TRADE?

1. In 1920, textile workers comprised about 25 percent of the country's industrial labor force and accounted for a similar proportion of value added in industry (Fishlow 1972, 323). In São Paulo, Dean (1969, 104–17) reports growth in processed foodstuffs

and footwear exploiting the labor and managerial skills accumulated in the early textile industry.

2. See chapter 3 for sources.

3. This section is based on Huberman and Meissner (2007).

4. Whatever its merits, Italy passed a law prohibiting downloading costs of accident compensation onto wages (U.S. Commissioner of Labor 1911, 1772).

5. German workers assumed 65 percent of total contributions to health insurance and 35 percent of old age; employers paid 90 percent of benefits for accident insurance (Khoudour-Castéras 2008, 223). In 1913, average social security contributions as a share of wages in Germany were 3.0 and 4.8 percent for blue- and white-collar employees (Broadberry and Burhop 2010, 412).

6. Chapter 4 describes the change in Germany's position on labor laws.

7. In response to international competition, the U.K. increased exports of printed and dyed goods to low-income markets (Marrison 1975).

8. The number of firms in the Swiss textile industry fell 20 percent, and workers by 10 percent, from 1880 to 1890 (Reichesberg 1911, 946).

9. The adoption of improved labor laws promoted the expansion of the informal sector in Indonesia in the mid 1990s, although compliance has since increased (Harrison and Scorse 2003). Freeman (2009) summarizes research on labor standards in developing countries.

10. This section draws on Huberman and Meissner (2010).

11. Mahaim (1905, 14–15) related deliberations at Berne.

12. To fix ideas about proportions, the U.K. employed about 2 million women in manufacturing in 1901 (Bairoch 1968, 98), and 320,000 women in cotton textiles in 1911 (U.K. 1911 census).

13. The 60 percent figure is for the U.K. (Boot and Maindonald 2008, 386). Many countries had a higher proportion of women employed in cotton textiles. Hours of work per day from Huberman (2004). The 10 percent figure understates the decline in labor input, because men's hours also contracted. See chapter 5.

14. See table 1.3 for factory inspection and employers' expenditures on accident insurance.

15. The sample of 2,884 country-pair years contains 90 instances of emulation in category 1 labor standards, and 151 in category 2.

16. In other (unreported) regressions, emulation was more likely if the country pair had similar levels of per capita income.

17. In a separate (unreported) multinomial estimation, bilateral distance and a border dummy were not statistically significant for high and low cost standards.

18. Regarding the diffusion of standards, the (unreported) period dummies for category 2 standards grow larger over time and are statistically significant, while none of the period dummies for category 1 are statistically important.

19. For a primer on the characteristics of exporting firms, see Greenway and Kneller (2007).

20. As an example, see Pavcnik's (2002) study of Chile in the early 1980s.

21. Figures from Van Houtte (1949, 263).

22. Into the 1930s, Belgium, along with Italy, had the highest proportion of young women employed in textiles in Europe (ILO 1937, 224).

23. Between 1890 and 1914, the average count spun, which amounted to an expanded range of products since the yarn combined labor and capital in new proportions, rose in France from nos. 50. to 80; in Germany, from nos. 30 to 40. Figures are average counts of new machinery orders (Saxonhouse and Wright 2004).

24. Agell and Lommerud (1997) describe a model in which workers, under the threat of unemployment, invest in human capital.

25. Edmonds and Pavcnik (2006) report a similar relation between trade and child labor in the 1990s.

26. I thank John Brown for suggesting Kertesz's (1917) study.

27. On capital deepening in mining after the introduction of the nine-hour work day, see Vandervelde (1911).

28. Numbers of items and destinations from Belgium, *Tableau general du commerce*, various years. See Degrève (1982) for a full list of export and import items.

29. Figures in this paragraph are from Cassiers (1989, 38–40).

30. Autor, Kerr, and Kugler (2007) propose an alternative model in which an exogenous increase in adjustment costs caused by regulation reduces short-term efficiency and, hence, total factor productivity.

31. The model is developed in Brown, Deardorff, and Stern (1996). The results go through when domestic and foreign goods are not perfect substitutes.

32. My translation of Mahaim (1905, 16).

33. For the U.S., which was a net exporter of manufactured goods, Irwin (2007, 601) found "little evidence on the ability to influence its terms of trade through policy measures."

34. An example off a capital-intensive labor standard is occupational safety legislation.

35. For Belgian prices, see figure 2–2. Tyszynski (1951) reports a 27 percent rise in European manufacturing prices from 1900 to 1913. Kindleberger (1956, 305) makes a claim similar to my own: Before 1914 "small countries which innovate or imitate in these income elastic goods had high export prices."

36. After 1900, terms of trade in the Old World rose, with the exception of the poor European periphery consisting of Italy, Portugal, Russia, and Spain (Blattman, Hwang, and Williamson 2007). In Australia, the decline began in 1903 (Gillitzer and Kearns 2005, 2). For the U.S., the picture is less clear, since it was a larger exporter of manufactured goods. Exports prices increased by 20 percent and import prices by 8 percent from 1900 to 1914 (U.S. Department of Commerce, 1975, series 226 and 238, 892–93).

37. The period's other trade shock was the opening of the Panama Canal in 1914.

38. Similarly, the share of Argentinean trade with Brazil peaked during the war (Albert 1988; McCrea, Van Metre, and Eder 1931, 72).

39. Miller (1981, 710) presents a more nuanced portrait: "Brazil manufacturers did benefit from the war, producing more and selling it at higher prices."

40. In 1915 the average textile establishment in São Paulo employed 595 workers, 25 percent greater than in the rest of the industry. In the non-tradable sector, metals and food processing, the average was about 35 workers (Lobo 1978, 608–10).

41. The order books underestimate the quality of Belgian production because the industry was older than Brazil's.

42. The *Monographies industrielles* (1902, 63) reported: "Au point de vue de la finesse des numéros fabriqués, la filature belge du coton a fait également de sérieux progrès. Alors que, il y a vingt ans, peu de nos filateurs dépassaient le no. 40A, plusieurs de nos établissements filent actuellement des numéros plus fins et l'un d'eux produit des fils allant jusqu'à 80A. Nous ajoutons qu'elle exporte une partie (7 à 8 pour cent) de ses produits en Hollande, en Suisse etc."

43. CIFTA (1925); Ribeiro (1988, 81); Von der Weid and Bastos (1986, 120).

44. For developments after 1943, see French (2004).

CHAPTER 7. THE LABOR COMPACT IN THE LONG TWENTIETH CENTURY

1. This chapter summarizes and extends Huberman and Minns (2007).

2. The unit of comparison in macroeconomic debates is generally hours of work per person. I prefer hours of full-time production workers, because it serves my objective of tracking differences across countries in labor supply over a long-term horizon. I am less interested in issues of labor force participation. Since the 1970s, definitions of full-time have differed across countries, but by this date the time series reveal distinct trends in Old and New Worlds. Anyway, definitions of full-time correspond closely to usual hours worked.

3. The Netherlands and the U.K. had large increases in part-time work (OECD 1998).

4. The New World in tables 7.1 to 7.3, and figure 7.1 comprises Australia, Canada, and the U.S.

5. French and Belgian workers viewed enviously the handful of U.S. firms that had introduced paid vacations before WWI (Hunnicutt 1988). Australia was the first country to institute paid days off on a broad scale (Coghlan 1918).

6. Atack, Bateman, and Margo (2003) observe that U.S. establishments before 1900 raised output by working more days and reducing daily hours, hence leaving total hours of operations unchanged.

7. The Canadian *Labour Gazette* (September 1935, Vol. XXXV, 743) reported the study.

8. About 5 percent of the gap between the two countries is explained by the shorter workweek; the remainder is explained by differences in labor force participation (Bell and Freeman 2001).

9. In the 1990s, the average of age of retirement in France and Germany was around 60 years; in the U.S., 63 years. Similarly, before 1914, the labor force participation rate of U.S. men aged 65 and older was greater than that of France, Germany, and the U.K. (Costa 1998, 29). In these decades, U.S. workers spent more years in school, but the gap in education was narrowing across regions. Fogel (2004) estimates that, in the U.S., the expected number of years in the labor force at time of entry was 40.1 in 1880 and 40.3 in 1995.

10. The irony is that Veblen was concerned about emulation of the super rich who distinguished themselves by their leisure time. For the bulk of workers, like those in the

Report, my intuition is that emulation was based on consumption standards set by the group that was above them in the distribution of income.

11. The incidence of long hours was different over the last one hundred years. In the U.S. in the early period, low-wage earners worked longer than high-income employees; in the later period, the relation was inverted (Costa 2000).

12. For these regressions, Old and New World countries (except for Latin America) are listed in table 7.3.

13. Regressions like those in table 7.4 may perform poorly because of a built-in spurious correlation. Daily earnings found in the report are themselves constructed from information on weekly earnings and on hours per week (Costa 2000, 165). To check for this possibility, I regressed hours on lagged wages. I am limited to U.K. observations because of data availability. The results did not change substantially. As an additional check, I used GDP per capita instead of wages. Again the results were similar to those reported in the table.

14. The demand for leisure varied within as well as between countries (Huberman and Minns 2007).

15. Figure 7.1 identifies the puzzle from a different optic. In 1870, the New World labored about 10 percent less than the Old, during a period in which its average GDP per capita was about one-third higher. In 2000, Belgium was richer than Chile by the same order of magnitude, but the average Belgian worked about 500 hours fewer, or about 25 percent less than a Chilean. The New World worked too long in 1870 given its level of income.

16. The large income effect in the early period is not surprising given the average length of the workday. Workers in the past had little opportunity to shift leisure over time and took the opportunity to labor fewer hours when they could as opposed to more days off or a shorter work life. Pencavel (1986) reports uncompensated labor supply elasticities in the range of 0.0 to −0.07 for the post 1945 period. See Costa (2000) for estimates for the U.S. in the 1890s.

17. When year dummies are omitted in table 7.5 column 2, the business cycle indicator is insignificant. I have excluded this variable in the next series of regressions.

18. I use this measure of inequality in chapter 6.

19. These figures are uncorrected for population. I am interested in whether the religious affiliation of the waves of settlers until 1870 affected work habits. Immigrants after this date may have had different affiliations than the representative worker in the New World in 1870, but only in the U.S. did the percentage of Protestants in the population actually fall (from 57 to 54 percent); in Australia and Canada the share was stable.

20. This effect is different from that associated with an increase in investments in human capital caused, say, by an exogenous increase in the demand for labor of a certain quality. The wage variable accounts for this. The regressions reported in the previous section omit the separate role of education as a transmitter of cultural values, and hence bias upward the estimated wage coefficients.

21. The schooling measure is primary-school students per 1000 children of ages 5–14 (Lindert 2004; Mitchell 1981). See appendix for values.

22. In other regressions, I used values for the percentage of Protestants in each country. The estimated coefficient was negative and insignificant.

CHAPTER 8. VANDERVELDE'S GIFT

1. On labor-market regimes, see Rosenbloom and Sundstrom (2011).
2. Citations in this paragraph are from the ILO (1956, 58, 60, 70).
3. Hiscox and Smyth (2008) present case studies of consumers' willingness to pay premium prices for improved labor conditions abroad.
4. For the group of countries above the world's median GDP per capita income in 2000, the correlation between levels of openness and employment protection laws is −0.13 (p = .12); the correlation between openness and social insurance is not different than zero. Measure of openness from the Penn World Tables; labor regulation from Botero et al. (2004). In line with these results, Lindert (2004) concludes that the costs of the welfare state have been overstated.

APPENDIX

1. For instance, following the 1905 Berne conference Belgium agreed to restrict women's work to 11 hours per day, but delayed passage until 1909. Certain aspects of the law were only implemented in 1911 (Lowe 1935, 126).
2. On centralization of Swiss and German factory laws, see Hennock (2007).
3. Huberman and Lewchuk (2003). For the U.S., Fishback, Holmes, and Allen (2009), and Holmes, Fishback, and Allen (2008) have assembled various indicators of labor regulation using different components and weights. They found a high correlation in the different measures.
4. Huberman and Meissner (2010) discuss the effects of sample selection in the model.
5. Trade data from Mitchell (1981); exchange rates from Obstfeld and Taylor (2004); GDP per capita from Maddison (1995, 2001). The ratio permits a linear in logarithms specification (Shirvani and Wilbratte 1997).
6. Atack and Bateman (1992, 803–4). I benefited from discussions with William Sundstrom on the reliability of the U.S. reports.
7. Until 1980, the data are from the ILO *Yearbook of Labour Statistics*; after 1980, from 'labor-related establishment surveys' in the ILO database LABORSTA.
8. I have not integrated observations from the Current Employment Statistics which reports 33 hours of work per week for Americans in 1990, or about five—unrealistic— hours shorter than the average workweek of Europeans.

References

OFFICIAL AND PRIMARY SOURCES

Belgium. *Annales parlementaires: Chambres des représentants* (BAP). 1884–85, 1894–95.

Belgium. 1919. *Recensement de l'industrie et du commerce. Résultats comparés: 1896–1910.* Office du Travail. Section de la Statistique. Brussels: Office de Publicité.

Belgium. *Tableau general du commerce avec les pays étrangers, 1870–1914.* Brussels: Ministre des Finances.

Brazil. Instituto Brasileiro de Geografia e Estatística (IBGE). Sector externo. Available at http://www.ibge.gov.br/seculoxx/economia/economia.shtm.

Canada. Department of Agriculture. *General Report of the Census of Canada, 1880–81.* Ottawa, 1885.

Canada. Department of Agriculture. *Census of Canada, 1890–91.* Ottawa, 1897.

Canada. Department of Labour. *Labour Gazette.* Ottawa, various years.

Canada. *Fielding Tariff Inquiry Commission, 1905–06.* Public Archives of Canada, Ottawa.

Centro Industrial do Brasil. Various reports, 1909, 1917. Rio de Janeiro.

Centro Industrial do Fiação e Tecelagem de Algodão do Rio de Janeiro (CIFTA). Various reports, 1913–24. Rio de Janeiro.

France. *Annuaire Statistique.* Paris, various years.

Institute Émile Vandervelde Bibliothèque et archives. Brussels.

International Federation of Textile Workers' Associations (IFTWA). *Reports of the International Congress, 1894–1924.* Manchester Metropolitan Museum, Manchester.

Parti Ouvrier Belge. *Rapports Annuels.* Brussels, various years.

Platt-Saco-Lowell Archives. DDPSL. Lancashire Record Office, Preston, Lancashire.

United Kingdom. Parliamentary Papers (PP). 1870. *Reports from Her Majesty's Diplomatic and Consular Agents.* Vol. LXVI.

U.K. PP. 1871. *Reports from Her Majesty's Diplomatic and Consular Agents.* Vol. LXVIII.

U.K. PP. 1893–94. *Commission on Labour, Foreign Reports,* Vol. XXXIX.

U.S. Commissioner of Labor. 1900. *Fifteenth Annual Report of the Commissioner of Labor: Wages in Commercial Countries.* 2 Vols. Washington, DC: GPO.

U.S. Commissioner of Labor. 1911. *Twenty-Fourth Annual Report of the Commissioner of Labor. Workmen's Insurance and Compensation Systems in Europe.* 2 Vols. Washington, DC: GPO.

ARTICLES, BOOKS, THESES, AND WORKING PAPERS

Abowd, John M., and Thomas Lemieux. 1991. "The Effects of International Competition on Collective Bargaining Outcomes: A Comparison of Canada and the U.S." In *Immigration, Trade, and the Labor Market,* edited by John M. Abowd and Richard Freeman. Chicago: University of Chicago Press. Pp. 343–68.

Acemoglu, Daron. 2002. "Directed Technical Change." *Review of Economic Studies* 69: 781–809.

Acemoglu, Daron. 2009. *Introduction to Modern Economic Growth.* Princeton: Princeton University Press.

Acemoglu, Daron, and James A. Robinson. 2006. *Economic Origins of Dictatorship and Democracy.* Cambridge, Mass.: MIT Press.

Addison, John T., and W. Stanley Sibert, editors. 1997. *Labor Markets in Europe: Issues of Harmonization and Regulation.* London: Dryden Press.

Adserà, Alícia, and Carles Boix. 2002. "Trade, Democracy, and the Size of the Public Sector: The Political Underpinnings of Openness." *International Organization* 56: 229–62.

Agell, Jonas. 1999. "On the Benefits from Rigid Labour Markets: Norms, Market Failures and Social Insurance." *Economic Journal* 108: F143–F164.

Agell, Jonas. 2002. "On the Determinants of Labour Market Institutions: Rent Seeking vs. Social Insurance." *German Economic Review* 3: 107–35.

Agell, Jonas, and Kjell Erik Lommerud. 1997. "Minimum Wages and the Incentives for Skill Formation." *Journal of Public Economics* 6: 25–40.

Aidt, T. S., Jaysari Dutta, and Elena Loukoianova. 2006. "Democracy Comes to Europe: Franchise Extension and Fiscal Outcomes 1830–1938." *European Economic Review* 50: 249–83.

Albert, Bill. 1988. *South America and the First World War: The Impact of the War on Brazil, Argentina, Peru, and Chile.* New York: Cambridge University Press.

Alesina, Alberto, and Edward L. Glaeser. 2004. *Fighting Poverty in the US and Europe: A World of Difference.* New York: Oxford University Press.

Alesina, Alberto, Edward L. Glaeser, and Bruce Sacerdote. 2005. "Work and Leisure in the United States and Europe: Why So Different?" In *NBER Macroeconomics Annual 2005,* edited by Mark Gertler and Kenneth Rogoff. Cambridge, Mass.: MIT Press. Pp. 1–64.

Alesina, Alberto, and Dani Rodrik. 1994. "Distributive Politics and Economic Growth." *Quarterly Journal of Economics* 109: 465–90.

Alesina, Alberto, and Joseph Zeira. 2006. "Technology and Labor Regulations." NBER working paper 12581.

Allen, Robert C. 2008. "A Review of Gregory Clark's *A Farewell to Alms: A Brief Economic History of the World.*" *Journal of Economic Literature* 46: 946–73.

Allen, Robert C. 2009. *The British Industrial Revolution in Global Perspective.* New York: Cambridge University Press.

Archer, Robin. 2007. *Why Is There No Labor Party in the United States?* Princeton: Princeton University Press.

Atack, Jeremy, and Fred Bateman. 1992. "How Long Was the Workday in 1880?" *Journal of Economic History* 52: 129–60.

Atack, Jeremy, Fred Bateman, and Robert A. Margo. 2003. "Productivity in Manufacturing and the Length of the Working Day: Evidence from the 1880 Census of Manufactures." *Explorations in Economic History* 40: 170–95.

Autor, David H., William R. Kerr, and Adriana D. Kugler. 2007. "Does Employment Protection Reduce Productivity? Evidence from US States." *Economic Journal* 117: F189–F217.

Avery, Donald. 1972. "Canadian Immigration Policy and the 'Foreign' Navy, 1896–1914." *Canadian Historical Association, Historical Papers:* 135–56.

Axelrod, Robert. 1970. *Conflict of Interest: A Theory of Divergent Goals with Application to Politics.* Chicago: Markham.

Bagwell, Kyle, and Robert W. Staiger. 2001. "The WTO as a Mechanism for Securing Market Access Property Rights." *Journal of Economic Perspectives* 15 : 69–88.

Bagwell, Kyle, and Robert W. Staiger. 2004. *The Economics of the World Trading System.* Cambridge, Mass.: MIT Press.

Baier, Scott L., Gerald P. Dwyer, and Robert Tamura. 2006. "How Important Are Capital and Total Factor Productivity for Economic Growth?" *Economic Inquiry* 44: 23–49. Data set available at www.jerrydwyer.com.

Bairoch, Paul, editor. 1968. *La population active et sa structure. International Historical Statistics, Vol. 1.* Brussels: Institut de sociologie, Université Libre de Bruxelles.

Bairoch, Paul. 1976. *Commerce extérieur et développement économique de l'Europe au XIXe siècle.* Paris: Mouton.

Bairoch, Paul. 1989. "European Trade Policy, 1815–1914." In *The Cambridge Economic History of Europe, Volume VIII, The Industrial Economies: The Development of Economic and Social Policies,* edited by Peter Mathias and Sidney Pollard. Cambridge: Cambridge University Press. Pp. 1–160.

Baldwin, Peter. 1990. *The Politics of Social Solidarity: Class Bases of the European Welfare State, 1875–1975.* New York: Cambridge University Press.

Bartolini, Leonardo, and Allen Drazen. 1997. "When Liberal Policies Reflect External Shocks, What Do We Learn?" *Journal of International Economics* 42: 249–73.

Baudoin, Lionel. 1905. *La réglementation légale du travail des femmes et des enfants dans l'industrie italienne.* Paris: H. Paulin.

Bayly, C. A. 2004. *The Birth of the Modern World, 1780–1914: Global Connections and Comparisons.* Malden, Mass.: Blackwell.

Beaulieu, Eugene, and J. C. Herbert Emery. 2001. "Pork Packers, Reciprocity, and Laurier's Defeat in the 1911 Canadian General Election." *Journal of Economic History* 61: 1083–1101.

Bell, Linda, and Richard B. Freeman. 1995. "Why Do Americans and Germans Work Different Hours? In *Institutional Frameworks and Labor Market Performance*, edited by Friedrich Butler, Wolfgang Franz, Ronald Schettkat, and David Soskice. London: Routledge. Pp. 101–31.

Bell, Linda, and Richard B. Freeman. 2001. "The Incentive for Working Hard: Explaining Hours Worked Differences in the US and Germany." *Labour Economics* 8: 181–202.

Berger, Suzanne. 2003. *Notre première mondialisation: Leçons d'un échec oublié*. Paris: Seuil.

Berman, Sheri. 2006. *The Primacy of Politics: Social Democracy and the Making of Europe's Twentieth Century*. New York: Cambridge University Press.

Bernard, Andrew B., J. Bradford Jensen, Stephen J. Redding, and Peter K. Schott. 2007. "Firms in International Trade." *Journal of Economic Perspectives* 21: 105–30.

Bernard, Andrew B., J. Bradford Jensen, Stephen J. Redding, and Peter K. Schott. 2009. "The Margins of US Trade." *American Economic Review* 99: 487–93.

Bernstein, Eduard. 1901. "Zum Kampf gegen die Zollschraube." *Sozialististische Monatshefte* 2.

Bertocchi, Graziella, and Chiara Strozzi. 2004. "Citizenship Laws and International Migration in Historical Perspective." CEPR discussion paper 4737.

Bertola, Giuseppe, Tito Boeri, and Giuseppe Nicoletti, editors. 2001. *Welfare and Employment in a United Europe*. Cambridge, Mass.: MIT Press.

Bértola, Luis, Cecilia Castelnovo, Javier Rodríguez, and Henry Willebald. 2010. "Between the Colonial Heritage and the First Globalization Boom: On Income Inequality in the Southern Cone." *Journal of Iberian and Latin American Economic History* 28: 307–41.

Besso, S. L. 1910. *The Cotton Industry in Switzerland, Vorarlberg, and Italy*. Manchester: Manchester University Press.

Betrán, Concha, and María A. Pons. 2004. "Skilled and Unskilled Labour Wage Differentials and Economic Integration." *European Review of Economic History* 8: 29–60.

Bhagwati, Jagdish N. 1996. "The Demands to Reduce Domestic Diversity Among Trading Nations." In *Fair Trade and Harmonization: Prerequisites for Free Trade? Economic Analysis, Vol.1*, edited by Jagdish Bhagwati and Robert Hudec. Cambridge, Mass.: MIT Press. Pp. 9–40.

Birchal, Sérgio de Oliveira. 1999. *Entrepreneurship in Nineteenth Century Brazil: The Formation of a Business Environment*. New York: St. Martin's.

Blanchard, Olivier. 1997. "The Medium Run." *Brookings Papers on Economic Activity* 28: 89–158.

Blanchard, Olivier. 2004. "The Economic Future of Europe." *Journal of Economic Perspectives* 18: 3–26.

Blattman, Christopher, Jason Hwang, and Jeffrey G. Williamson. 2007. "Winners and Losers in the Commodity Lottery: The Impact of Terms of Trade Growth and Volatility in the Periphery, 1870–1939." *Journal of Development Economics* 82: 156–79.

Blau, Francine, and Lawrence Kahn. 1996. "Wage Structure and Gender Earnings Differentials: An International Comparison." *Economica* 63: S29–62.

Blomme, Jan. 1993. *The Economic Development of Belgian Agriculture 1880–1980: A Quantitative and Qualitative Analysis*. Leuven: Leuven University Press.

Boeri, Tito. 2009. "Immigration to the Land of Redistribution." IZA working paper 4273.

Boix, Carles. 2003. *Democracy and Redistribution*. New York: Cambridge University Press.

Boix, Carles. 2006. "Between Redistribution and Trade: The Political Economy of Protectionism and Domestic Compensation." In *Globalization and Egalitarian Redistribution*, edited by Pranab Bardhan, Samuel Bowles, and Michael Wallerstein. Princeton: Princeton University Press. Pp. 192–16.

Boot, H. M., and J. H. Maindonald. 2008. "New Estimates of Age-and Sex-Specific Earnings and the Male-Female Earnings in the British Cotton Industry, 1833–1906." *Economic History Review* 6: 380–408.

Bordo, Michael, Barry Eichengreen, and Douglas Irwin. 1999. "Is Globalization Today Really Different from Globalization a Hundred Years Ago?" *Brookings Trade Forum 1999*. Brookings: Washington, DC. Pp. 1–50.

Bortz, Jeffrey. 2000. "The Revolution, the Labor Regime and Conditions of Work in the Cotton Textile Industry in Mexico." *Journal of Latin American Studies* 32: 671–703.

Botero, Juan, Simeon Djankov, Rafael La Porta, Florencio Lopez-de-Silanes, and Andrei Shleifer. 2004. "The Regulation of Labor." *Quarterly Journal of Economics* 119: 1339–82.

Bourguignon, François, and Christian Morrison. 2002. "Inequality Among World Citizens, 1890–1992." *American Economic Review* 92: 727–44.

Bowles, Samuel. 2006. "Egalitarian Redistribution in Globally Integrated Economies." In *Globalization and Egalitarian Redistribution*, edited by Pranab Bardhan, Samuel Bowles, and Michael Wallerstein. Princeton: Princeton University Press. Pp. 120–47.

Bowles, Samuel, and Yongjin Park. 2005. "Emulation, Inequality, and Work Hours: Was Thorstein Veblen Right?" *Economic Journal* 115: F397–F412.

Boyer, George. 2007. "The Convergence of Living Standards in the Atlantic Economy, 1870–1930." In *The New Comparative Economic History: Essays in Honor of Jeffrey G. Williamson*, edited by Timothy J. Hatton, Kevin H. O'Rourke, and Alan M. Taylor. Cambridge, Mass.: MIT Press. Pp. 317–42.

Boyer, George, and Timothy J. Hatton. 2002. "New Estimates of British Unemployment, 1870–1913." *Journal of Economic History* 62: 643–75.

Broadberry, Stephen, and Carsten Burhop. 2010. "Real Wages and Labor Productivity in Britain and Germany, 1871–1938: A Unified Approach to the International Comparison of Living Standards." *Journal of Economic History* 70: 400–27.

Brown, Andrew G., and Robert M. Stern. 2008. "What Are the Issues in Using Trade Agreements to Improve International Labor Standards?" *World Trade Review* 7: 331–57.

Brown, Drusilla K. 2001. "Labor Standards: Where Do They Belong on the International Trade Agenda?" *Journal of Economic Perspectives* 15: 89–112.

Brown, Drusilla K., Alan V. Deardorff, and Robert M. Stern. 1996. "International Labor Standards and Trade: A Theoretical Analysis." In *Fair Trade and Harmonization: Prerequisites for Free Trade? Economic Analysis, Vol.1*, edited by Jagdish Bhagwati and Robert Hudec. Cambridge, Mass.: MIT Press. Pp. 225–80.

Brown, John C. 1995. "Imperfect Competition and Anglo-German Trade Rivalry: Markets for Cotton Textiles Before 1914." *Journal of Economic History* 5: 494–527.

Bulmer-Thomas, Victor. 2003. *The Economic History of Latin America since Independence.* New York: Cambridge University Press.

Burgoon, Brian. 2001. "Globalization and Welfare Compensation: Disentangling the Ties That Bind." *International Organization* 55: 509–51.

Burgoon, Brian, and Phineas Baxandall. 2004. "Three Worlds of Working Time: The Partisan Politics of Work Hours in Industrialized Countries." *Politics & Society* 32: 439–73.

Butler, Kim D. 1998. *Freedoms Given, Freedoms Won: Afro-Brazilians in Post-Abolition Sao Paulo and Salvador.* New Brunswick, N.J.: Rutgers University Press.

Buyst, Erik. 2007. "Changes in the Occupational Structure of Belgium: New Estimates for the 1846–1910 Period." Unpublished manuscript, Centre for Economic Studies, University of Leuven.

Caballero, Ricardo J., and Mohamad L. Hammour. 1998. "Jobless Growth: Appropriability, Factor Substitution, and Unemployment." *Carnegie-Rochester Conference Series on Public Policy* 48: 51–94.

Cameron, David R. 1978. "The Expansion of the Public Economy: A Comparative Analysis." *American Political Science Review* 72: 1243–61.

Campbell, George (Duke of Argyll). 1867. *The Reign of Law.* London: Alexander Strahan.

Casella, Alessandra. 2005. "Free Trade and Evolving Standards." In *Fair Trade and Harmonization: Prerequisites for Free Trade? Economic Analysis, Vol. 1,* edited by Jagdish Bhagwati and Robert Hudec. Cambridge, Mass.: MIT Press. Pp. 119–56.

Cassiers, Isabel. 1980a. "Le rôle de l'État à l'apogée du libéralisme 1850–1886." *Contradictions* 23–24: 121–43.

Cassiers, Isabel. 1980b. "Une fonction importante de l'État libéral: la création et la gestion des chemins de fer 1850–1914." *Contradictions* 23–24: 153–64.

Cassiers, Isabel. 1989. *Croissance, crise et régulation en économie ouverte: La Belgique entre les deux guerres.* Brussels: De Boeck Université.

Catão, Luis A. V., and Solomos N. Solomou. 2005. "Effective Exchange Rates and the Classical Gold Standard Adjustment." *American Economic Review* 95: 1259–75.

Chatelain, L. 1908. *La protection internationale ouvrière.* Paris: Arthur Rousseau.

Clapham, John H. 1961. *The Economic Development of France and Germany, 1815–1914.* Cambridge University Press.

Clark, Gregory. 1987. "Why Isn't the Whole World Developed? Lessons from the Cotton Mills." *Journal of Economic History* 47: 141–74.

Clark, Gregory. 2007. *A Farewell to Alms: A Brief Economic History of the World.* Princeton: Princeton University Press.

Clark, W. A. 1909. *Cotton Goods in Latin America: Part 1, Cuba, Mexico, and Central America.* Washington, DC: GPO.

Clark, W. A. 1910. *Cotton Goods in Latin America: Part II, Brazil, Colombia, and Venezuela.* Washington, DC: GPO.

Clarke, Peter. 1978. *Liberals and Social Democrats.* Cambridge: Cambridge University Press.

Clayton, Richard, and Jonas Pontusson. 1998. "Welfare State Retrenchment Revisited." *World Politics* 51: 67–98.

Coghlan, T.A. 1918. *Labour and Industry in Australia, Part IV.* London: Oxford University Press.

Colistete, Renato P. 2007. "Productivity, Wages, and Labor Politics in Brazil, 1945–1962." *Journal of Economic History* 67: 93–128.

Conrad, Sebastien. 2008. "Globalization Effects: Mobility and Nation in Imperial Germany, 1880–1914." *Journal of Global History* 3: 43–66.

Conybeare, John A. C. 1987. *Trade Wars: The Theory and Practice of International Commercial Rivalry.* New York: Columbia University Press.

Costa, Dora. L. 1998. *The Evolution of Retirement: An American Economic History, 1880–1990.* Chicago: University of Chicago Press.

Costa, Dora L. 2000. "The Wage and the Length of the Workday: From the 1890s to 1991." *Journal of Labor Economics* 18: 156–91.

Crafts, N. F. R. 1997. "The Human Development Index and Changes in Standards of Living: Some Historical Comparisons." *European Review of Economic History* 1: 299–322.

Craven, Paul. 1980. 'An Impartial Umpire': Industrial Relations and the Canadian State 1900–1911. Toronto: University of Toronto Press.

Craven, Paul, and Tom Traves. 1979. "The Class Politics of the National Policy." *Journal of Canadian Studies* 14: 63–76.

Cross, Gary. 1988. "Worktime in International Discontinuity, 1886–1940." In *Worktime and Industrialization: An International History*, edited by Gary Cross. Philadelphia: University of Pennsylvania Press.

Crowley, Terry. 1995. "Rural Labour." In *Labouring Lives: Work and Workers in Nineteenth-Century Ontario*, edited by Paul Craven. Toronto: University of Toronto Press. Pp. 13–104.

Cunningham, Hugh, and Pier Paolo Viazzo. 2001. *Child Labor in Historical Perspective, 1800–1985: Case Studies from Europe, Japan, and Colombia.* Florence: UNICEF.

Dales, John H. 1966. *The Protective Tariff in Canada's Economic Development.* Toronto: University of Toronto Press.

Daudin, Guillaume, Matthias Morys, and Kevin H. O'Rourke. 2010. "Globalization, 1870–1914." In *The Cambridge Economic History of Modern Europe, Volume 2: 1870 to the Present*, edited by Stephen Broadberry and Kevin H. O'Rourke. New York: Cambridge University Press. Pp. 30–58,

Daunton, Martin. 2010. "Creating Legitimacy: Administering Taxation in Britain, 1815–1914." In *Paying for the Liberal State: The Rise of Public Finance in Nineteenth-Century Europe*, edited by José Luís Cardoso and Pedro Lains. New York: Cambridge University Press, Pp. 27–56.

Dean, Warren, 1969. *The Industrialization of São Paulo, 1880–1945.* Austin: University of Texas Press.

Degrève, Daniel. 1982. *Le commerce extérieur de la Belgique, 1830–1913–1939: Présentation critique des données statistiques.* Brussels.

de Herdt, René. 2001. "Child Labour in Belgium, 1800–1914." In *Child Labour in Historical Perspective 1800–1985*, edited by Hugh Cunningham and P. P. Viazzo. Florence: UNICEF and Instituto degli Innocenti.

de la Garza Toledo, Enrique. 2003. "Free Trade and Labor Relations in México." In *International Labour Standards: Globalization, Trade, and Public Policy*, edited by Robert J. Flanagan and William B. Gould IV. Stanford: Stanford University Press. Pp. 227–61.

Delevingne, Malcolm. 1934. "The Pre-War History of International Labor Legislation." In *The Origins of the International Labor Organization, Vol. 1*, edited by J. T. Shotwell. New York: Columbia University Press. Pp. 19–53.

De Long, J. Bradford. 1986. "Senior's 'Last Hour': Suggested Explanation of a Famous Blunder." *History of Political Economy* 2: 325–33.

Denoon, Donald, Phillipa Mein-Smith, and Marivic Wyndham. 2000. *A History of Australia, New Zealand and the Pacific*. London: Blackwell.

de Vries, Jan. 2008. *The Industrious Revolution: Consumer Behavior and the Household Economy 1650 to the Present*. New York: Cambridge University Press.

Diaz Alejandro, Carlos F. 1970. *Essays on the Economic History of the Argentine Republic*. New Haven: Yale University Press.

DiNardo, John, Nicole Fortin, and Thomas Lemieux. 1996. "Labour Market Institutions and the Distribution of Wages, 1973–1992: A Semiparametric Approach." *Econometrica* 64: 1001–46.

Dobbin, Frank, Beth Simmons, and Geoffrey Garrett. 2007. "The Global Diffusion of Public Policies: Social Construction, Coercion, Competition, or Learning." *Annual Review of Sociology* 3: 449–72.

Doepke, Matthias, and Fabrizio Zilibotti. 2005. "The Macroeconomics of Child Labor Regulation." *American Economic Review* 95: 1492–1524.

Donald, Moira. 2001. "Workers of the World Unite? Exploring the Enigma of the Second International." In *The Mechanics of Internationalism: Culture, Society, and Politics from the 1840s to the First World War*, edited by Martin H. Geyer and Johannes Paulmann. London: Oxford University Press. Pp. 177–204.

Dormois, Jean-Pierre. 2009. *La défense du travail national? L'incidence du protectionnisme sur l'industrie en Europe, 1870–1914*. Paris: PUPS.

Drezner, Daniel W. 2001. "Globalization and Policy Convergence." *International Studies Review* 3: 53–78.

Drummond, Ian. 1987. *Progress Without Planning: The Economic History of Ontario from Confederation to the Second World War*. Toronto: University of Toronto Press.

Dudzik, Peter. 1987. *Innovation und Investition. Technische Entwicklung und Unternehmerentscheide in der schweizerischen Baumwollspinnerei, 1800 bis 1916*. Zurich: Chronos.

Dutton, Paul V. 2002. *Origins of the French Welfare State: The Struggle for Social Reform in France, 1914–1947*. New York: Cambridge University Press.

Eddie, Scott M. "Economic Policy and Economic Development in Austria-Hungary, 1867–1913." In *The Cambridge Economic History of Europe, Vol. VIII*, edited by Peter Mathias and Sidney Pollard. Cambridge: Cambridge University Press. 1989. Pp. 814–86.

Edmonds, Eric, and Nina Pavcnik. 2006. "International Trade and Child Labor: Cross-country Evidence." *Journal of International Economics* 68: 115–140.

Edrington, Josh, Jenny Minier, and Kenneth R. Troske. 2009. "Where the Girls Are: Trade and Labor Market Segregation in Colombia." IZA discussion paper 4131.

Ehrenberg, Ronald, G. 1994. *Labor Markets and Integrating National Economies.* Washington, DC: Brookings.

Eichengreen, Barry. 1992. *Golden Fetters: The Gold Standard and the Great Depression, 1919–1939.* New York: Oxford University Press.

Eichengreen, Barry. 1996. "Institutions and Economic Growth: Europe after World War II." In *Economic Growth in Europe since 1945,* edited by Nicholas Crafts and Gianni Toniolo. New York: Cambridge University Press. Pp. 38–72.

Eichengreen, Barry. 2007. *The European Economy since 1945: Coordinated Capitalism and Beyond.* Princeton: Princeton University Press.

Elliot, Kimberly Ann, and Richard B. Freeman. 2003. *Can Labor Standards Improve Under Globalization?* Washington, DC: Institute for International Economics.

Ely, Richard. 1888. *Problems of To-day: A Discussion of Protective Tariffs, Taxation, and Monopolies.* New York: T. Y. Crowell.

Emery, J. C. Herbert, Kris Inwood, and Henry Thille. 2007. "Heckscher-Ohlin in Canada: New Estimates of Regional Wages and Land Prices." *Australian Economic History Review* 47: 95–120.

Engerman, Stanley J. 2003. "The History and Political Economy of International Labor Standards." In *International Labor Standards: History, Theory, and Policy Options,* edited by Kaushik Basu, Henrik Horn, Lisa Roman, and Judith Shapiro. Oxford: Blackwell. Pp. 9–83.

Epifani, Paolo, and Gino Gancia. 2009. "Openness, Government Size, and the Terms of Trade." *Review of Economic Studies* 76: 629–68.

Esping-Andersen, Gøsta. 1990. *The Three Worlds of Welfare Capitalism.* Princeton: Princeton University Press.

Esping-Andersen, Gøsta. 2001. "Comments." In *Welfare and Employment in a United Europe,* edited by Giuseppe Bertola, Tito Boeri, and Giuseppe Nicoletti. Cambridge, Mass.: MIT Press. Pp. 127–46.

Fahrmeir, Andreas. 2001. "Passport and the Status of Aliens." In *The Mechanics of Internationalism: Culture, Society, and Politics from the 1840s to the First World War,* edited by Martin H. Geyer and Johannes Paulmann. London: Oxford University Press. Pp. 93–120.

Farnie, Douglas A., and David J. Jeremy, editors. 2004. *The Fibre That Changed the World: The Cotton Industry in International Perspective, 1600–1990s.* Oxford: Oxford University.

Feldman, David. 2003. "Was the Nineteenth Century a Golden Age for Immigrants? The Changing Articulation of National, Local and Voluntary Controls." In *Migration Control in the North Atlantic World: The Evolution of State Practices in Europe and the United States from the French Revolution to the Inter-war Period,* edited by Andreas Fahrmeir, Olivier Faron, and Patrick Weil. New York: Berghahn. Pp. 167–77.

Ferrie, Joseph. 2005. "The End of American Exceptionalism? Mobility in the U.S. since 1850." *Journal of Economic Perspectives* 19: 199–215.

Finbow, Robert G. 2006. *The Limits of Regionalism: NAFTA's Labour Accord.* Burlington, VT: Ashgate.

Finch, Winston, and Gustavo Franco. 2000. "Aspects of the Brazilian Experience with the Gold Standard." In *Monetary Standards in the Periphery: Paper, Silver, and Gold, 1854–1933*, edited by Pablo Martín Aceña and Jaime Reis. London: Macmillan. Pp. 152–74.

Findlay, Ronald, and Kevin H. O'Rourke. 2007. *Power and Plenty: Trade, War, and the World Economy in the Second Millennium*. Princeton: Princeton University Press.

Fine, Sidney. 1969. *Laissez-faire and the General Welfare State: A Study of Conflict in American Thought, 1865–1901*. Ann Arbor: University of Michigan.

Fishback, Price. 1998. "Operations of 'Unfettered' Labor Markets: Exit and Voice in American Labor Markets at the Turn of the Century." *Journal of Economic Literature* 36: 722–65.

Fishback, Price. 2007. "The Progressive Era." In *Government and the American Economy: A New History*, edited by Price Fishback et al. Chicago: University of Chicago Press. Pp. 288–322.

Fishback, Price, Rebecca Holmes, and Samuel Allen. 2009. "Lifting the Curse of Dimensionality Measures of the Labor Legislation Climate in the States during the Progressive Era." *Labor History* 50: 313–46.

Fishback, Price, and Shawn Kantor. 1995. "Did Workers Pay for the Passage of Worker Compensation Laws?" *Quarterly Journal of Economics* 110: 713–42.

Fishback, Price, and Shawn Kantor. 2000. *A Prelude to the Welfare State: The Origins of Workers' Compensation*. Chicago: University of Chicago Press.

Flanagan, Robert J. 2003. "International Labor Standards and International Competitive Advantage." In *International Labour Standards: Globalization, Trade, and Public Policy*, edited by Robert J. Flanagan and William B. Gould IV. Stanford: Stanford University Press. Pp. 15–61.

Fletcher, Roger A. 1983. "The Free Trade Internationalism of Eduard Bernstein, 1899–1914." *American Historical Review* 88: 561–78.

Fletcher, Roger A. 1984. *Revisionism and Empire: Socialist Imperialism in Germany, 1897–1914*. London: Allen & Unwin.

Fogel, Robert W. 2000. *The Fourth Great Awakening and the Future of Egalitarianism*. Chicago: University of Chicago Press.

Fogel, Robert W. 2004. *The Escape from Hunger and Premature Death, 1700–2100: Europe, America, and the Third World*. New York: Cambridge University Press.

Follows, J. W. 1951. *Antecedents of the International Labour Organization*. Oxford: Oxford University Press.

Fontaine, Arthur. 1920. "A Review of International Labour Legislation." In *Labour as an International Problem*, edited by E. John Solano. London: Macmillan. Pp. 161–97.

Fowler, Alan. 2003. *Lancashire Cotton Operatives and Work, 1900–1950: A Social History of Lancashire Cotton Operatives in the Twentieth Century*. Aldershot, U.K.: Ashgate.

Francke, Ernest. 1909. "International Labour Treaties." *Economic Journal* 19: 212–33.

Frankema, Ewout. 2009. *Has Latin America Always Been Unequal? A Comparative Study of Asset and Income Inequality in the Long Twentieth Century*. Boston: Brill.

Freeman, Richard. 1995. "Are Your Wages Set in Beijing?" *Journal of Economic Perspectives* 9: 15–32.

Freeman, Richard B. 2007. "Labor Market Institutions Around the World." NBER working paper 13242.

Freeman, Richard B. 2009. "Labor Regulations, Unions, and Social Protection in Developing Countries: Market Distortions or Efficient Institutions." NBER working paper 14789.

French, John D. 2004. *Drowning in Laws: Labor Law and Brazilian Political Culture.* Chapel Hill: University of North Carolina Press.

Freund, Caroline, and Bineswaree Bolaky. 2008. "Trade, Regulations, and Income." *Journal of Development Economics* 87: 309–21.

Frieden, Jeffry A. 2006. *Global Capitalism: Its Fall and Rise in the Twentieth Century.* New York: Norton.

Friedman, Gerald. 1998. *State-Making and Labor Movements: France and the United States, 1876–1914.* Ithaca: Cornell University Press.

Friedman, Gerald. 2003. "Industrial Relations." In *The Oxford Encyclopedia of Economic History, Vol. 3,* edited by Joel Mokyr. New York: Oxford University Press. Pp 45–49.

Fuchs, Frieda. 2001. "Institutions, Values and Leadership in the Creation of the Welfare States: A Comparison of Protective Labor Legislation in Britain and France." Ph.D. diss., Harvard University.

Fuchs, Frieda. 2005. "The Effects of Protective Labor Legislation on Women's Wages and Welfare: Lessons from Britain and France." *Politics and Society* 33: 595–636.

Fudge, Judy, and Eric Tucker. 2000. "Pluralism or Fragmentation?: The Twentieth-Century Employment Law Regime in Canada." *Labour/Le Travail* 46: 251–306.

Furlogh, Ellen. 1998. "Making Mass Vacations: Tourism and Consumer Culture in France, 1930s to 1970s." *Comparative Studies in Society and History* 40: 247–86.

Garrett, Geoffrey. 1998. *Partisan Politics in the Global Economy.* New York: Cambridge University Press.

Garry, L. S. 1920. *Textile Markets of Brazil.* Washington, DC: GPO.

George, Henry. 1886. *Protection or Free Trade: An Examination of the Tariff Question with Special Regard to the Interest of Labor.* New York.

Gerschenkron, Alexander. 1943. *Bread and Democracy in Germany.* Berkeley: University of California Press.

Gillitzer, Christian, and Jonathan Kearns. 2005. "Long-term Patterns in Australia's Terms of Trade." RBA Research discussion paper 2005–01.

Glaeser, Edward L., and Andrei Shleifer. 2003. "The Rise of the Regulatory State." *Journal of Economic Literature* 41: 401–25.

Glyn, Andrew. 2006. *Capitalism Unleashed: Finance, Globalization, and Welfare.* Oxford: Oxford University Press.

Goldberg, Pinelopi Koujianou, and Nina Pavcnik. 2007. "Distributional Effects of Globalization in Developing Countries." *Journal of Economic Literature* 45: 39–82.

Goldin, Claudia. 1990. *Understanding the Gender Gap: An Economic History of Women.* New York: Oxford University Press.

Goldin, Claudia. 1994. "The Political Economy of Immigration Restriction in the United States, 1890–1921." In *The Regulated Economy: A Historical Approach to Political*

Economy, edited by Claudia Goldin and Gary D. Libecap. Chicago: University of Chicago Press. Pp. 223–57.

Goldin, Claudia. 2000. "Labor Markets in the Twentieth Century." In *The Cambridge Economic History of the United States, Vol. III, The Twentieth Century*, edited by Stanley J. Engerman and Robert E. Gallman. New York: Cambridge University Press. Pp. 549–625.

Goldin, Claudia, and Lawrence F. Katz. 2008. *The Race Between Education and Technology*. Cambridge, Mass.: Harvard University Press.

Gómez-Galvarriato (Freer), Aurora. 1999. "The Impact of the Revolution: Business and Labor in the Mexican Textile Industry, Orizaba, Veracruz 1900–1930." Ph.D. diss., Harvard University.

Gómez-Galvarriato, Aurora. 2002. "Measuring the Impact of Institutional Change in Capital-Labor Relations in the Mexican Textile Industry, 1900–1930." In *The Mexican Economy, 1870–1930: Essays on the Economic History of Institutions, Revolution, and Growth*, edited by Jeffrey L. Bortz and Steven Haber. Stanford: Stanford University Press. Pp. 289–323.

Gómez-Galvarriato, Aurora, and Jeffrey G. Williamson. 2008. "Was It Prices, Productivity or Policy? The Timing and Pace of Latin American Industrialization after 1870." NBER working paper 13990.

Gong, Guan, and Wolfgang Keller, W. 2003. "Convergence and Polarization in Global Income Levels: A Review of Recent Results on the Role of International Technology Diffusion." *Research Policy* 32: 1055–79.

Goossens, Martine, Stefaan Peeters, and Guido Pepermans. 1988. "Interwar Unemployment in Belgium." In *Interwar Unemployment in International Perspective*, edited by Barry Eichengreen and Timothy J. Hatton. Dordrecht: Kluwer. Pp. 289–324.

Goulart, Pedro, and Arjun S. Bedi. 2007. "A History of Child Labour in Portugal." Institute of Social Studies, working paper 448.

Gourevitch, Peter. 1986. *Politics in Hard Times: Comparative Responses to Economic Crises*. Ithaca: Cornell University Press.

Goutor, David. 2007. *Guarding the Gates: The Canadian Labour Movement and Immigration, 1872–1934*. Vancouver: UBC Press.

Graebner, William. 1977. "Federalism in the Progressive Era: A Structural Interpretation of Reform." *Journal of American History* 64: 331–57.

Graves, Robert, and Alan Hodge. 1940. *The Long Week-end: A Social History of Great Britain, 1918–1939*. New York: W. W. Norton.

Gravil, Roger. 1975. "Anglo-U.S. Trade Rivalry in Argentina and the D'Abernon Mission of 1929." In *Argentina in the Twentieth Century*, edited by David Rock. London: Duckworth. Pp. 41–66.

Green, Alan G. 2000. "Twentieth-Century Canadian Economic History." In *The Cambridge Economic History of the United States, Vol. III, The Twentieth Century*, edited by Stanley L. Engerman and Robert E. Gallman. New York: Cambridge University Press. Pp. 191–247.

Green, Alan G., and David A. Green. 1993. "Balanced Growth and the Geographical Distribution of Immigrant Arrivals to Canada, 1900–1912." *Explorations in Economic History* 20: 31–59.

Green, Alan G., and Mary MacKinnon. 1988. "Interwar Unemployment and Relief in Canada." In *Interwar Unemployment in International Perspective*, edited by Barry Eichengreen and Timothy J. Hatton. Dordrecht: Kluwer. Pp. 353–96.

Greenway, David, and Richard Kneller. 2007. "Firm Heterogeneity, Exporting and Foreign Direct Investment." *Economic Journal* 117: F134–F161.

Greenwood, Jeremy, and Guillaume Vandenbroucke. 2005. "Hours Worked: Long-run Trends." NBER working paper 11629.

Gregory, R. G., V. Ho, L. McDermott, and J. Hagan. 1988. "The Australian and US Labour Markets in the 1930s." In *Interwar Unemployment in International Perspective*, edited by Barry Eichengreen and Timothy J. Hatton. Dordrecht: Kluwer. Pp. 397–429.

Gruner, Erich. 1998. *Arbeiterschaft und Wirtschaft in der Schweiz, 1880–1914*. Zurich: Verlag.

Gutman, H. G. 1973. "Work, Culture, and Society in Industrializing America, 1815–1919." *American Historical Review* 78: 531–88.

Habakkuk, H. J. 1962. *American and British Technology in the Nineteenth Century: The Search for Labour-Saving Inventions*. Cambridge: Cambridge University Press.

Haber, Stephen. 1992. "Business Enterprise and the Great Depression in Brazil: A Study of Profits and Losses in Textile Manufacturing." *Business History Review* 66: 353–63.

Haber, Stephen. 1997. "The Efficiency Consequences of Institutional Change: Financial Market Regulation and Industrial Productivity Growth in Brazil, 1866–1934." In *Latin America and the World Economy since 1800*, edited by John H. Coatsworth and Alan M. Taylor. Stanford: Stanford University Press. Pp. 243–59.

Haber, Stephen. 2006. "The Political Economy of Industrialization." In *The Cambridge Economic History of Latin America, Vol. II, The Long Twentieth Century*, edited by Victor Bulmer-Thomas, John H. Coatsworth, and Roberto Cortés Conde. New York: Cambridge University Press. Pp. 537–84.

Hacker, Jacob S., and Paul Pierson. 2002. "Business Power and Social Policy: Employers and the Formation of the American Welfare State." *Politics and Society* 30: 277–325.

Hagemann, Harold. 2001. "The Verein für Sozialpolitik: From Its Foundation until World War I." In *The Spread of Political Economy and the Professionalisation of Economists*, edited by M. M. Augello and M. E. L. Guidi. London: Routledge. Pp. 152–75.

Haggard, Stephen, and Robert R. Kaufman. 2008. *Development, Democracy and Welfare States: Latin America, East Asia and Eastern Europe*. Princeton: Princeton University Press.

Hahner, Jane E. 1977. "Women and Work in Brazil, 1850–1920: A Preliminary Investigation." In *Essays Concerning the Socioeconomic History of Brazil and Portuguese India*, edited by Dauril Allen and Warren Dean. Gainesville: University of Florida Press. Pp. 87–117.

Hall, Peter. 1997. "The Role of Interests, Institutions, and Ideas in the Comparative Political Economy of the Industrialized Nations." In *Comparative Politics: Rationality, Culture, and Structure*, edited by Mark Lichbach and Alan Zuckerman. New York: Cambridge University Press. Pp. 175–207.

Hannah, Leslie. 2008. "Logistics, Market Size, and Giant Plants in the Early Twentieth Century: A Global View." *Journal of Economic History* 68: 46–80.

Harrington, Michael. 1998. "Trade and Social Insurance: The Development of National Unemployment Insurance in Advanced Industrial Democracies." Ph.D. diss., University of California at Los Angeles.

Harris, Jose. 1984. *Unemployment and Politics: A Study in English Social Policy, 1880–1914.* New York: Oxford University Press.

Harris, Jose. 1993. *Private Lives, Public Spirit: Britain 1970–1914.* Harmondsworth: Penguin.

Harris, Jose. 2002. "From Poor Law to Welfare State? A European Perspective." In *The Political Economy of British Historical Experience, 1688–1914,* edited by Donald Winch and Patrick K. O'Brien. Oxford: Oxford University Press. Pp. 409–38.

Harrison, Ann E. 2007. "Globalization and Poverty: An Introduction," In *Globalization and Poverty,* edited by Ann E. Harrison. Chicago: University of Chicago Press. Pp. 1–32.

Harrison, Ann E., and Jason Scorse. 2003. "Globalization's Impact on Compliance with Labor Standards." *Brookings Trade Forum 2003.* Washington, DC. Pp. 45–82.

Hatton, Timothy J., and Jeffrey G. Williamson. 1998. *The Age of Mass Migration: Causes and Economic Impact.* New York: Oxford University Press.

Hatton, Timothy J., and Jeffrey G. Williamson. 2005. *Global Migration and the World Economy: Two Centuries of Policy and Performance.* Cambridge, Mass.: MIT Press.

Haupt, George. 1986. *Aspects of International Socialism 1871–1914.* New York: Cambridge University Press.

Hay, J. R. 1977. *The Origins of the Liberal Welfare Reforms, 1906–1914.* London: Macmillan.

Helpman, Elhanan. 2004. *The Mystery of Economic Growth.* New York: Cambridge University Press.

Helpman, Elhanan, and Oleg Itskhoki. 2008. "Labor Market Rigidities, Trade and Unemployment." Unpublished manuscript, Harvard University.

Hennock, E. P. 1987. *British Social Reform and German Precedents: The Case of Social Insurance 1880–1914.* Oxford: Oxford University Press.

Hennock, E. P. 2007. *The Origin of the Welfare State in England and Germany, 1850–1914.* New York: Cambridge University Press.

Herbert, Ulrich. 2001. *Geschichte der Ausländerpolitik in Deutschland: Saisonarbeiter, Zwangsarbeiter, Gastarbeiter, Flüctlinge.* Munich: C. H. Beck.

Hicks, Alex. 1999. *Social Democracy and Welfare Capitalism.* Ithaca: Cornell University Press.

Hilden, Patricia. 1993. *Women, Work, and Politics. Belgium, 1830–1914.* Oxford: Clarendon Press.

Hiscox, Michael J. 2002. *International Trade and Political Conflict: Commerce, Coalitions, and Mobility.* Princeton: Princeton University Press.

Hiscox, Michael J., and Nicholas F. B. Smyth. 2008. "Evidence from Field Experiments in Social Product Labelling." Unpublished manuscript, Harvard University.

Hobsbawm, Eric J., editor. 1982. *The History of Marxism, Vol. 1: Marxism in Marx's Day.* Bloomington: Indiana University Press.

Holmes, Rebecca, Price Fishback, and Samuel Allen. 2008. "Measuring the Intensity of State Labor Regulation during the Progressive Era." In *Quantitative Economic History: The Good of Counting,* edited by Joshua Rosenbloom. New York: Routledge. Pp. 119–45.

Holzinger, Katharina, Christoph Knill, and Thomas Sommerer. 2008. "Environmental Policy Convergence: The Impact of International Harmonization, Transnational Communication, and Regulatory Competition." *International Organization* 62: 538–87.

Horlings, Edwin. 1997. "The International Trade of a Small and Open Economy. Revised Estimates of the Imports and Exports of Belgium, 1835–1990." *NEHA—Jaarboek* 65: 110–42.

Hourwich, Isaac A. 1911. "The Economic Aspects of Immigration." *Political Science Quarterly* 26: 615–42.

Huberman, Michael. 1997. "An Economic and Business History of Worksharing: The Bell Canada and Volkswagen Experiences." *Business and Economic History* 26: 404–15.

Huberman, Michael. 2004. "Working Hours of the World Unite? New International Evidence of Worktime, 1870–1913." *Journal of Economic History* 64: 964–1001.

Huberman, Michael. 2005. "Are Canada's Labor Standards Set in the Third World?: Historical Trends and Future Prospects." C. D. Howe Commentary, no. 209.

Huberman, Michael. 2008. "Ticket to Trade: Belgian Labour and Globalization Before 1914." *Economic History Review* 61: 326–59.

Huberman, Michael, and Wayne Lewchuk. 2003. "European Economic Integration and the Labour Compact, 1850–1913." *European Review of Economic History* 7: 3–41.

Huberman, Michael, and Christopher M. Meissner. 2007. "Are Your Labor Standards Set in China? Evidence from the First Great Wave of Globalization, 1870–1914." Unpublished manuscript, Université de Montréal.

Huberman, Michael, and Christopher M. Meissner. 2010. "Riding the Wave of Trade: Explaining the Rise of Labor Regulation in the Golden Age of Globalization." *Journal of Economic History* 70: 657–85. (A longer version appears as NBER working paper 15374.)

Huberman, Michael, and Chris Minns. 2007. "The Times They Are Not Changin': Days and Hours of Work in Old and New Worlds, 1870–2000." *Explorations in Economic History* 44: 538–67.

Huberman, Michael, and Chris Minns. 2008. "Labor Regulation and the Wage Gap in Old and New Worlds During the First Great Wave of Globalization." Unpublished manuscript, Université de Montréal.

Huberman, Michael, and Denise Young. 1999. "Cross-Border Unions: Internationals in Canada, 1901–1914." *Explorations in Economic History* 36: 204–31.

Humair, Cédric. 2004. *Développement économique et État central (1815–1914). Un siècle de politique douanière suisse au service des élites.* Berne: Lang.

Hunnicutt, Benjamin. 1988. *Work Without End: Abandoning Shorter Hours for the Right to Work.* Philadelphia: Temple University Press.

Hunt, E. H. 1985. *British Labour History, 1815–1914.* London: Weidenfeld and Nicolson.

Hutchins, B. L., and A. Harrison. 1903. *A History of Factory Legislation.* Westminster: P. S. King & Son.

International Association for Labor Legislation (IALL). 1907. *Report of the 4th General Meeting of the Committee of the IALL.* Geneva, September 26–29, 1906. London: Labour Representative Printing & Publishing.

IALL. 1911. *First Comparative Report on the Administration of Labour Laws: Inspection in Europe.* London: P. S. King & Son.

International Labour Office (ILO). 1937. *The World Textile Industry: Economic and Social Problems,* 2 vols. Geneva: ILO.

ILO. 1939. *The Organisation of Labour Inspection in Industrial and Commercial Undertakings.* Geneva: ILO.

ILO. 1956. *Social Aspects of European Economic Co-operation.* Studies and Reports, new series, no. 46. Geneva: ILO.

Irwin, Douglas A. 1993. "Multilateral and Bilateral Trade Policies in the World Trading System: An Historical Perspective." In *New Dimensions in Regional Integration,* edited by Jaime de Melo and Arvind Panagariya. New York: Cambridge University Press. Pp. 90–128.

Irwin, Douglas A. 1996. *Against the Tide: An Intellectual History of Free Trade.* Princeton: Princeton University Press.

Irwin, Douglas A. 2002. "Interpreting the Tariff-Growth Correlation of the Late Nineteenth Century." *American Economic Review* 91: 165–69.

Irwin, Douglas A. 2007. "Tariff Incidence in America's Gilded Age." *Journal of Economic History* 67: 582–607.

Iversen, Torben. 2005. *Capitalism, Democracy and Welfare.* Cambridge: Cambridge University Press.

Iversen, Torben, and Thomas R. Cusack. 2000. "The Causes of Welfare State Expansion: Deindustrialization or Globalization?" *World Politics* 5: 313–49.

Jacks, David S., Christopher M. Meissner, and Dennis Novy. 2008. "Trade Costs, 1870–2000." *American Economic Review* 98: 529–34.

Jacks, David S., Christopher M. Meissner, and Dennis Novy. 2010. "Trade Costs in the First Wave of Globalization." *Explorations in Economic History* 47: 127–42.

Jacoby, Sandford. 1985. *Employing Bureaucracy: Managers, Unions, and the Transformation of Work in American Industry, 1900–1945.* New York: Cambridge University Press.

Jay, Raoul. 1891. *La limitation légale de la journée de travail en Suisse.* Paris: Larose.

Jay, Raoul. 1910. *La protection légale des travailleurs: Premiers éléments de la législation ouvrière.* Second edition. Paris: L. Larose and L. Ténin.

Jenson, Jane. 1989. "Paradigms and Political Discourse: Protective Legislation in France and the United States before 1914." *Canadian Journal of Political Science* 22: 235–58.

Jewkes, John, and E. M. Gray. 1935. *Wages and Labour in the Lancashire Cotton-Spinning Industry.* Manchester: Manchester University Press.

Jousse, Emmanuel. 2007. *Réviser le marxisme? D'Édouard Bernstein à Albert Thomas.* Paris: L'Harmattan.

Katzenstein, Peter. 1985. *Small States in World Markets: Industrial Policy in Europe.* Ithaca: Cornell University Press.

Kaufman, Bruce E. 2004. *The Global Evolution of Industrial Relations: Events, Ideas and the IIRA.* Geneva: International Labour Office.

Keay, Ian. 2000. "Canadian Manufacturers' Relative Productivity Performance, 1907–90." *Canadian Journal of Economics* 33: 1049–68.

Keck, Margaret E., and Kathryn Sikkink. 1998. *Activists Beyond Borders: Advocacy Networks in International Politics.* Ithaca: Cornell University Press.

Kemp, Tom. 1989. "Economic and Social Policy in France." In *The Cambridge Economic History of Europe, Vol. VIII, The Industrial Economies: The Development of Economic and Social Policies,* edited by Peter Mathias and Sidney Pollard. Cambridge: Cambridge University Press. Pp. 691–751.

Kertesz, Adolf. 1917. *Die Textilindustrie sämtlicher Staaten.* Braunschweig: F. Viehweg.

Khoudour-Castéras, David. 2008. "Welfare State and Labor Mobility: The Impact of Bismarck's Social Legislation on German Emigration Before World War I." *Journal of Economic History* 68: 211–48.

Kindleberger, Charles P. 1956. *The Terms of Trade: A European Case Study.* New York: John Wiley & Sons.

Korpi, Walter. 1983. *The Democratic Class Struggle.* London: Routledge & Kegan Paul.

Kossmann, E. H. 1978. *The Low Countries: 1780–1940.* Oxford: Clarendon Press.

Kreuger, Alan B. 2000. "From Bismarck to Maastricht: The March to European Union and the Labor Compact." *Labour Economics* 7: 117–34.

Kreuger, Alan B. 2007. "International Labor Standards and Trade." In *Annual World Bank Conference on Development Economics,* 1996, edited by Michael Bruno and Boris Pleskovic. Washington, DC: The World Bank. Pp. 281–302.

Krugman, Paul R. 2008. "Trade and Wages Reconsidered." *Brookings Papers on Economic Activity:* 103–54.

Lake, David A. 2009. "Open Economy Politics: A Critical Review." *Review of International Organization* 4: 219–44.

Lamb, P. N. 1967. "Crown Land Policy and Government Finance in NSW, 1856–1900." *Australian Economic History Review* 7: 38–68.

Lampe, Markus. 2009. "Effects of Bilateralism and the MFN Clause on International Trade: Evidence from the Cobden-Chevalier Network, 1860–1975." *Journal of Economic History* 69: 1012–41.

Landes, David S. 1999. *The Wealth and Poverty of Nations: Why Some Are So Rich and Some So Poor.* New York: W. W. Norton.

Lawrence, Robert Z. 2008. *Blue-Collar Blues: Is Trade to Blame for Rising US Income Inequality?* Washington, DC: Peterson Institute for International Economics.

Lazer, David. 1999. "The Free Trade Epidemic of the 1860s and Other Outbreaks of Economic Discrimination." *World Politics* 51: 447–83.

Leff, Nathaniel H. 1982. *Underdevelopment and Development in Brazil. Vol. 1: Economic Structure and Change, 1822–1947.* London: Allen & Unwin.

Lemieux, Thomas. 2008. "The Changing Nature of Wage Inequality." *Journal of Population Economics* 21: 1432–75.

Lewis, Arthur J. 1978. *The Evolution of the International Economic Order.* Princeton: Princeton University Press.

Lewis, Colin. 1975. "Anglo-American Trade, 1845–1965." In *Argentina in the Twentieth Century,* edited by David Rock. London: Duckworth. Pp. 114–35.

Lindert, Peter H. 2004. *Growing Public: Social Spending and Economic Growth since the Eighteenth Century.* New York: Cambridge University Press.

Lindert, Peter H. 2006. "What Is Happening to the Welfare State?" In *The Global Economy in the 1990s: A Long-Run Perspective,* edited by Paul W. Rhode and Gianni Toniolo. New York: Cambridge University Press. Pp. 234–62.

Lindert, Peter H., and Jeffrey G. Williamson. 2003. "Does Globalization Make the World More Unequal?" In *Globalization in Historical Perspective,* edited by Michael D. Bordo, Alan M. Taylor, and Jeffrey G. Williamson. Chicago: University of Chicago Press. Pp. 227–76.

Lobo, Eulália Maria Lahmeyer. 1978. *História do Rio de Janeiro, do capital comercial ao capital industrial e financeiro, 2° vol.* Rio de Janeiro: IBMEC.

Long, Jason, and Joseph P. Ferrie. 2007. "The Path to Convergence: Intergenerational Occupational Mobility in Britain and the U.S. in Three Eras." *Economic Journal* 117: C61–C71.

López-Córdova, José Ernesto, and Christopher M. Meissner. 2003. "Exchange Rate Regimes and International Trade: Evidence from the Classical Gold Standard." *American Economic Review* 97: 344–53.

López-Córdova, José Ernesto, and Christopher M. Meissner. 2008. "The Impact of International Trade on Democracy: A Long-Run Perspective." *World Politics* 60: 539–75.

Lowe, Boutelle E. 1935. *The International Protection of Labor: International Labor Organization, History and Law.* New York: Macmillan.

Ludwig, Armin K. 1985. *Brazil: A Handbook of Historical Statistics.* Boston: G. K. Hall.

Lyons, Francis S. L. 1963. *Internationalism in Europe, 1815–1914.* Leyden: A. W. Sythoff.

MacKinnon, Mary. 1996. "New Evidence on Canadian Wage Rates." *Canadian Journal of Economics* 28: 114–31.

Maddison, Angus, 1995. *Monitoring the World Economy, 1820–1992.* Paris: OECD.

Maddison, Angus. 2001. *The World Economy: A Millennial Perspective.* Paris: OECD.

Mah, J. H. 1997. "Core Labor Standards and Export Performance in Developing Countries." *The World Economy* 20: 773–85.

Mahaim, Ernest. 1895. "Economics and Social Science in Belgium." *Economic Journal* 5: 462–71.

Mahaim, Ernest. 1905. "La conférence de Berne concernant la protection ouvrière." *Revue économique internationale*: 1–29.

Mahaim, Ernest. 1910. *Les abonnements d'ouvriers sur les lignes de chemins de fer belges et leurs effets sociaux.* Brussels: Misch and Thron.

Mandelbaum, Michael. 2002. *The Ideas That Conquered the World: Peace, Democracy, and Free Markets in the Twenty-first Century.* New York: Public Affairs.

Maram, Sheldon L. 1977. "Labor and the Left in Brazil, 1890–1921: A Movement Aborted." *Hispanic American Historical Review* 57: 254–72.

Mares, Isabela. 2003. *The Politics of Social Risk: Business and Welfare State Development.* New York: Cambridge University Press.

Marrison, Andrew. 1975. "Great Britain and Her Rivals in the Latin-American Cotton Piece-Goods Market, 1880–1914." In *Great Britain and Her World: Essays in Honour of W. O. Henderson*. Manchester: Manchester University Press. Pp. 309–49.

Marx, Karl 1977. "Speech on Free Trade [1848]." In *Karl Marx: Selected Writings*, edited by David McLellan. Oxford: Oxford University Press.

Marx, Karl 1981. *Capital Vol. III* [1886]. New York: Vantage.

Mascarenhas, G. M. 1972. *Centenário da Fábrica do Cedro, 1872–1972*. Belo Horizonte.

Maskus, Keith E. 2004. "Trade and Competitiveness Aspects of Environmental and Labor Standards in East Asia." In *East Asia Integrates: A Trade Policy Agenda for Shared Growth*, edited by Kathie Krumm and Homi Kharas. Washington, DC: The World Bank. Pp. 163–85.

Matessini, F., and B. Quintieri. 2006. "Does a Reduction in the Length of the Working Week Reduce Unemployment? Some Evidence From the Italian Economy During the Great Depression." *Explorations in Economic History* 43: 413–37.

Mayda, Anna Maria, Kevin H. O'Rourke, and Richard Sinnott. 2007. "Risk, Government, and Globalization: International Survey Evidence." NBER working paper 13037.

Mazur, Jay. 2000. "Labor's New Internationalism." *Foreign Affairs* 79: 79–93.

McBriar, A. M. 1962. *Fabian Socialism and English Politics, 1884–1914*. Cambridge: Cambridge University Press.

McCrea, Roswell, Thurman W. Van Metre, and George Jackson Eder. 1931. "International Competition in the Trade in Argentina." *International Conciliation* (June): No. 271.

McLean, Iain. 2001. "Irish Potatoes, Indian Corn and British Politics: Interests, Ideology, Heresthetic and the Repeal of the Corn Laws." In *International Trade and Political Institutions: Instituting Trade in the Long Nineteenth Century*, edited by Fiona McGillivray, Iain McLean, Robert Pahre, and Cheryl Schonhardt-Bailey. Cheltenham, U.K.: Edward Elgar. Pp. 99–145.

McLean, Ian W. 2007. "Why Was Australia So Rich? " *Explorations in Economic History* 44: 233–55.

Meissner, Christopher M. 2005. "A New World Order: Explaining the International Diffusion of the Gold Standard, 1870–1913." *Journal of International Economics* 66: 385–406.

Melitz, Marc J. 2003. "The Impact of Trade on Intra-Industry Reallocations and Aggregate Industry Productivity." *Econometrica* 71: 1695–1725.

Messerlin, Patrick, and Stephane Becuwe. 1986. "Intra-industry Trade in the Long Run: The French Case, 1850–1913." In *Imperfect Competition and International Trade*, edited by David Greenway and P. K. M. Tharakan. Atlantic Highlands, N.J.: Humanities Press. Pp. 191–215.

Métin, Albert. 1908. *Les traités ouvriers: Accords internationaux de prévoyance et de travail*. Paris: Armand Colin.

Milhaud, Edgard. 1899. *Le Congrès socialiste de Stuttgart*. Paris: Georges Bellais.

Miller, Rory. 1981. "Latin American Manufacturing and the First World War: An Exploratory Essay." *World Development* 9: 707–16.

Mitchell, Brian. 1981. *European Historical Statistics, 1750–1975*. New York: Facts On File.

Moehling, Carolyn. 1999. "State Child Labor Laws and the Decline of Child Labor Law." *Explorations in Economic History* 36: 72–106.

Monographies industrielles. 1902. *Aperçu économique, technologique et commercial. VIII: Industries textiles. Filature mécanique du coton, du lin, du chanvre et du jute.* Brussels: Société belge de librairie.

Moriguchi, Chiaki. 2005. "Did American Welfare Capitalists Breach Their Implicit Contracts During the Great Depression? Preliminary Findings from Company-level Data." *Industrial and Labor Relations Review* 59: 51–81.

Morrisson, Christian. 2000. "Historical Perspectives on Income Distribution." In *Handbook of Income Distribution, Vol. 1,* edited by Anthony B. Atkinson and François Bourguignon. Amsterdam: Elsevier. Pp. 217–60.

Moynihan, Daniel Patrick. 1960. "The United States and the International Labor Organization, 1889–1934." Ph.D. diss., Tufts University.

Mulligan, Casey E., and Andrei Shleifer. 2004. "Population and Regulation." NBER working paper 10234.

Murphy, Kevin M., Andrei Shleifer, and Robert W. Vishny. 1989. "Industrialization and the Big Push." *Journal of Political Economy* 97: 1003–26.

Murray, B. K. 1980. *The People's Budget 1909/10: Lloyd George and Liberal Politics.* Oxford: Oxford University Press.

Musacchio, Aldo. 2009. *Experiments in Financial Democracy: Corporate Governance and Financial Development in Brazil, 1882–1950.* New York: Cambridge University Press.

Neuville, Jean. 1979. *Naissance et croissance du syndicalisme.* Brussels: Vie Ouvrière.

Newbery, David M., and Joseph E. Stiglitz. 1984. "Pareto Inferior Trade." *Review of Economic Studies* 51: 1–12.

Noiriel, Gérard. 2001. *État, nation, et immigration: Vers une histoire du pouvoir.* Paris: Belin.

Noiriel, Gérard, and Michel Offerlé. 1997. "Citizenship and Nationality in Nineteenth-Century France." In *European Integration in Social and Historical Perspective: 1850 to the Present,* edited by Jytte Klausen and Louise A. Tilly. Lanham, Md.: Rowman & Littlefield. Pp.71–84.

Nugent, Walter. 1995. *Crossings: The Great Transatlantic Migrations, 1870–1914.* Bloomington: Indiana University Press.

Nye, John V. C. 2007. *War, Wine, and Taxes: The Political Economy of Anglo-French Trade, 1689–1900.* Princeton: Princeton University Press.

Obstfeld, Maurice, and Alan M. Taylor. 2004. *Global Capital Markets: Integration, Crisis, and Growth.* New York: Cambridge University Press.

Odell, Ralph M. 1911. *Cotton Goods in Spain and Portugal.* Washington, DC: GPO.

OECD. 1998. *Employment Outlook.* Paris: OECD.

O'Rourke, Kevin H. 2000. "Tariffs and Growth in the Late 19th Century." *Economic Journal* 110: 456–483.

O'Rourke, Kevin H., and Alan M. Taylor. 2007. "Democracy and Protectionism." In *The New Comparative Economic History: Essays in Honor of Jeffrey G. Williamson,* edited by Timothy J. Hatton, Kevin H. O'Rourke, and Alan M. Taylor. Cambridge, Mass.: MIT Press. Pp. 193–216.

O'Rourke, Kevin H., and Jeffrey G. Williamson. 1999. *Globalization and History; The Evolution of a Nineteenth-Century Atlantic Economy.* Cambridge, Mass.: MIT Press

O'Rourke, Kevin H., and Jeffrey G. Williamson. 2002. "The Heckscher-Ohlin Model Between 1400 and 2000: When It Explained Factor Price Convergence, When It Did Not, and Why?" In *Bertil Ohlin: A Centennial Celebration (1989–1999)*, edited by Ronald Findlay, Lars Jonung, and Mats Lundahl. Cambridge, Mass.: MIT Press. Pp. 429–62.

Osterhammel, Jürgen, and Niels P. Petersson. 2005. *Globalization: A Short History.* Princeton: Princeton University Press.

Ostry, Bernard. 1960. "Conservatives, Liberals and Labour in the 1870s." *Canadian Historical Review* 41: 93–127.

Pahre, Robert. 1998. "Reactions and Reciprocity: Tariffs and Trade Liberalization from 1815 to 1914." *Journal of Conflict Resolution* 42: 467–92.

Pahre, Robert. 2001. "Most-Favored-Nation Clauses and Clustered Negotiations." *Industrial Organization* 55: 859–90.

Pahre, Robert. 2007. *Politics and Trade Cooperation in the Nineteenth Century. The 'Agreeable Customs' of 1815–1914.* New York: Cambridge University Press.

Pavcnik, Nina. 2002. "Trade Liberalization, Exit, and Productivity Improvements: Evidence from Chilean Plants." *Review of Economic Studies* 69: 245–76.

Pearse, Arno S. 1923. *Brazilian Cotton.* Manchester: International Federation of Master Cotton Spinner's & Manufacturers.

Pencavel, John. 1986. "Labor Supply of Men: A Survey." In *Handbook of Labor Economics, Vol. 1.*, edited by Orley Ashenfelter and Richard Layard. Amsterdam: North Holland. Pp. 4–102.

Persson, Torsten, and Guido Tabellini. 2004. "Constitutions and Economic Policy." *Journal of Economic Perspectives* 18: 75–98.

Pierson, Paul. 1996. "The Politics of the Welfare State." *World Politics* 48: 143–79.

Polanyi, Karl. 1944. *The Great Transformation.* New York: Farrar & Rinehart.

Polasky, Janet. 1995. *The Democratic Socialism of Émile Vandervelde: Between Reform and Revolution.* Oxford: Berg.

Pontusson, Jonas. 2005. *Inequality and Prosperity: Social Europe vs. Liberal America.* Ithaca: Cornell University Press.

Pope, Clayne. 2000. "Inequality in the Nineteenth Century." In *The Cambridge Economic History of the United States, Vol. II, The Nineteenth Century,* edited by Stanley J. Engerman and Robert E. Gallman. New York: Cambridge University Press. Pp. 109–42.

Potter, D. Shena. 1910. "The Movement for International Labour Legislation." *Economic Journal* 20: 347–57.

Prados de la Escosura, Leandro. 2007. "Inequality and Poverty in Latin America: A Long-Run Exploration." In *The New Comparative Economic History,* edited by Timothy J. Hatton, Kevin H. O'Rourke, and Alan M. Taylor. Cambridge, Mass.: MIT Press. Pp. 291–315.

Prescott, Edward C. 2004. "Why Do Americans Work So Much More than Europeans?" *Federal Reserve Bank of Minneapolis Quarterly Review* 28: 2–13.

Price, George M. 1923. "Administration of the Labor Laws and Factory Inspection in Certain European Countries." *Monthly Labor Review* 16: 1153–71.

Puissant, Jean. 1979. *L'évolution du mouvement ouvrier socialiste dans le Borinage.* Brussels: Palais des Académies.

Putnam, Robert D. 1988. "Diplomacy and Domestic Politics: The Logic of Two-Level Games." *International Organization* 42: 427–60.

Rae, John. 1894. *Eight Hours for Work.* London: Macmillan.

Rahikainen, Marjatta. 2001. "Child Labour Legislation in Nineteenth Century Finland." *Scandinavian Economic History Review* 49: 41–62.

Rajan, Raghuram G., and Luigi Zingales. 2003. "The Great Reversals: The Politics of Financial Development in the Twentieth Century." *Journal of Financial Economics* 69: 5–50.

Razo, Armando, and Stephen Haber. 1998. "The Rate of Growth of Productivity in Mexico, 1850–1933: Evidence from the Cotton Textile Industry." *Journal of Latin American Studies* 30: 481–517.

Redfield, Arthur H. 1920. *Brazil: A Study of Economic Conditions since 1913.* Washington, DC: GPO.

Rees, Albert. 1973. *The Economics of Work and Pay.* New York: Harper & Row.

Reichesberg, Naum. 1911. *Handwörterbuch der schweizerischen Volkswirtschaft, Sozialpolitik und Verwaltung.* Bern: Verlag Encyklopädie.

Report of the Proceedings of the International Trade Congress. 1908. London: Cobden Club.

Ribeiro, Maria Alice Rosa. 1988. *Condições de trabalho na indústria têxtil paulista (1870–1930).* São Paulo: Hucitec.

Rist, Charles. 1897. "La durée du travail dans l'industrie française de 1820 à 1970." *Revue d'économie politique:* 371–73.

Rivera-Batiz, Luis A., and Maria-Angels Oliva. 2003. *International Trade: Theory, Strategies, and Evidence.* New York: Oxford University Press.

Rodgers, Daniel T. 1978. *The Work Ethic in Industrial America, 1850–1920.* Chicago: University of Chicago Press.

Rodgers, Daniel T. 1998. *Atlantic Crossings: Social Politics in a Progressive Age.* Cambridge, Mass.: Harvard University Press.

Rodgers, Gerry. 2011. "India, the ILO, and the Quest for Social Justice since 1919." *Economic & Political Weekly* 46: 45–52.

Rodgers, Gerry, Eddy Lee, Lee Swepston, and Jasmien Van Daele. 2009. *The International Labor Organization and the Quest for Social Justice.* Ithaca: ILR Press.

Rodríguez García, Magaly. 2006. "Early Views on Internationalism: Marxist Socialists vs Liberals." *Revue Belge de Philologie et d'Histoire* 84: 1049–74.

Rodrik, Dani. 1996. "Labor Standards in International Trade: Do They Matter and What Do We Do About Them?" In *Emerging Agenda for Global Trade: High Stakes for Developing Countries*, edited by Robert Z. Lawrence, Dani Rodrik, and John Whalley. Washington, DC: Johns Hopkins University Press. Pp. 35–79.

Rodrik, Dani. 1997. *Has Globalization Gone Too Far?* Washington: Institute for International Economics.

Rodrik, Dani. 1998. "Why Do More Open Economies Have Bigger Governments?" *Journal of Political Economy* 106: 997–1032.

Rodrik, Dani. 2007. *One Economics, Many Recipes: Globalization, Institutions, and Economic Growth.* Princeton: Princeton University Press.

Rodrik, Dani. 2011. *The Globalization Paradox: Democracy and the Future of the World Economy.* New York: W. W. Norton.

Rogowski, Ronald. 1987. "Political Cleavages and Changing Exposure to Trade." *American Political Science Review* 81: 1121–37.

Rogowski, Ronald. 1989. *Commerce and Coalitions: How Trade Affects Domestic Political Alignments.* Princeton: Princeton University Press.

Rolin-Jaequemins, M. G. 1890. "La conférence de Berlin sur la législation du travail et le socialisme dans le droit international." *Revue de Droit International et de Législation Comparée* 22: 4–28.

Rose, Sonya O. 1992. *Limited Livelihoods: Gender and Class in Nineteenth-Century England.* Berkeley: University of California Press.

Rosenbloom, Joshua L., and William A. Sundstrom. 2011. "Labor-Market Regimes in U.S. Economic History." In *Economic Evolution and Revolution in Historical Time,* edited by Paul W. Rhode, Joshua L. Rosenbloom, and David F. Weiman. Stanford: Stanford University Press. Pp. 277–310.

Rosenstein-Rodan, Paul. 1943. "The Problems of Industrialisation of Eastern and South-Eastern Europe." *Economic Journal* 53: 202–11.

Rouillard, Jacques. 1974. *Les travailleurs du cotton au Québec, 1900–1915.* Montreal: Les Presses de l'Université du Québec.

Rudra, Nita. 2008. *Globalization and the Race to the Bottom in Developing Countries. Who Really Gets Hurt?* New York: Cambridge University Press.

Rueschemeyer, Dietrich, Evelyne H. Stephens, and John D. Stephens. 1992. *Capitalist Development and Democracy.* Chicago: University of Chicago Press.

Sabel, Charles, and Jonathan Zeitlin. 1985. "Historical Alternatives to Mass Production. Politics, Markets, and Technology in Nineteenth-century Industrialization." *Past & Present* 108: 133–76.

Sánchez-Alonso, Blanca. 2006. "Labor and Immigration." In *The Cambridge Economic History of Latin America, Vol. II, The Long Twentieth Century,* edited by Victor Bulmer-Thomas, John H. Coatsworth, and Roberto Cortés Conde. New York: Cambridge University Press. Pp. 377–426.

Sanders, Elizabeth. M. 1999. *Roots of Reform: Farmers, Workers, and the American State, 1877–1917.* Chicago: University of Chicago Press.

Saramago, José. 2003. *The Cave.* Orlando, Fla.: Harcourt.

Saul, S. B. 1960. *Studies in British Overseas Trade, 1870–1914.* Liverpool: Liverpool University Press.

Saxonhouse, Gary, and Gavin Wright. 2004. "Technological Evolution in Cotton Spinning, 1878–1933." In *The Fibre That Changed the World: The Cotton Industry in International Perspective, 1600–1990s,* edited by Douglas A. Farnie and David J. Jeremy. Oxford: Oxford University Press. Pp. 129–52.

Saxonhouse, Gary, and Gavin Wright. 2010. "National Leadership and Competing Technological Paradigms: The Globalization of Cotton Spinning, 1878–1933." *Journal of Economic History* 70: 535–66.

Scholliers, Peter. 1996. *Wages, Manufacturers and Workers in the Nineteenth Century Factory: The Voortman Cotton Mill in Ghent*. Oxford: Berg.

Scholliers, Peter. 2001. "Mots et pratiques. L'industrie cotonnière gantoise, les crises et la perception patronale de la concurrence internationale, 1790–1914." *Revue d'histoire du XIXe siècle* 23: 121–42.

Schön, Lennart. 2010. "The Rise of the Fiscal State in Sweden, 1800–1914." In *Paying for the Liberal State: The Rise of Public Finance in Nineteenth-Century Europe*, edited by José Luís Cardoso and Pedro Lains. New York: Cambridge University Press. Pp. 162–87.

Schonhardt-Bailey, Cheryl. 2006. *From the Corn Laws to Free Trade: Interests, Ideas, and Institutions in Historical Perspective*. Cambridge, Mass.: MIT Press.

Sen, Amartya. 2004. "How to Judge Globalism." In *The Globalization Reader*, edited by Frank J. Lechner and John Boli. Second edition. Malden, Mass.: Blackwell. Pp. 16–21.

Shepsle, Kenneth A. 1985. "Comment." In *Regulatory Policy and Social Science*, edited by Roger G. Noll. Berkeley: University of California Press. Pp. 231–37.

Shirvani, Hassan, and Barry Wilbratte. 1997. "The Relationship Between the Real Exchange Rate and the Trade Balance: An Empirical Reassessment." *International Economic Journal* 11: 39–50.

Shotwell, James T. 1934. *The Origins of the International Labour Organization*. New York: Columbia University Press.

Silver, Barbara J. 2003. *Forces of Labor: Workers' Movements and Globalization since 1870*. New York: Cambridge University Press.

Silverman, Dan. P. 1971, "The Economic Consequences of Annexation: Alsace-Lorraine and Imperial Germany, 1871–1918." *Central European History* 4: 34–53.

Simmons, Beth A., Frank Dobbin, and Geoffrey Garrett. 2008. "Introduction: The Diffusion of Liberalization." In *The Global Diffusion of Markets and Democracy*, edited by Beth Simmons, Frank Dobbin, and Geoffrey Garrett. New York: Cambridge University Press. Pp. 1–63.

Singh, Nirvikar. 2003. "The Theory of International Trade Standards from an Economic Perspective." In *International Labor Standards: History, Theory, and Policy Options*, edited by Kaushik Basu, Henrik Horn, Lisa Romain, and Judith Shapiro. Malden, Mass.: Blackwell. Pp. 107–81.

Sinn, Hans-Werner. 2007. *Can Germany Be Saved? The Malaise of the World's First Welfare State*. Cambridge, Mass.: MIT Press.

Slaughter, Matthew J. 2001. "International Trade and Labor Demand Elasticities." *Journal of International Economics* 54: 27–56.

Smith, Michael S. 1980. *Tariff Reform in France, 1860–1900. The Politics of Economic Interest*. Ithaca: Cornell University Press.

Smits, Jan-Pieter, Edwin Horlings, and Jan Luiten van Zanden. 2000. "Dutch GNP and Its Components, 1800–1913." Groningen Growth and Development Centre.

Stedman Jones, Garth. 1983. *Languages of Class: Studies in English Working Class History, 1832–1982*. Cambridge: Cambridge University Press.

Steenson, Gary. 1991. *After Marx, Before Lenin: Marxism and Socialist Working-class Parties in Europe, 1889–1914*. Pittsburgh: University of Pittsburgh Press.

Stein, Stanley J. 1957. *The Brazilian Cotton Manufacture: Textile Enterprise in an Underdeveloped Area, 1850–1950*. Cambridge, Mass.: Harvard University Press.

Stewart, M. L. 1989. *Women, Work and the French State: Labour Protection and Social Patriarchy, 1879–1919*. Montreal: McGill-Queen's University Press.

Stigler, George J. 1982. *The Economist as Preacher and Other Essays*. Chicago: University of Chicago Press.

Stiglitz, Joseph E. 2006. *Making Globalization Work*. New York: W. W. Norton.

Strikwerda, Carl. 1997. "Reinterpreting the History of European Integration: Business, Labor, and Social Citizenship in Twentieth-Century Europe." In *European Integration in Social and Historical Perspective: 1850 to the Present*, edited by Jytte Klausen and Louise A. Tilly. Lanham, Md.: Rowman & Littlefield. Pp. 51–70.

Strikwerda, Carl. 1998. "France and the Belgian Immigration of the Nineteenth Century." In *The Politics of Immigrant Workers: Labor Activism and Migration in the World Economy since 1830*, edited by Camille Guerin-Gonzáles and Carl Strikwerda. New York: Holmes & Meier. Pp.111–44.

Summerhill, William R. 2003. *Order Against Progress: Government, Foreign Investment, and Railroads in Brazil, 1854–1913*. Stanford: Stanford University Press.

Summers, Lawrence. 2008. "Preserving the Open Economy at Times of Stress." *Financial Times*, 21 May. http://blogs.ft.com/wolfforum/2008/05/preserving-the-open-economy-at-times-of-stress.

Suzigan, Wilson. 1986. *Indústria brasileira: Origem e Desenvolvimento*. São Paulo: Brasiliense.

Swank, Duane. 2006. "Conditional Diffusion Model of the Spread of Neoliberalism." *International Organization* 60: 847–82.

Swenson, Peter. 2002. *Capitalists Against Markets: The Making of Labor Markets and Welfare States in the United States and Sweden*. New York: Oxford University Press.

Swenson, Peter. 2004. "Varieties of Capitalist Interests: Power, Institutions, and the Regulatory Welfare State in the United States and Sweden." *Studies in American Political Development* 18: 1–29.

Tabellini, Guido. 2005. "Culture and Institutions: Economic Development in the Regions of Europe." CESifo working paper 1492.

Taylor, Alan M., and Jeffrey G. Williamson. 1997. "Convergence in the Age of Mass Migration." *European Review of Economic History* 2: 27–63.

Taylor, K. A., and H. Michell. 1931. *Statistical Contributions to Canadian Economic History, Vol. II, Statistics of Foreign Trade*. Toronto: Hunter-Rose Co.

Temin, Peter. 1997. "The Golden Age of European Growth." *European Review of Economic History* 1: 127–49.

Thelen, Kathleen. 2004. *How Institutions Evolve: The Political Economy of Skills in Germany, Britain, Japan, and the United States*. New York: Cambridge University Press.

Tilly, Charles. 1995. "Globalization Threatens Labour's Rights." *International Labour and Working Class History* 4: 1–24.

Toniolo, Gianni, and Giovanni Vecchi. 2007. "Italian Children at Work." Understanding Children's Work Project, working paper 35.

Trentmann, Frank. 1997. "Wealth vs Welfare: The British Left Between Free Trade and National Political Economy Before the First World War." *Historical Research* 70: 70–96.

Trentmann, Frank. 2008. *Free Trade Nation: Commerce, Consumption, and Civil Society in Modern Britain.* Oxford: Oxford University Press.

Trentmann, Frank, and Martin Daunton. 2004. "Worlds of Political Economy: Knowledge, Practices and Contestation." In *Worlds of Political Economy: Knowledge and Power in the Nineteenth and Twentieth Centuries*, edited by Frank Trentmann and Martin Daunton. Basingstoke: Palgrave Macmillan. Pp. 1–23.

Tyszynski, H. 1951. "World Trade in Manufactured Commodities, 1899–1950." *The Manchester School of Economic and Social Studies* 19: 222–304.

United Nations. 1951. *Labour Productivity of the Cotton Textile Industry in Five Latin-American Countries.* Department of Economic Affairs. New York: United Nations.

United States. Department of Commerce. 1989. *Historical Statistics of the United States, Colonial Times to 1870.* New York: Kraus Publications.

University of Groningen. 2010. "Total Economy Database." Available at http://www.ggdc.net/databases/ted.htm.

Urquhart, M. C., and K. A. H. Buckley. 1983. *Historical Statistics of Canada.* Second Edition. Ottawa: Statistics Canada.

van Beers, Cees. 1998. "Labour Standards and Trade Flows of OECD Countries." *The World Economy* 2: 57–73.

van Daele, Jasmien. 2005. "Engineering Social Peace: Networks, Ideas, and the Founding of the International Labour Organization." *International Review of Social History* 50: 435–66.

van den Eeckhout, Patricia. 1993. "Family Income in Ghent Working Class Families, c. 1900." *Journal of Family History* 18: 87–110.

van der Linden, Marcel. 2003. *Transnational Labor History: Explorations.* Aldershot, U.K: Ashgate.

Vandervelde, Émile. 1889. *Les difficultés de l'assurance ouvrière en Belgique.* Brussels: Veuve Monnom.

Vandervelde, Émile. 1895. *Le socialisme agricole.* Brussels: Bibliothèque de Propagande Socialiste.

Vandervelde, Émile. 1897. *Les lois sociales en Belgique.* Brussels: Bibliothèque de Propagande Socialiste.

Vandervelde, Émile. 1899. *L'influence des villes sur les campagnes.* Brussels: L'Institut des Sciences Sociales.

Vandervelde, Émile. 1910. *L'exode rural et le retour aux champs.* Paris: Félix Alcan.

Vandervelde, Émile. 1911. "La journée de neuf heures dans les mines." *Revue d'économie politique.* 185–209.

Vandervelde, Émile. 1920. "Labour Reforms in Belgium." In *Labour as an International Problem*, edited by E. John Solano. London: Macmillan. Pp. 105–31.

Vandervelde, Émile, and Jules Destrée. 1898. *Le socialisme en Belgique*. Paris.

van Houtte, F-X. 1949. *L'évolution de l'industrie textile en Belgique et dans le monde de 1800 à 1939*. Leuven: E. Nauwelaerts.

van Molle, Leen. 1989. *Katholieken en Landbouw: Landbouwpolitiek in België*. Leuven.

Vanthemsche, Guy. 1990. "Unemployment Insurance in Interwar Belgium." *International Review of Social History* 35: 349–76.

van Zanden, Jan Luiten, and Marten Prak. 2006. "Towards an Economic Interpretation of Citizenship: The Dutch Republic between Medieval Communities and Modern Nation States." *European Review of Economic History* 10: 111–47.

van Zanden, Jan Luiten, and Arthur van Riel. 2010. "The Development of Public Finance in the Netherlands, 1815–1914." In *Paying for the Liberal State: The Rise of Public Finance in Nineteenth-Century Europe*, edited by José Luís Cardoso and Pedro Lains. New York: Cambridge University Press. Pp. 57–81.

Veblen, Thorstein. 1953. *The Theory of the Leisure Class: An Economic Study of Institutions [1899]*. New York: Mentor Books.

Versiani, Flavio R. 1971. "Technical Change, Equipment Replacement, and Labor Absorption: The Case of the Brazilian Textile Industry." Ph.D. diss., Vanderbilt University.

Villa, Pierre. 1993. *Une analyse macroéconomique de l'économie française au XXᵉ siècle*. Paris: CNRS.

Vogel, David. 1995. *Trading Up: Consumer and Environmental Regulation in a Global Economy*. Cambridge, Mass.: Harvard University Press.

Volden, Craig. 2006. "States as Policy Laboratories: Emulating Success in the Children's Health Insurance Program." *American Journal of Political Science* 50: 294–312.

Volodine, Andre I. 2007. "Russian Factory Inspection (1882–1918): *Cui Bono?*" Unpublished manuscript, Moscow State University.

von der Weid, Elisabeth, and Ana Marta Rodrigues Bastos. 1986. *O fio da meada: Estratégia de expansão de uma indústria têxtil: Companhia América Fabril, 1878–1930*. Rio de Janeiro: FCRB-CNI.

von Laue, Theodore H. 1960. "Factory Inspection under the 'Witte System': 1892–1903." *American Slavic and East European Review* 19: 347–62.

Voth, Hans Joachim. 2000. *Time and Work in England, 1750–1830*. Oxford: Clarendon Press.

Webb, Sidney, and Beatrice Webb. 1902. *Industrial Democracy*. New edition in one vol. London: Longmans Green.

Webber, Jeremy. 1995. "Labour and the Law." In *Labouring Lives: Work and Workers in Nineteenth-Century Ontario*, edited by Paul Craven. Toronto: University of Toronto Press. Pp, 105–203.

Weber, Eugen. 1976. *Peasants into Frenchman: The Modernization of Rural France, 1870–1914*. Stanford: Stanford University Press.

Weill, Claudie. 1978. "Le débat sur les migrations ouvrières dans la Deuxième Internationale." *Pluriel*: 55–73.

Weinstein, Barbara. 1996. *For Social Peace in Brazil: Industrialists and the Remaking of the Working Class in São Paulo, 1920–1964*. Chapel Hill: University of North Carolina Press.

Weir, David R. 1992. "A Century of U.S. Unemployment, 1890–1990: Revised Estimates and Evidence for Stabilization." *Research in Economic History* 14: 301–41.

Williamson, Jeffrey G. 1995. "The Evolution of Global Labor Markets since 1830: Background Evidence and Hypotheses." *Explorations in Economic History* 32: 141–96.

Williamson, Jeffrey G. 1998. "Globalization, Labor Markets, and Policy Backlash in the Past." *Journal of Economic Perspectives* 12: 51–72.

Williamson, Jeffrey G. 2002. "Land, Labor, and Globalization in the Third World, 1870–1940." *Journal of Economic History* 62: 55–85.

Williamson, Jeffrey G. 2006. *Globalization and the Poor Periphery Before 1950*. Cambridge, Mass.: MIT Press.

Wise, B. R. 1892. *Industrial Freedom: A Study in Politics*. London: Cassell.

Witte, Els, Jan Craeybeckx, and Alain Meynen. 2000. *Political History of Belgium from 1830 Onwards*. Brussels: VUB Press.

Wood, Louis Aubrey. 1975. *A History of Farmers' Movements in Canada [1924]*. Toronto: University of Toronto Press.

Wright, Gavin. 2006. "Productivity Growth and the American Labor Market: The 1990s in Historical Perspective." In *The Global Economy in the 1990s: A Long-Run Perspective*, edited by Paul Rhode and Gianni Toniolo. New York: Cambridge University Press. Pp. 139–60.

Zacher, Mark W., and Richard A. Matthew. 1995. "Liberal International Theory: Common Threads, Divergent Strands." In *Controversies in International Relations Theory: Realism and the Neoliberal Challenge*, edited by Charles Kegley. New York: St. Martin's. Pp. 107–50.

Zamagni, Vera. 1993. *The Economic History of Italy, 1860–1990*. Oxford: Oxford University Press.

Zepeda, Eduardo, Timothy A. Wise, and Kevin P. Gallagher. 2009. "Rethinking Trade Policy for Development: Lessons from Mexico under NAFTA." Policy Outlook, Carnegie Endowment for Social Peace.

Zolberg, Aristide R. 2006. *A Nation by Design: Immigration Policy in the Fashioning of America*. Cambridge, Mass.: Harvard University Press.

INDEX

accident insurance (accident compensation): adoption, 26, 42, 59, 114, 174, 186 n. 23; compliance, 18; convergence in, 122–25; cost of, 18, 122, 198 n. 5; and labor treaties, 58; results, 36, 58, 120, 121

Acemoglu, Daron, 55, 59, 190 n. 12

agriculture: agricultural and food prices, 2, 51, 52, 57, 190 n. 6; coalition of farmers and labor, 50; landowners, 2, 3; share of GDP, 36; share of labor force in, 44

Allen, Robert C., 89, 191 n. 18

Alsace-Loraine, 34–35

ancien régime, 2, 57

Argentina, 126, 134, 136, 147

Australia: federal structure, 13, 173; hours of work, 109, 144, 148; inequality, 105; labor regulation, 19, 63, 147, 149; political coalitions in, 63; political voice in, 43, 48; redistribution, 63; wages, 100; welfare state, 19

Austria-Hungary: and IFTWA, 68; labor regulation, 10, 121; labor treaties, 77, 80

Bagwell, Kyle (Bagwell-Staiger model), 41, 67, 77

Bairoch, Paul, 7, 108

Belgian Labor Party (Parti Ouvrier Belge, POB), 1, 11, 50, 54; and free trade, 53, 56–58; and labor compact, 57, 58; militancy of, 62; and political coalitions, 57, 59; and women, 196 n. 27 *See also* Vandervelde, Émile

Belgium: agriculture, 2, 51, 53, 58; attitudes toward free trade, 52–53; commercial policy, 2; cotton industry, 29, 93, 111, 126; emigration, 75; exports, 51, 118, 122, 126–27; factor endowments, 51; hours of work, 114, 144, 166; and IALL, 73; and IFTWA, 68; labor compact, 20, 166; labor militancy, 52, 62–63; labor regulation, 55, 93; political parties, 52, 56, 59; social entitlements, 59; tariff debate of 1894, 56–59; terms of trade, 132–33; trade agreements, 51; train network, 53–54; unemployment, 52, 102; wages, 52, 54, 93, 106; welfare state, 19, 59. *See also* Belgian Labor Party; Vandervelde, Émile

Bell, Linda, 139, 148, 154

Berlin, International Conference, 13, 74–75, 173

Bernstein, Eduard, 11, 63, 186 nn. 16, 21

Milton Keynes UK
Ingram Content Group UK Ltd.
UKHW012134010724
444852UK00008B/52